earnestly yours

earnestly yours

Selected Addresses of Dr. Ernest L. Wilkinson
University President
Attorney
Churchman
Patriot
Civic Leader

EDITED BY
Edwin J. Butterworth and David H. Yarn

Published by
Deseret Book Company
Salt Lake City, Utah
1971

Library of Congress No. 75-159394
SBN No. 87747-390-0

LITHOGRAPHED BY

IN THE UNITED STATES OF AMERICA

Dedicated to my wife and sweetheart,
Alice Ludlow Wilkinson, whose equanimity,
poise, affection, and encouragement have
always made life worth while despite the
vicissitudes of the moment.
                    —Ernest L. Wilkinson

Dr. Ernest L. Wilkinson

INTRODUCTION

On the third floor of the Abraham O. Smoot Administration and General Services Building at Brigham Young University is an entire room filled with filing cabinets containing decades of correspondence of the University's president, Dr. Ernest L. Wilkinson. Thousands of these letters bear the complimentary close, "Earnestly and faithfully yours." While it is obviously a play on words, the phrase is without doubt genuine and appropriate: Ernest is indeed earnest.

Dr. Wilkinson's speeches selected for this volume are only a small part of more than three hundred major addresses he has presented before civic clubs, professional groups, university audiences, and church congregations. Unlike the utterances of other men in prominent positions which are limited to their specialties, the speeches of Dr. Wilkinson cover a wide range, reflecting his prodigious output as an attorney, university president, patriot, civic leader, and churchman.

All who know him will agree that his talks usually run very long and for two good reasons: (1) he has a lot to say, and (2) he cannot escape the compulsion of the attorney to get all of the facts into the record. In view of this reality, some complete speeches have been included; other selections are excerpts or sections of longer addresses.

Notwithstanding the substantial nature of his discourses, his audiences are seldom inattentive. Dr. Wilkinson speaks with a deep, resonant voice, reflecting a fierce sincerity. Not all of his listeners may agree with him, but his speeches usually are a lively occasion.

When Dr. Wilkinson took over the reins of Brigham Young University in 1951, he already had built a successful career, financial security, and a national reputation as an attorney.

He began the practice of the law from 1928 to 1935 as an associate of Honorable Charles Evans Hughes, later Chief Justice of the United States Supreme Court. Later he moved to Washington, D.C., where he organized his own law firm, of which he is still the senior partner.

As attorney for the Ute Indians he handled one case lasting over 16 years in which he put in evidence testimony and exhibits aggregating over 34,000 pages. That case, together with three others, resulted in four judgments totalling $31,500,000. One of these, totalling $24,000,000, still is the largest single judgment ever rendered against the United States.

In a subsequent proceeding before the same court to determine the attorneys' fees to which Dr. Wilkinson and his associates were entitled, the Honorable Owen J. Roberts, who had resigned as an Associate Justice of the Supreme Court of the United States, paid Dr. Wilkinson a compliment of having handled the claims "with all of the skill of a great advocate and a great trial lawyer. As I cast the horoscope of these cases . . . had I been the lawyer . . . I would not have known how to proceed."

The Honorable Homer Cummings, Attorney General of the United States, testified that the main case which Dr. Wilkinson and his associates handled "ought not to be called a case. It is a life-long venture. . . . I don't think any disinterested person can trace the history of this case without doffing its hat to a counsel who prevailed against such odds. It's an amazing experience."

The Honorable Seth Richardson, who had been Assistant Attorney General in charge of defending Indian tribal claims against the government, testified that although he had actively and strenuously practiced law for nearly half a century and had tried almost every known kind of a case, including Indian cases, the amount of service rendered by Dr. Wilkinson and his associates "almost staggers our imagination . . . I never saw anything like this in my life. . . . To me the amount of services rendered here is almost impossible for the ordinary mind to grasp."

Pointing out that at one time Dr. Wilkinson set himself a goal of recovering $30 million, Mr. Richardson testified: ". . . is is an extraordinary thing to look at $30 million as a goal over the rough pathway that this suit had to go, and then come out with $32 million. . . . That is two million above perfection." Stating he was testifying without any monetary compensation, he concluded: "I will tell you what I did. I got a copy of it (Wilkinson's affidavit of services) and took it to the two attorneys in our office that are now working on Indian cases and said, "Boys, the time you spend reading this is the most valuable time you can spend in the next two years. You nor I never had an opportunity to contact human work in the profession of law that compares with this case. It is the most extraordinary thing I ever saw."

With this national reputation as an attorney he became president of BYU in 1951.

In the next twenty years he gained national fame for a second career as he built BYU into the largest private university in the United States (on a basis of full-time students), and enrollment grew from 4,654 in 1950 to 25,021 in 1970, accompanied by an amazing building program.

He was born in Ogden, Utah, May 4, 1899, a son of Robert and Cecilia Anderson Wilkinson, his father a native of Scotland and his mother of Danish ancestry. He received his early education in Ogden schools and Weber College, was graduated from Brigham Young University in 1921, and served as a private in the U.S. Army in 1918.

He was graduated from George Washington University Law School, summa cum laude, 1926, and received the degree of doctor of juridical science at Harvard University, 1927.

It was at BYU that he met Alice Ludlow, who later became his wife. They have three sons and two daughters, all of whom attended BYU.

The oldest son, Ernest Ludlow, the father of five boys, is now a distinguished physician in Salt Lake City, specializing in cardiology, and is the representative for Utah of the American Heart Association. The second son, David Lawrence, is a successful lawyer in Los Angeles. The third son, Douglas Dwight, is now attending University of Utah Law School. The oldest daughter, Marian, is the mother of three daughters and the wife of a bishop (Gordon Jensen) in Sunnyvale, California, and active in Church and civic affairs. The younger daughter, Alice Ann, is the mother of three boys and one daughter, the wife of a leading lawyer in Salt Lake City (John Knight Mangum), and a civic leader in Salt Lake City. Four of them graduated from BYU, and the fifth obtained her husband there.

He was a member of the faculty of Weber College, 1921-23; Business High School, Washington, D.C., 1923-26; superintendent of Camp Good Will, Washington, 1925. He was admitted to Washington, D.C., Bar, 1926; Utah Bar, 1927; New York Bar, 1928; and held a professorship in law at New Jersey Law School, 1927-1933.

While in the East he served as president of Manhattan Queens Branch, The Church of Jesus Christ of Latter-day Saints; Bishop of Queens Ward, and a member of the Washington Stake Presidency.

President Wilkinson took office at BYU in February 1951 and his resignation was accepted by the Board of Trustees on March 9, 1971, effective at the end of that school year. He was then assigned to a major role in the establishment of a new BYU College of Law. His 20-year administration was interrupted only once, in 1964 when he unsuccessfully ran for the U.S. Senate.

The campus has grown into a spacious, beautiful plant of more than 100 major, permanent buildings, more than 80 of which were constructed during the Wilkinson administration.

He considers as probably the greatest accomplishment during his administration the organization on campus of wards and stakes of The Church of Jesus Christ of Latter-day Saints, which he proposed to the Church leaders.

When he first became president there was one branch of the Church on campus; there are now ten stakes with 98 wards.

President Wilkinson also has placed great emphasis on scholarship at BYU and during his administration the curriculum has been completely revised. The original five colleges were expanded to 13, with addition of such new areas as Family Living, General College, Humanities, Industrial and Technical Education, Nursing, and Engineering Sciences, etc. To the bachelor's and master's degrees were added the associate and doctor's degrees. The school changed from the quarter system to the semester system, scholarships were expanded, and the Honors Program was established for gifted students.

Under his aegis many other improvements have thrived, such as Army and Air Force ROTC, the weekly Forum of great speakers, Lyceum program of great concerts, Indian Education Program, intramural sports, youth leadership courses, Master of Business Administration program, Institute of Government Service, Institute of Mormon Studies, Institute of Book of Mormon Studies, Asian Studies, Latin American Studies, and many others.

For all of these improvements he always gives the Board of Trustees credit. However, in recognition of his accomplishments, the BYU Board of Trustees named the spacious student activities building "Ernest L. Wilkinson Center" at dedication ceremonies on April 3, 1965. The Board also conferred on him the honorary degree of doctor of laws in 1957, and he received the honorary degree of doctor of public service from the University of Ft. Lauderdale in June 1970.

In addition to being president of BYU, he was chancellor of the Unified Church School System from 1953 to 1964 which consisted of a junior college, 161 institutes of religion near universities and colleges, 1,658 seminaries of religion near high schools, LDS Business College, the Brigham Young University Laboratory School, and two academies and 24 elementary schools in Mexico.

A figure of national importance, Dr. Wilkinson was a

member of the National Committee of Army and Navy
Chaplains, 1947-50; member of the Governor's committee
representing Utah to the White House Conference on
Education, 1955; delegate to the Republican National
Conventions, 1956, 1960 and 1968; member of the
Resolutions Committee, Republican National Conven-
tion, 1960 and 1968; member, U.S. Chamber of Commerce
committees on Government Expenditures, 1952-58, and
on National Defense, 1959. For sometime he has been an
Overseer of Freedoms Foundation at Valley Forge and is
at present President of The National Right to Work
Legal Defense Foundation.

He served as president of the American Association of
Independent College and University Presidents in 1968-9,
and in that capacity testified in behalf of private universities and colleges before the Senate Finance Committee to
preserve financial aids to education during hearings
for the Tax Reform Bill.

High honor came to Dr. Wilkinson in 1961 when he
was awarded the George Washington Medal by the Freedoms Foundation for his address to the National Chamber
of Commerce on free enterprise, and in 1963 at a public
dinner at Hotel Utah he received the highest award of the
American Coalition of Patriotic Societies. The Freedoms
Foundation awarded him another medal in February 1971
for his address "Academic Anarchy vs. University Management" given before the Oakland Rotary Club.

He has served also as a member of the Board of Direc-
tors, Deseret News Publishing Co., Beneficial Life Insurance
Co., Radio Service Corp. of Utah, Ellison Ranching Co.,
Rolling Hills Orchard, Utah Foundation, and Foundation
for Economic Education. He has been a member of the
National Ad Hoc USO Survey Committee; committee
member, International Council for the Hall of Free
Enterprise for the 1964-65 New York World's Fair; chair-
man of Utah County United Fund; member, National
Speakers Bureau, American Medical Association; the
Accreditation Commission for Business Schools; and
National Right to Work Committee.

The numerous statements of such a distinguished career cannot be condensed into a volume of this size. However, in this sampling much of the detail, statistics, and business of the moment have been deleted to leave basic ideas representative of an unusual man. Not all of the material is concerned with the development of ideas or opinions, but some has been included also to give the biographical flavor of a dynamic life.

Edwin J. Butterworth
David H. Yarn

TABLE OF CONTENTS

AUTOBIOGRAPHICAL
REMARKS

Section 1

Dr. Ernest L. Wilkinson reports to Ute Indian Council on award of $32,000,000 claim.

Dr. Ernest L. Wilkinson, center, is introduced as new president of Brigham Young University by Church President George Albert Smith, right, and his counselor, J. Reuben Clark, Jr., at the Diamond Jubilee convocation at Brigham Young University October 16, 1950.

UP FROM HELL'S HALF ACRE

(Opening address of the year to Brigham Young University student body, September 22, 1966 in George Albert Smith Fieldhouse.)

At the beginning of this school year I bring you the personal greetings of President David O. McKay. He wants you to know he loves you and as President of the Board of Trustees of this University, will be watching with pride your activities and your accomplishments. We were honored this summer to be able to drive him, Sister McKay and their daughter around the campus—even drove him onto the stage of the Concert Hall in the Franklin S. Harris Building. As we drove off the stage he said he had now seen about everything, that life was so easy now that one could play to an audience while still riding in a horse and buggy propelled by gas. As I took him back to his home in the Hotel Utah he said, "You not only have the greatest student body led by the finest faculty, but you now have the most beautiful campus. This has been one of the most memorable days of my life."

I have the privilege also of greeting you in behalf of your devoted teachers. As I addressed them last week I pointed out that they represent not only a community of scholars but, more importantly, a congregation of disciples, for at this institution there is a fusion of secular and re-vealed knowledge that is unique among the major universities of the world.

I had the privilege on Thursday of shaking hands with over 6,000 of you who are freshmen and transfer students. I always enjoy this, primarily because I like your youthful, radiant enthusiasm, but secondarily because I have traveled in every state of the Union and delivered addresses of one kind or another in most of them. I didn't know I had travelled so much until this last summer United Air Lines delivered me a plaque attesting to the fact I had flown a million miles.

You are in the most distinctive and potentially dynamic student body in the world. By the time registration closes there will be nearly 20,000 of you. Before the year is finished there will be over 6,000, or nearly one-third, who will be returned missionaries. Where else could you girls find such a happy hunting ground? Where else could we find such a mature and seasoned student body? No wonder that our graduates—their skills developed and their testimonies strengthened—are in demand wherever ability and integrity are required.

We welcome you to a University where you will all be treated as equals, regardless of the economic, social or religious status of your parents. The son of a father who has a Cadillac, which it will take him three years to pay for, will be treated no better than the son of a father who has a Volkswagen all paid for. In fact, the latter may get his check from home more regularly. Here you are all children of God limited only by your own abilities and energies, and your own self-motivation.

Those of you who have entered BYU in the Honors Program are among the best students to register any place in the nation this year. The general level of the student body is impressively high. A score on your entering tests which would have put you at the 84th percentile in 1956 would have dropped to the 72nd by 1960. Last year, that same score would have placed you no higher than the 51st percentile.

This description of your intellectual competence reminds me of the true story told of Nobel Waite, at one time a stake president in Los Angeles. A very distinguished man, a member of his stake, called on him stating he had a real, personal problem to solve. "You know, President Waite," he began, "my wife and I and three of our children are graduates of an educational institution in Utah a little north of the BYU and we have been very loyal to that institution. I am very much troubled this morning because our youngest daughter insists on going to the BYU." Quick as a flash President Waite replied, "She's the smartest child you have."

My associates in the administration have urged me this morning to relate some of my personal experiences and tell something of my own life. I have hesitated to do so because I don't want them to have something which they can use against me and because it is generally considered poor taste to talk about one's self. Nevertheless, I am going to follow their suggestions.

I start out with the story of a young man whom I knew as a youngster and whom I have kept in touch with the rest of my life. I do it to show you how you can rise above your environment, throw off bad companions and bad habits and become a relatively good citizen under the dynamic influence of a church school, similar to the one in which you now find yourselves.

This young man was raised in Ogden where I was raised. I'm afraid he grew up in about the worst environment in the city. The area around his home was known as "Hell's Half Acre." The only thing wrong with this description was that it contained more than one-half acre. Across the street was a section known as Devil's Square. Just how they distinguished one from the other I can't recall. Two blocks in the other direction was a race track where all the human vermin generally associated with gambling and racing hung out. There were not many boys of this youngster's age in this environment, so he associated with men many years his senior, and also partook of some of their vices.

The chief Sunday preoccupation for a large element of the neighborhood consisted of "cock fights." Game roosters bred and carefully raised for their fighting quality would be equipped with $1\frac{3}{4}$-inch steel spurs on each leg and then pitted against each other in a cock fight until one or the other was physically incapacitated or dead. It would have been bad enough to have permitted them to fight with their own spurs, but to equip them with steel spurs was merciless.

As a youngster, never lazy, and always curious to know what was going on in his surroundings, my young friend joined a group of these cock fighters, and with money which he saved from a paper route, purchased a few game cocks and went into partnership with some grown men who frequented the cockpits.

One dark morning about 4 a.m. there was an exchange of shots outside the young man's home in which one man was seriously wounded. When daylight came and the facts could be knitted together, the following story was revealed.

The richest man in Ogden was David Eccles. He had received a blackmail note directing him to deliver a certain sum of money in gold coin to the corner outside this young man's home at 4 a.m. that morning. Failure to do so would result in his death. This place had been designated because it was the only corner on the street where there was a street light and the blackmailers wanted to be able to see Eccles when he appeared.

Eccles instead engaged a very courageous detective who, impersonating him, carried a bag over his back with washers in it instead of gold coin and a sawed off shot-gun under his overcoat. As the detective approached this lighted corner, the blackmailers detected the subterfuge and shot the officer down. The detective managed to fire a few shots himself, however, and one of the blackmailers was slightly wounded in the leg.

This wound was the cause of his apprehension and conviction as a blackmailer for which he served time in the Utah State Prison. The blackmailer turned out to be the game chicken partner of the young man of whom I am speaking.

Shortly thereafter the police stopped the cock fights, and this young man began to pal with a group somewhat nearer to his own age, but still older than he. They had a hangout where they met every night, played cards, smoked and engaged in sex stories, although this young man never fully participated as did the others. But he longed for association with others, and this is where he found it.

As previously stated, he carried a paper route for the Deseret News, which was 12 miles or more in length and which he sometimes had to navigate in deep snow. After this paper route, which would take until 8 or 9 p.m. to complete, he would stop at this hangout for an evening of mental and social dissipation.

The one bright spot in this young man's family life was his mother—who all through his childhood was president of either the Primary Association or Relief Society. His father at this stage in his life, while a hard worker, was completely inactive in the Church. One Saturday, however, a new bishop got hold of his father and told him they were going to build a new ward meeting house adjoining their old one and asked him if he would bring his team and scraper and help excavate the basement. In those days the members of the ward often built their own meeting houses. The next morning, which was Sunday, when the bishop showed up for church at the old meeting house, this boy's father was there with his team and nearly had the basement of the new meeting house dug. It was known thereafter as the ward with a Sunday basement in it.

About this time his mother persuaded her son to attend Weber Academy, a church school such as you have here, except it was the equivalent of a high school. This new influence brought an abrupt change in this young man's life. He immediately saw the error of his ways and where his associations could lead him. He couldn't resist the all pervasive spiritual environment of that school. It changed his whole life.

But he had a terrible struggle separating himself from his old gang. One day in school he resolved he would never go to their den again, but when he passed their hang-out that night he couldn't muster enough will power to pass by, and so he went in. This resolve and failure to abide by it carried on for days. One day he had been particularly inspired by one of his teachers and that night with all the resolve he could muster he pedaled right by the hangout and never returned. All this was the result of his church school training.

He started going to Sunday School regularly. At 15 years of age he was made assistant superintendent of the Sunday School. He applied himself in his school work, became both editor of the school paper and president of the student body. Later he came to BYU and here met the girl of his dreams who became the mother of his five children, four of whom have graduated from this institution and the fifth of whom is on a mission and will return here to graduate.

As you may have guessed by now, the young man who was raised in Hell's Half Acre, who engaged in cock-fighting, associated with criminals, spent his time with pals who had no real purpose in life, and who could have followed in their footsteps is, I admit today, the person who is standing before you. On the other hand, one of his boyhood pals is now in prison for murder. Out of deep gratitude to my mother, to my Heavenly Father, and the profound influence of a church school, I acknowledge my blessings. What could have been a life of iniquity has become one of opportunity and happiness.

I make this confession to you today because if there are any of you who find that you are slaves to pernicious habits, or have associations which you must sever, or new resolutions which you must effect, I offer myself as an example that it can be done. And your whole life will be changed. I don't want you to get the impression that I changed in the twinkling of an eye from sinner to saint. Changes do not often take place that abruptly, and I do not now claim to be ready to be taken up.

There have been many times in my life when I have been tempted to stray from the path of rectitude and righteousness. And I have sometimes detoured from the straight line. But the Good Lord has whispered to me so plainly that I have even heard my name called, and I have quickly returned to the path which I am sure nearly all of you are treading today.

I now want to bear my testimony as to the value of assuming responsibility and grasping all opportunities that present themselves. My father, despite his shortcomings and inactivity for sometime in the Church, was the hardest working man I have ever known. He emigrated to this country from Scotland with his father and an older brother, when he was 10 years of age. All three of them immediately went to work to save enough money to send for the mother in the family and 8 other children. Under these conditions he obtained only three years of grammar school training. Without an understanding of the American way of life he at one time was the Socialist candidate for mayor of Ogden. I remember him taking me at one time to hear Eugene V. Debs, then the Socialist candidate for president of the United States. His remedy for the world's ills was for all of us to join one big union. In my youth I thought this was a great ideal. I now know it would spell the end of our country.

While my father had practically no education himself, and frankly didn't profess to think much of education, my mother believed in it intensely. And when Father turned his pay check over to my mother (as most husbands do) she spent it mainly on the education of her children, for three out of five brothers graduated from college, and our only sister has had educational and other experiences excelling a college education.

In order to see that his children obtained the education our saintly mother desired, Father, until he was 70 years of age, generally held two full-time jobs simultaneously—one beginning early in the morning, the other beginning in the afternoon and continuing until midnight. Until he was 81 years of age he worked hard at physical labor. When he was 82, and working on the west coast, he obtained a job as a shoveler of coal on a steamer

bound for New York, via the Panama Canal, and showed
up one day in our home in New York completely un-
announced.

The rest of his days he lived with us, spending his
last nine years on this campus. He always referred to you
students as scholars. One day in the first part of September,
he asked me when the scholars would return. I replied that
I didn't know whether we would have any. This puzzled
him for days because he couldn't distinguish between a
scholar and one who merely paid tuition.

My father died at the age of 95, having worked harder
but living longer than any of his four brothers. I say this
because I don't want you to get the opinion that hard work
hurts anyone. The reverse is true. I have related this
about my father because I want you to know I have great
gratitude and love for him. To him I am sure I owe in
large part my zest and capacity for work.

Unfortunately, however, he was a very poor business
man. His life's ambition was to own a large farm or ranch.
But my mother knew from his failure in managing a small
farm, he would never succeed in managing a larger one,
so she spent all of his money on the education of his
children and he never got his farm.

This doesn't mean he didn't try. I remember once
when I was in my young teens and we had our first automobile, which was a truck, Father took me with him to
Manti to see a farm he wanted to buy. When we got
there, we didn't have enough money to go to a hotel, so
we slept out in an alfalfa patch across from the temple.
What he intended to use for money to purchase the farm
my mother and I never knew.

Because of my father's lack of business judgment,
and the great difficulty which my mother had in making up
her mind, it fell my lot, in my early teens to make many
decisions for the family. This was very difficult for me
because, like my father, I had developed an inferiority
complex and was frightened to death of business transac-
tions.

I recall at one time being sent to a bank by my mother

to borrow a relatively small amount of money. I think I walked back and forth past the door of the bank 10 times or more before I dared go in. Contrary to what most people think, this timidity has continued with me and even now I have to summon all my courage to meet people whom I greatly respect or to transact certain business. I think I would have overcome this had I served a mission, which I very much wanted to do. I even suggested the same to my bishop. But he was of the old school who thought missions were largely to reform young men and told me that in view of the record I was making in school he would not send me.

I mention these experiences, some of which seem humorous now, but which were very serious when they occurred, because many of you will now have to make decisions, some for the first time. Don't shrink from it; seize the opportunity, but do it cautiously and prayerfully, with all the advice you can get. But I repeat, don't shun it.

I have sometimes wrestled with myself all night making decisions, but this is a part of the learning process. I take great satisfaction from a statement that the late President Heber J. Grant continuously used which originated with Emerson: "That which we persist in doing becomes easier to do, not that the nature of the thing has changed, but that our ability to do has increased."

I promise you that through your making one decision it will be easier to make another. The same thing holds for participating in any pursuit of life—in academic and afterwards in business or professional affairs. I remember the first time I ever debated in high school. I was so frightened I started shaking in the morning before the debate and continued shaking the balance of the day after the debate. The first law school exam I took was in the evening. I didn't sleep the rest of the night. So if you have similar experiences remember that the rest of us have had to pay the same price.

Now I want to give you my testimony as to the value of hard work. I have already expressed my gratitude to my father for the example he set for me. That hard work enabled me to get my degree at the "Y" in three years. Don't try to do it now, for as I have suggested above, the standards are much, much higher. It might now take me five.

When I attended George Washngton University law school I was honored, not because of any brilliance, but because of hard work to graduate at the head of my class. I am sure there were many others more competent than I.

Because of my academic record at George Washington I was then awarded a scholarship for graduate work at Harvard Law School. The rules of Harvard were that a doctoral candidate should have years of experience in the teaching of law. Over the protest of Professor Felix Frankfurter, who later became an Associate Justice of the Supreme Court, Dean Pound waived this requirement in my case. But when I registered I found myself in a class of Frankfurter, who had thought I was not competent to enter. This was a very uncomfortable position.

Each student in his class was required to write a thesis on some phase of administrative law. He then interrogated the student for three hours before the class. I worked hard on this thesis but even so didn't know what was in store for me. After three hours of gruelling I was sure I would never get a doctoral degree, since the rule of the school was that such a degree was given only to those maintaining a straight "A" average. The next week, when this class met again, Frankfurter, without any warning, gruelled me for another three hours. Then I was sure I was through. The third week (something unheard of) he was back to the attack—altogether nine hours of exhaustive interrogation. By this time I was sure I had flunked.

When time for examinations came, I was required to go to his office to ask for an extension of two days to get in my thesis so I could study for another exam. I think I walked by his door 20 times before I dared enter. When I did, I stuttered out my request, to which he replied, "Wilkinson, you tell your other teacher you are not taking his exam, that you don't need to, because I am giving you double credit in administrative law." My effort, not my brilliance, had paid off.

Brother Covey has already informed you of the compliment the judges of the United States Court of Claims paid me when they awarded my associates and me a legal fee of $2,800,000. They made findings of fact in which they discovered, on the basis of time devoted to my law office (for I made a record of every 15 minute period) that I had crowded 26 years of work into 16 years.

I want to bear you my testimony that if you develop the habit of work, it will be the most invigorating, satisfying, relaxing and greatest blessing of your life. The opportunity to work is God's greatest gift to man, and this means six days of each week. Many of us remember that we are to rest the seventh, but forget that the Lord told us "six days shalt thou labor." I can't urge upon you enough the necessity for your studying hard on Saturday. You will never be successful here or in any profession or business on a 40-hour week.

May I now bear to you my testimony on the validity of tithing. At the conclusion of my third year of law at the George Washington University, I had been blessed with the receipt of a scholarship at Harvard University for advanced study. I accordingly made arrangements to go to Harvard for an additional year of legal training. Preparatory to leaving Washington, I figured up my income and found that I was short some $230 in that year in the payment of tithing. Not wanting to leave Washington without making a full accounting to my branch president, I went to a strange bank in Washington, D.C., to see if I couldn't borrow $230. I approached the lending officer with a great deal of apprehension. He did not know me, and I had established no credit at the bank. Indeed, I had no credit to establish. I thought the best thing to do under the circumstances was to tell him frankly why I needed the money. As I concluded, the banker looked at me and said, "Young man, if you have enough character in you to consider that tithing is an obligation for which you need to borrow money, this bank will be happy to make the loan. We have no doubt you will repay it."

Armed with a clear conscience, I went to Harvard

Law School. After having been there for less than one
month, I received a letter informing me that a distinguished singer from the West had begun suit against the
Boston Transit Company for partial loss of her singing
voice due to the negligence of this streetcar company.
The complaint was that she had been riding in a streetcar
down one of the hills of Boston when the brakes gave way.
She had been thrown out of her seat and suffered an
abrasion to her shin, the shock of which had impaired
her singing voice. The letter concluded by saying that
she had engaged some attorneys in Boston, who apparently
were not very enthusiastic about the case, and asked if I
would consent to be associated with them in the prosecution
of the case.

Skeptical as I could be about the merits of such a
case, I nevertheless went to Boston to call on these attorneys, for every young lawyer likes his first case. But I found
they were even more skeptical about the merits of the
case than I. Indeed, the trial was to come on in a couple
of weeks, and they were about ready to back out. They
had been to some eminent doctors in the town who refused to testify because they thought there was no causal
connection between the shin injury and the impairment
of the voice. I told them I would think it over for a day or
so. Actually, I wanted to think of some good reason for
not taking the case. But on going home I did some praying
about the matter, for I had great respect for this singer
and did not believe she would make a fictitious claim.

After a couple of days of thinking and praying, but
still being of the opinion that there was no way of justify-
ing this particular suit, I started to go through Harvard
Square to the attorneys' office to tell them that I thought
the case was hopeless. As I proceeded through the Square
on that day, I ran into an old school teacher of mine, a
graduate of BYU who had become head of the phonetics
laboratory at Ohio State University—what at that time
was probably the leading phonetics laboratory in the
country. I immediately proceeded to tell him of this
strange law case and I asked him whether, in view of his

expertness in the field of phonetics, he thought an abrasion on the shin could cause the loss of voice. He looked at me and said, "Ernest, now I know why I stayed over in Harvard today. I was all set to go last night. I had no particular reason for staying around another day but just felt that for some reason I ought to stay. Now I know I was needed in this particular case." He further said, "If you will come with me down to the Boston Public Library, I will get you one copy of a famous book—there are only three copies in this country—which documents the history of about one hundred cases where highly strung artists have had their artistic talents impaired through a slight body injury." Responding with alacrity, I went to the library with him where we obtained a documented book. My former teacher agreed to remain and testify, and he became the leading witness in the case. As a result we obtained a well-deserved, large judgment for this famous singer, out of which I received a fee that helped me very materially to finish my training at Harvard Law School. Call it coincidence if you want, but I am simple enough to believe otherwise.

I came to BYU campus first in 1918 during World War I in the uniform of my country. A dread influenza epidemic, with which our medical profession did not then know how to cope, spread throughout the two companies of soldiers quartered on this hill. The Maeser Building was the only academic edifice then in existence on the upper campus. I was one of the first stricken with that disease, which took more American lives than were sacrificed on the battlefields of France. As a fellow member of my company who also held the priesthood placed his hands on my head and blessed me that I would recover (and we all did), I promised my Heavenly Father that if He would spare my life, I would serve this institution if ever the opportunity presented itself. Little did I realize that about thirty years later I would be appointed president of Brigham Young University, and that my office would consist of the room where I was restored to health. I humbly hope that in that capacity I have kept my promise.

In the name of Jesus Christ, Amen.

DISCOURSES ON PATRIOTISM, FREE ENTERPRISE, AND LAW AND ORDER

Section 2

President of the United States Harry S. Truman talks with Church President David O. McKay and BYU President Ernest L. Wilkinson during a visit to Brigham Young University Oct. 7, 1952.

Richard M. Nixon, when he was Vice-President of the United States, enters George Albert Smith Fieldhouse at BYU with President Ernest L. Wilkinson on Oct. 17, 1958.

AN APPEAL FOR PATRIOTISM

(*On May 2, 1963, Dr. Wilkinson was awarded the Merit Medallion of the American Coalition of Patriotic Societies, the highest honor of a federation of 125 groups with over three million membership, at a dinner in his honor at Hotel Utah in Salt Lake City, which was attended by hundreds of religious, business, governmental, and educational leaders. The presentation was made by Hon. Hugh C. Mitchell, state senator from North Carolina, who also presented Dr. Wilkinson with a certificate of appreciation from the Patterson School for Boys.*)

Mr. Chairman, Mr. Toastmaster, President and Mrs. McKay, Governor and Mrs. Clyde, other distinguished guests, and my many, many friends.

I am deeply honored, Senator Mitchell, for the award of the Order of Merit and the Certificate of Appreciation from the Patterson School for Boys which you have been kind and generous enough to tender me tonight. So many of my friends who really know of my unworthiness have been asking as to why I have been singled out for this award that I had hoped you might disclose the uninformed person who nominated me and the equally uninformed persons who voted for the nomination. But since you have failed to give me any information as to how my selection was manipulated, I can only conclude that it must have been accomplished by a combination of disillusioned and disenfranchised Jeffersonian Democrats and Taft Republicans, who, not being able to win any elections, decided that this might be a good occasion to talk about patriotism.

I am overwhelmed by the presence of so many of you, my friends, here tonight. If my father, whom we buried three years ago at the age of 95, had ever thought

anyone would pay $6.00 to honor his son he would have
been sure, an unreconstructed Democrat as he was, that
the country had either "gone to the dogs" or it was the
result of Democratic prosperity. I hope that none of you
have come in on a modern credit card. You know, in my
father's day $6.00 would have purchased a lot of bread
and milk for the family—milk at 5¢ a quart and flour
at $2.00 for a 50 lb. bag.

An immigrant from Scotland with only three years
of schooling, he spent a good part of his life holding
down two 8-hour jobs in order to save enough that he
could buy a farm. But my mother was the chancellor
of the exchequer in our family and she spent it not in the
acquisition of a farm but in the procurement of an
education for all of her children.

I remember as a youngster about 1914 when we
acquired our first automobile, which was a truck, my
father took me to Manti where he wanted to look at a
farm which he yearned very much to purchase. On the
way down he remembered that my mother had talked
him out of the few dollars he had saved for that trip in
order to buy some school books for my brothers and sis-
ters. So my father and I decided that we would go on
without our meals that day, and we also slept out that
night in an alfalfa patch across from the Manti Temple
under the majestic stars. I learned more that night about
the unrelated subjects of astronomy and hunger than I
have ever learned since. The stars were beautiful but they
provided no calories for a young man's stomach.

Without even enough to buy a night's lodging, my
father never succeeded in purchasing that farm, but I
have been grateful all my life for the example he set for
me, as well as for his saving and my mother's spending
proclivities—he made it and she spent it—an experience
which all of us husbands have come to experience and
endure.

Indeed, not until late in life did my father achieve
his ambition to be a farmer, but my mother constantly
achieved her ambition of seeing her children educated.

That meant more to her than anything she could ever do for herself. So first of all tonight I want to thank my mother and father for what little I have accomplished. They did not always agree with respect to the education of their children, but their disagreements in some way, at least as far as my brothers and sister are concerned, produced results. I only hope that through helping others I can in part repay them for what they did for me.

I would not have you think from this that we were the poorest of the poor, for I suppose that for those days we were average citizens with the ordinary problems of a medium-sized family of seven children. I am sure that we could not qualify under the story that the late Tony Lund, leader of the Tabernacle Choir, used to tell about his early days in Sanpete County. Tony said, "Ve vas poor. Oh, ve vas poor! Ve vas so poor dat all ve had vas pie plant and polygamy." But I do acknowledge with gratitude my early days in a humble home immortalized, however, by a mother who thought that humble circumstances were no bar to her children doing just as well as those on the sophisticated side of the tracks. It may be that this background has something to do with my firm conviction that "desire" is more important than "money" in obtaining an education and that the difference between one who obtains his education by his own and his family's efforts as compared with one who obtains it as a subsidy from the state, is comparable, in general, to the difference between our Revolutionary heroes and the paid Hessian soldiers!

I want also to acknowledge my indebtedness to my sweetheart, without whose help, affectionate understanding, and constant forgiveness I would never have succeeded at all. During most of my law practice and during my "easy" days at the BYU she has seldom seen me until late at night. Yet she has seldom complained and has been entirely responsible for the proper training of our five children, who are improvements on the old paternal generation. Indeed, I think she has done much better than if I had been around to interfere with her—

as I understand some husbands do. Lately, since she has been on the General Relief Society Board of her Church and participating in quarterly stake conferences at many places throughout the country, the tables have been turned. Instead of her being the widow I have become the widower in the family.

Her graciousness, which admittedly I do not possess, is illustrated by the fact that when I returned to become President of BYU I met one of my friends in this hotel. He had just read of my appointment. His frank and meaningful comment was conspicuous not only by what he did but did not say:

"Alice," he said, "will surely make a lovely president's wife." She has and she is.

Because this dinner is given under the auspices of the American Coalition of Patriotic Societies, I have been informed it is appropriate for me to pay reverence to the American patriots of the past for the purpose of reflecting on our own patriotic duties of today.

A month before the fateful conflict at Lexington and Concord in 1775, Patrick Henry, the great Virginia orator, declared words as real and true for our own day of peril as for his:

Is life so dear, or peace so sweet, as to be purchased at the price of chains and slavery? Forbid it, Almighty God! I know not what course others may take; but as for me, give me liberty or give me death!

Within a short time, however, after the War for Independence had broken out, many Americans became discouraged by the bad turn of events. But at this darkest point of the revolutionary struggle, Tom Paine gave great heart to Americans with these eloquent words from his pamphlet, *The Crisis:*

These are the times that try men's souls. The summer soldier and the sunshine patriot will, in this crisis, shrink from the service of their country; but he that stands it *now* deserves the love and thanks of man and woman.

Fortunately we had many heroes who did not shrink from the service of their country. When George Washington called for volunteers to go behind British lines to determine British strategy, Nathan Hale, a school teacher, fully aware of the tremendous risk, volunteered for the secret mission. Apprehended and convicted by the enemy, he bravely faced his execution by hanging, and uttered these imperishable words:

I only regret that I have but one life to lose for my country.

The fiercest naval battle of the War for Independence was fought in 1779 between *Bonhomme Richard*, the flagship of John Paul Jones, and Britain's *Serapis*. A British convoy of several valuable vessels was the prize and the two battleships fought all day. Jones' refusal to surrender—"I have not yet begun to fight!"—made him famous for all time. Faced with that heroic determination, the battered and broken *Serapis* struck her colors in the moonlight.

Under the shadow of threatening Civil War, another great patriot, Sam Houston, was to reap temporary hatred but eternal honor as he fought to keep his beloved Texas in the Union. As governor of the state he had been so instrumental in creating, he waged a tremendous struggle in 1860 to prevent Texan secession. He fought bravely and almost alone, and lost. But heedless of personal or political danger, he arose from a sickbed to make one final appeal for the Union:

I am denounced now. Be it so! Men who never endured the privation, the toil, the peril that I have for my country call me a traitor because I am willing to yield obedience to the Constitution and the constituted authorities. What are the people who call me a traitor? Are they those who march under the national flag and are ready to defend it? That is my banner! And so long as it waves proudly o'er me, even as it has waved amid stormy scenes where these were not, I can forget that I am called a traitor.

While Sam Houston was not successful then, time has vindicated not only his patriotism, but also his judgment, and the city of Houston, Texas, seventh in size of all our cities, now proudly bears his name.

There are, of course, hundreds of examples of the great patriots of the past and their legacy to us. Like

the senators in the golden days of Greece who served
without compensation, George Washington and Herbert
Hoover honored their high public trust so much that they
refused compensation while serving in the White House.

Nor has this patriotism been confined to those who
have represented us in battle or in public office. Andrew
Carnegie, who like my father was an immigrant boy from
Scotland, but who, unlike my father, amassed a fortune,
gave most of his away in the founding of libraries
throughout the country. His gratitude to his God and his
second homeland brought to America what at that time
was the most generous act of philanthropy in history.
His own patriotic code was described by him in these
words:

> This, then, is held to be the duty of the man of wealth: First,
> to set an example of modesty, unostentatious living, shunning
> display or extravagance; to provide moderately for the legitimate
> wants of those dependent upon him; and, after doing so, to consider
> all surplus revenues which come to him simply as trust funds, which
> he is called upon to administer, and strictly bound as a matter of
> duty to administer in the manner, which in his judgment, is best
> calculated to produce the most beneficial results for the community
> —the man of wealth thus becoming the mere trustee and agent for
> his poorer brethren, bringing to their service his superior wisdom,
> experience, and ability to administer, doing for them better than
> they would or could do for themselves.

Carnegie's patriotism consisted in giving his fortune
for the enlightenment of mankind.

These great patriots of the past displayed that spirit
of enterprise, that vision, that industry, and that rugged
independence which have been characteristic of our
America since its birth. Those qualities have brought us,
within a relatively short span of time, from the feeble-
ness of national infancy into the strength and glory of a
great, free republic.

Unfortunately, in some quarters today, the ideals of
patriotism are glossed over or ridiculed. *This Week* magazine recently made a survey of school history books issued
before 1920 compared with those issued since that time.
Patrick Henry's statement appeared in 12 of the 14 earlier

texts and in only 3 of the 45 recent ones. Nathan Hale's utterance appeared in 11 of the prior texts and only one of the recent ones. John Paul Jones' statement appeared in 9 of the old books and in none of the new. (April 1963 *Reader's Digest* article by Charles H. Brower "Let's Dare to be Square.")

George Bernard Shaw, the famous but cynical playwright and Fabian Socialist, once declared: "Patriotism is a pernicious, psychopathic form of idiocy." Thorstein Veblen, the so-called liberal American economist, who also believes that the free enterprise system of our founding fathers should be transplanted by a modern socialistic state, has said: "Into the cultural and technological system of the modern world, the patriotic spirit fits like dust in the eyes and sand in the bearings." Sad to say, there is an increasing number of Americans who agree with these opinions and find patriotism unfashionable.

Why has this deplorable philosophy developed among many in our society today? Perhaps we have become blinded by the "things of the world" and have allowed ourselves to become corrupt and cynical about our liberties, our civic virtue, public service, and public dedication. Too often we use the wrong standards in gauging our love of country. We talk today in terms of the "gross national product" and burdensome taxation, rather than in terms of "national honor," "voluntary giving" and development of integrity and individual and national character. Some of us may think that Americanism can be measured in terms of the number of bathtubs, cars, telephones, etc. that we possess. Heaven help us the moment a majority thinks in those terms!

Of course, we should be proud of our outstanding economic ingenuity which has produced under a free enterprise system remarkable riches, and remarkable advancements that stir the envy and the desire of the whole world. But if we rest on the laurels of our economic achievements, we are doomed. Such glory is not enough. When Rome was decaying within she thought she was invincible, because there were still the Roman legions,

the Roman swords, and Roman culture and law everywhere in the ancient world. But Rome was doomed, and
why? Because she had lost the sense of mission, the sense
of dedication above personal self. Hence, decay and corruption were inevitable. It was the boast of proud Augustus Caesar that he found a Rome of brick and left it a
Rome of marble. But he also found the Romans free.
He left them slaves. He found Romans hard-working,
self-reliant and self-supporting. He left them indolent,
dependent on the state for their sustenance and for subsidies.

Unfortunately, some of the influences which preceded
the downfall of Rome are evident today. Modern man
finds himself becoming softer in both physical and moral
fibre. He too often develops a vast contempt for work,
wanting a 6-hour day. He is often corrupted by the artificial and easy environment of urban life. Government
falsely tells him he is the equal of all other men, and science tells him that he is becoming totally exempt from
physical labor. The ideal of a mission or a dedication in
life is often fleeting rapidly away. We engage in self-
pampering and rationalization, and have a cynical dis-
regard for patriotic sentiment. Hence, "our boy is stuck
in the army," instead of "our boy is serving his country."
Sad to state, it seems that many of our countrymen have
forgotten Plato's famous admonition to the effect that
man is happiest when he pursues service to the point where
worldly matters become of little importance.

What can be done to halt the threatening decline,
the faltering image of America? I have no automatic
panaceas to offer, but I should like to suggest some lines
of thought for your serious study and possible action.

First, we should do all we can to minimize the corrosive influence of a society regnant with materialism. I
do not mean by this that we should curtail our commerce or business activities. It is important that we expand rather than contract our free enterprise economy.
But we should never let the *products* of our fabulous system become the *objects* of our worship. Nor should we

ever forget that the true greatness of our people will ever reside in the humble homes of our people rather than the marble splendor of our government buildings in Washington. When I learned that the recent marble Senate office building in Washington will cost $555,556 for the offices of a single senator who is being supported by taxes levied on all our people, many who cannot afford a $10,000 home, I cannot help but wonder whether the citadel of our federal government has become our master rather than our servant. I wonder also whether this marble, as in the days of Rome, is being purchased at the sacrifice of the self-reliance and well being of our people.

Second, just as Nathan Hale regretted that he had but one life to *lose* for his country, the duty of a patriot today is to regret that he has but one life to *live* for his country. For it is equally as important that we live to improve and enrich and ennoble our country as it is to die to prevent the destruction of our country. In this respect I fully subscribe to the exhortation of President Kennedy in his Inaugural Address when he summoned us to duty with these words:

> And so my fellow Americans, ask not what your country can do for you; ask what you can do for your country.

My only regret is that we are not following this admonition as a national policy. Instead, one of the campaign slogans of one of our national parties in a recent election was "What's in it for you?"

In my judgment the true patriot of today is he who at great risk of losing his present fortune, and with little likelihood of obtaining any added take-home pay, creates new industries and provides new jobs and employment for the growing army of the unemployed, many of whom are unemployed as a result of governmental policies which stifle growth. It does not consist in the acquisition of tax exempt securities and clipping coupons. It means, as it meant to Andrew Carnegie, that we are only stewards of the riches which God, by the use of our talents, has permitted us to acquire and that we should use them for

the benefit of our fellowmen—not, however, by confiscatory tax of the State, but rather by the spirit of adventure
and sacrifice and the joy of giving, which is the essence
of religion. The late Woodrow Wilson once gave expression to the same thought when he said the thing that
had made America great is not what it had done under
compulsion of law, but what it had done of its own
volition. We need to preserve and practice that free
volition.

Third, as patriots we should always remember that
the preservation of the American way of life and of our
liberties likewise means the preservation for ourselves
and our posterity of our property rights which are continually being eroded away. For there is no fundamental distinction between property and human rights.
The best statement on this subject of which I know is one
made by George Sutherland, an alumnus of Brigham
Young University, who became one of our distinguished
senators and the only man from this state ever to grace
the seats of the United States Supreme Court. In his address given to the American Bar Association, of which
he was president, he said:

> . . . Property, per se, has no rights; but the individual—the
> man—has three great rights, equally sacred from arbitrary inter-
> ference; the right to his life, the right to his liberty, the right to
> his property . . . To give a man his life but deny him his liberty,
> is to take from him all that makes his life worth living. To give him
> his liberty but take from him the property which is the fruit and
> badge of his liberty is to still leave him a slave.

May I ask you whether you consider your home a property right or a human right. Well, under our law it is a
property right and yet if we were ever deprived of the
right to own our own home we would all consider it a
loss of a human right.

Finally, we need to be rebaptized in the political
faith of our fathers and have a clear recognition, as stated
by President Grover Cleveland, that while it is our duty to
support our country it is never the duty of our country
to support us. These beliefs must be accepted as an in-

herent part of our faith, for I submit that man cannot either be vassals or mendicants of the state and still preserve the independence of thought and action that characterize a truly religious man.

I suggest that it is not without significance that concomitant with Great Britain's entry into socialism, the Church of England adopted an official report stating that the work of the churches must start from the premise that Britain is a pagan nation—over one-half of the population of that country belonged to no church. They had substituted the false god of socialism. And after socialism is once accepted it continues and has continued regardless of party.

Let us, therefore, as fellow Americans, proceed from this occasion with a new sense of dedication to our country. Let us not be ashamed that we love these United States of America and that we would exert any effort or endure any sacrifices for the sake of our country.

And so, Senator Mitchell, in the name of these patriotic principles which I have enumerated, I humbly accept the "Order of Merit" which you have conferred, pledging my feeble efforts to continue to proclaim them wherever and whenever time and strength will permit. As to the Certificate of Appreciation from the Patterson School for Boys, I only hope that my life will be an example for the boys attending that and similar institutions to rise to greater endeavor.

To all of you here tonight I express my deep gratitude for your presence—an honor from my neighbors and friends which I know I do not deserve. May God bless you for your kindness!

THE CHANGING NATURE OF AMERICAN GOVERNMENT FROM A CONSTITUTIONAL REPUBLIC TO A WELFARE STATE

(*An address given to the Brigham Young University student body, April 21, 1966*)

I approach this responsibility, which I have been invited by the forum committee to undertake, with humility and great concern because, as president of this institution, I am charged by the Board of Trustees with the awesome mandate of making sure that the truth, as revealed and understood by the Lord's prophets, is taught at this institution. When, therefore, as today, it becomes my responsibility to appear on this platform, I must be certain, as I am, that what I say conforms to the views of the living Prophet, even though my subject is not strictly of a theological nature.

I therefore plead with each of you this morning to give me of your faith and prayers that I may be faithful to my trust.

The Prophet Joseph once said that it was the duty of the prophets to advise us on temporal as well as spiritual matters and that the two are inseparably connected. President John Taylor also advised that the elders of Israel should

. . . understand that they have something to do with the world politically as well as religiously, that it is as much their duty to study correct political principles as well as religious.[1]

---
[1] *Journal of Discourses*, 9:340.

3

Besides the preaching of the Gospel, we have another mission, namely, the perpetuation of the free agency of man and the maintenance of liberty, freedom, and the rights of man.[2]

I know that there are some who try to differentiate between advice given by our leaders on religious matters and advice which they allege pertains to political matters, claiming that we do not need to follow the Prophet when he advises us on political matters. Of course we don't; neither are we required to follow him on spiritual matters; neither are we required to keep the Ten Commandments, for the Lord himself has given us our free agency. But if we are faithful members of the Church, and if we want the blessings of liberty for ourselves and our posterity, we are under the same moral obligation to follow his advice on political as on religious matters.

There are others who say that our leaders should confine themselves merely to discussions of the Standard Works of the Church. In one of the early meetings of our Church, one brother, in the presence of the Prophet Joseph, preached that doctrine, stating that "those who give revelations should give revelations according to those books" and "confine (themselves) to them." When he concluded, Brother Joseph turned to Brother Brigham and said, "Brother Brigham, I want you to take the stand and tell us your views with regard to the living oracles and the written word of God." Brother Brigham took the stand, and he took the Bible, and laid it down; he took the Book of Mormon, and laid it down; and he took the Book of Doctrine and Covenants, and laid it down before him, and he said: "There is the written word of God to us, concerning the work of God from the beginning of the world almost, to our day, And now," said he, "when compared with the living oracles, those books are nothing to me; those books do not convey the word of God direct to us now, as do the words of a Prophet . . . in our day and generation. I would rather have the living oracles than all the writing in the books. . . ." When he was through, Brother Joseph said to the congregation:

[2]*Ibid.*, 233:63.

"Brother Brigham has told you the word of the Lord,
and he has told you the truth."[3]

With this responsibility upon me, I propose today to
discuss certain public trends which are contrary to the
teachings of all the prophets of our Church and which
threaten the foundations of our Republic. I do this in
conformity with the special statement which President
McKay made to the general priesthood meeting at the
last conference of the Church, in which he said in part:

. . . Church members are at perfect liberty to act according to
their own consciences in the matter of safeguarding our way of life. . . .
They are free to participate in non-Church meetings which are held to
warn people of the threat of communism or any other theory or
principle which will deprive us of our free agency or individual
liberties vouchsafed by the Constitution of the United States.

The Church, out of respect for the rights of all of its members
to have their political views and loyalties, must maintain the strictest
possible neutrality. We have no intention of trying to interfere with
the fullest and freest exercise of the political franchise of our members
under and within our Constitution which the Lord declared "I
established . . . by the hands of wise men whom I raised up unto this
very purpose."

. . . we are continually being asked to give our opinion concerning various patriotic groups or individuals who are fighting
Communism and speaking up for freedom. Our immediate concern,
however, is not with parties, groups, or persons, but with principles.

We therefore commend and encourage every person and every
group who are sincerely seeking to study Constitutional principles
and awaken a sleeping and apathetic people to the alarming conditions which are rapidly advancing among us. We wish all our citizens
throughout the land were participating in some type of organized
self-education in order that they could better appreciate what is
happening and know what they can do about it.

Supporting the FBI, the police, the congressional committees
investigating communism, and various organizations which are attempting to awaken the people through educational means, is a
policy we warmly endorse for all people.

No member of this Church can be true in his faith, nor can any
American be loyal to his trust, while lending aid, encouragement, or
sympathy to any of these false philosophies; for if he does, they will
prove snares to his feet.[4]

[3]Wilford Woodruff, *Conference Report 10*, 97:232.

[4]Statement of President David O. McKay at the General Priesthood Session
of the General Conference of The Church of Jesus Christ of Latter-day Saints, April 9,
1966.

Please note that while the Prophet was speaking specifically of communism, he denounced not only communism but "any other theory or principle which will deprive us of our free agency."

I propose today to speak of one of those philosophies—the paternalism which leads inevitably to the "welfare state"—which debases and deprives man of his free agency, and which, unless arrested, will ultimately spell the doom of our Republic.

Elder Romney just recently spoke on the closely related subject of socialism, and what he said applies in general to my subject also. I choose this subject because, apart from living the gospel, there is nothing that is of as much importance to us at this time, for we are living in a political rather than a religiously organized society and everything the government does affects our lives. In the words of President McKay, we have an obligation to know "what is happening and what we can do about it."

I am aware that in theory, socialism is generally defined as "state ownership and operation of the production and distribution of goods." Stated another way, it means complete governmental ownership and management of all land and other property in the nation. We, of course, do not have complete socialism of that nature in our country, but since we are traveling in that general direction via the welfare state, I will sometimes use that term as a single indicator of the adverse trend we are taking.

At the present time, for instance, about 25 per cent of our utilities are owned by the government, and vast housing projects are governmental in nature. The government also owns and operates tens of thousands of businesses in direct competition with the taxpayers who pay for these government operations. Furthermore, approximately 40 cents of every dollar in this country is taken for taxation, and when taxes get that high, it doesn't make much difference whether the individual or the government owns the property, for the profits therefrom are going to the government anyway. In this respect, it is appropriate to quote some definitions:

If you want your father to take care of you, that's paternalism.
If you want your mother to take care of you, that's maternalism.
If you want the government to take care of you, that's socialism.
If you want your comrades to take care of you, that's communism.

But—if you want to take care of yourself, that's Americanism!

Any government with the power to give you anything you want is strong enough to take away everything you have.[5]

Some other definitions, which, while rather oversimplified, still point out humorously the differences existing in certain political and economic terms, are:

Socialism:	If you have two cows, the government takes one and gives it to your neighbor.
Communism:	If you have two cows, the government takes both and gives you some milk.
Facism:	If you have two cows you keep the cows, and give the milk to the government, and the government then sells you some of the milk.
Nazism:	If you have two cows, the government shoots you and keeps the cows.
Capitalism:	If you have two cows, you sell one and buy a bull![6]

Last year at the commencement exercises I gave an address on "The Decline and Possible Fall of the American Republic" in which I quoted from the Prophet Joseph and succeeding prophets (President Brigham Young, John Taylor, Joseph F. Smith, Heber J. Grant, George Albert Smith and David O. McKay), denouncing the general concepts of socialism and the welfare state. Because time will not permit me to repeat all those quotations, I respectfully refer you to that address which can be obtained at the Bookstore, or the Extension Publications Sales Area in the Herald R. Clark Building. I urge you to obtain that talk, not because I gave it, but because it contains a careful documentation of the advice given us by our prophets.

I will here content myself by merely saying that Joseph Smith categorically declared he did not believe in

[5]Anonymous.
[6]Anonymous.

"socialism";[7] President Brigham Young denounced socialism or the welfare state by saying, "It is a poor, unwise and
very imbecile people who cannot take care of themselves";[8]
President John Taylor described it as a "species of robbery";[9] President Heber J. Grant characterized it by saying,
"The Spirit that would have us get something for nothing
is from the lower regions";[10] and President David O.
McKay warned, "It is not the government's duty to
support you."[11]

Suffice it here to say that so far as I have been able
to ascertain, our prophets, their counselors and members
of the Council of the Twelve Apostles have been unani-
mous in condemning communism, socialism, and any
other ism which exalts the power of the state over the
liberty of the individual. These leaders have differed in
their political allegiances, but they have never differed
in their condemnation of the demoralizing influence on
individual character of any of these state isms.

In an address given at the Semi-Annual Conference
of the Church last October, President McKay said:

> Force rules the world today. . . . Unwise legislation, too often
> promoted by political expediency, if enacted, will seductively under-
> mine man's right of free agency, rob him of his rightful liberties,
> and make him a cog in the crushing wheel of regimentation.[12]

Elder Harold B. Lee gave utterance to the same
thought when he said:

> I want to say with all the sincerity within my soul that there
> is more guarantee of security in the intelligent will, initiative and
> determined independence of the American youth today than in all
> the laws that Congress may make intended to provide us with in-
> surance from the "cradle to the grave." Men who are dreaming of
> that kind of a security are not the kind that pioneered this country
> and explored the unknown. They are not the ones who built the
> world of today nor will they be the builders of the "new" world of
> tomorrow of which they speak. They are, as someone has said,
> "Only tenants in houses of other men's dreams."[13]

[7]History of the Church, 6:33.
[8]Journal of Discourses, 1870, 14:21.
[9]John Taylor, Government of God, 1852, p. 23.
[10]Albert E. Bowen, The Church Welfare Plan, 1946, p. 70.
[11]Church News Section, Deseret News, March 14, 1953, pp. 4, 15.
[12]Ibid., October 9, 1965, pp. 7-8.
[13]Ibid., June 23, 1945. Elder Lee's quote is from George Sokolsky.

With all of these prophetic utterances being condem-
natory of the current trend in our nation I come directly
to the prophecy attributed to the Prophet Joseph that
the Constitution of the United States would hang by a
single thread, but be saved by the Elders of Israel.

The first reference to substantiate this important
prophecy was given in a sermon by President Brigham
Young in the Old Tabernacle on the Temple Block on
Independence Day, July 4, 1854. In the course of his
address he said: "Will the Constitution be destroyed? No.
It will be held inviolate by this people; and as Joseph
Smith said, 'the time will come when the destiny of this
nation will hang upon a single thread, and at this critical
juncture, this people will step forth and save it from the
threatened destruction.' It will be so." (*Journal History*, July
4, 1854—Quoted *Deseret News* on December 15, 1948,
Christmas News.)

On February 6 and 7 of the following year, 1855, a
celebration was held in the Social Hall, by the surviving
members of the Mormon Battalion to commemorate their
long march to the Pacific, made in 1846-47. On this occasion President Jedediah M. Grant spoke of the same
prophecy in the following language: "We are friendly to
our country, and when we speak of the flag of our Union,
we love it, and we love the rights the Constitution guar-
antees to every citizen. What did the Prophet Joseph say?
When the Constitution shall be tottering, we shall be the
people to save it from the hand of the foe." (*The Mormon
Battalion*, Tyler, p. 350.)

Three years later, on January 3, 1858, Orson Hyde
was speaking in the Old Tabernacle in Salt Lake City. At
that time he made this significant statement: "It is said
that Brother Joseph in his lifetime declared that the Elders
of this Church should step forth at a particular time when
the Constitution should be in danger, and rescue it and
save it. This may be so; but I do not recollect that he said
exactly so. I believe he said something like this—that the
time would come when the Constitution and the country
would be in danger of an overthrow; and said he, 'If the

Constitution be saved at all, it will be by the Elders of this Church.' I believe this is about the language, as nearly as I can recollect it." (*Journal of Discourses*, Vol. 6: 152.)

Two years later, Eliza R. Snow, president of the Relief Society, gave her version of the prophecy in these words: "I heard the Prophet Joseph Smith say . . . that the time would come when this nation would so far depart from its original purity, its glory and love of freedom, and its protection of civil rights and religious rights, that the Constitution of our country would hang as it were by a thread. He said also that this people, the Sons of Zion, would rise up and save the Constitution and bear it off triumphantly." (*Deseret News Weekly*, Jan. 19, 1870, p. 556.)

Notwithstanding all these warnings of the prophets against the welfare state, we have for a period of at least 30 years been proceeding just about as fast as it is possible for a nation to proceed in the direction of the welfare state. Instead of believing that we are personally responsible, as individuals, for our own economic condition, we have fast been surrendering that responsibility to the state. It was about 20 years ago that Norman Thomas, a perennial Socialist candidate for President, refused to run again because he said the other parties were adopting socialistic principles anyway and that Socialists could obtain more success simply by joining the major parties. Maynard Kreuger, former Socialist candidate for Vice-President, also took the same general position, but specifically urged Socialists to join the "labor coalition" inside the Democratic Party.[14] At the same time, Earl Browder, head of the Communist Party in the United States, asserted that socialism or the welfare state had progressed further in the United States than in Great Britain, even under the Labor Party.[15]

The advice of Thomas and Kreuger to join the other parties has undoubtedly contributed to the fact that

---

[14]*U.S. News & World Report*, April 1, 1955, p. 57.

[15]Earl Browder, *State Capitalism and Progress* (Part I of *Keynes, Foster and Marx;* 2 Parts; Yonkers, New York, Earl Browder, 1950), pp. 29-30.

within the last 30 years America has enacted more
socialist-type legislation than during the entire previous
history of the Republic.

Although President John Kennedy, in his Inaugural
Address of 1961, exhorted us to "ask not what your
country can do for you, but what you can do for your
country,"[16] he immediately proposed to Congress a massive
welfare program, predicated on what the government could
do for us, including:

1. A massive and expensive program of federal aid to
   education;
2. An extension of unemployment compensation
   benefits;
3. A plan for federal aid to so-called "depressed
   areas";
4. A program for distributing food to the so-called
   "needy" through a food stamp plan;
5. A government medicare plan through Social
   Security;
6. An increase in the minimum wage level;
7. A broad, new federal housing program;
8. A new cabinet post for housing and urban problems;
9. A vigorous policy of government intervention in
   labor-management disputes (with obviously strong
   prejudice in favor of labor union interests);
10. A return to and extension of the public power
    planning of the "New Deal" whereby public
    power, finances by you and me as tax payers, is
    to be preferred to private power, which provides
    the taxes;
11. A fantastically irresponsible agricultural program
    providing government control over the farmer,
    while still offering him the juicy bribe of price
    supports;
12. And many other welfare programs.

---

[16]*Congressional Record*, Vol. 107, Part 1, pp. 10, 13. (Inaugural Address,
President John F. Kennedy, January 20, 1961.)

President Kennedy was unsuccessful in persuading Congress to pass most of these welfare state measures. But his successor, President Johnson, has prevailed upon Congress to approve practically all of them—together with others gleaned from his own fertile imagination—so that today we have largely turned our backs on the Republic of our fathers which was founded upon freedom of choice and political and economic freedoms as well.

If you think I am too harsh in characterizing our government as a welfare state, let me quote from President Johnson's own words in 1964, stating what he intended to do. I quote him word for word:

> We are going to try to take all of the money that we think is unnecessarily being spent and take it from the "haves" and give it to the "have nots" that need it so much.[17]

That is a statement of socialism and the welfare state in full bloom! That is a statement that the government is no longer our servant, but has become our master.

Now what has happened in our country during the time we have been plunging toward socialism? Are we actually at that point where the Constitution may be hanging by a single thread and we need to step in to save it?

One does not need to look very far or long in America to see evidences of the serious moral decay which has always preceded the downfall of any nation, for we should constantly remember that "Righteousness exalteth a nation; but sin is a reproach to any people."[18]

1. Increase in Crime: Crime is on the increase every year. The FBI estimates that serious crimes in this country may increase from 2,500,000 in 1964 to 4,000,000 by 1970.[19]

2. Juvenile Delinquency: From 1940 to 1948 juvenile

---

[17]*Ibid.*, Vol. 110, Part 5, p. 6142. (White House Speech to Senior Citizens. March 24, 1964.)

[18]*Proverbs*, 14:34.

[19]*Uniform Crime Reporting*, 1964 Preliminary Annual Release (for release Wednesday a.m., March 10, 1965), issued by J. Edgar Hoover, Director, FBI, U.S. Department of Justice, Washington, D.C., p. 1.

delinquency increased four times as fast as the growth in population.[20]

3. Divorce: One out of every four marriages in America now ends in divorce.

4. Welfare Rolls: From 1954 to 1964 the per cent of people on welfare rolls increased nearly three times as fast as the growth in population.[21]

5. Illegitimacy: President David O. McKay, at our last conference, pointed out that the increase in illegitimacy is alarming; that by 1970 ten million Americans will have been born out of wedlock.[22]

6. Civil Disobedience: Over the last few years we have had an alarming number of major riots, as in the Watts

---

[20]Utah State Legislative Council (Subcommittee on Juvenile Delinquency—in cooperation with Utah Training Center for the Prevention and Control of Juvenile Delinquency), "Juvenile Delinquency in Utah—A Survey of Problems and Resources," November, 1964, p. 8. (Mimeobrochure.)

[21]From 1954 to 1964 the population of the United States increased from 162,400,000 to 192,100,000, or 18 percent. During this same decade the number of people on relief in our country increased from 5,500,000 to 7,800,000, or 42 per cent. In New York City alone an additional 6,000 persons go on relief each month.

The cost for these welfare rolls in New York City have also increased rapidly, rising from $2.7 billion in 1954 to $5.1 billion in 1964, an increase of 90 per cent in the last ten years. From 1954 to 1964 the number of welfare cases in this area has increased 104 per cent from 1,984,000 in 1954 to 4,056,000 in 1964.

The immense cost of these federal, state, and local "public-aid payments" has increased from $1,200,000,000 in 1946 to $5,100,000,000 in 1964, and this *does not* include the $25,000,000,000 spent in 1964 in such related programs as Social Security pensions, unemployment compensation, and aid to veterans. (*U.S. News & World Report*, March 8, 1965, p. 40.)

The abuses of public welfare programs are scandalous. Not long ago two women and a girl of 14 appeared in a Philadelphia, Pennsylvania, courtroom. The women were the girls' mother and grandmother. All lived together in a small apartment, all were unmarried, and all had been made pregnant by the same man. They were in court to testify against him. One more common fact linked them: public welfare was supporting all three, and public welfare would support their children. ((Why the Dole Doesn't Work," *Reader's Digest,* March, 1965, p. 79.)

Rhode Island reports that one of its welfare families has drawn $50,000 from the public coffers, with no end in sight.

In Philadelphia, one hard core relief clan, with all the generations and the aunts and uncles, cost taxpayers $16,000 a year in welfare funds. ("Why the Dole Doesn't Work," *Reader's Digest,* March, 1965, p. 80.)

Cecil Moore, a Negro lawyer and the head of the NAACP in Philadelphia, says, "Go down into the area of my city where most of the relief people live. Hardly anyone there has any pride in himself. That's what public assistance has done for them. To me, relief is a self-perpetuating degradation, the worst thing that could have happened to my race." ("Why the Dole Doesn't Work. *Reader's Digest,* March, 1965, p. 83.)

[22]Church News Section, *Deseret News,* April 16, 1966, p. 6.

area of Los Angeles; civil disobedience regrettably seems to be the order of the day.

This alarming increase in crime and social disorder parallels and therefore strongly suggests a correlation with the growth of the welfare state. For after all, this trend is predicated on the pernicious philosophy that we should surrender to the power and policy of Caesar rather than rely upon the love of God and our individual efforts for the solution to all of our problems—that the government by mandate of law, rather than the individual by industrious righteous living, can cure all the ills of the world. You will recall that a similar plan for spiritual exaltation was rejected in the pre-existent world. Unfortunately, our country is now accepting a governmental mandate, not unlike the plan of Lucifer, for our economic way of life.

Major Trends of the Welfare State

Time will permit me only to discuss four major trends of the welfare state, which, if permitted to continue, could spell the end of our Constitution and Republic. And even as to them my discussion must be in summary fashion.

I.   Income Tax and Its Abuse.

The first of these is the income tax and its abuse. Our federal government needed a Constitutional amendment to permit such a tax, the Supreme Court having previously held, in several decisions, that it was alien to our form of government. A review of the debates in Congress reveals that when the amendment itself and the first income tax law were enacted, many senators voted in favor on the theory that such a tax would never be levied "in time of peace" but that it was necessary "to provide an income adequate for the carrying on of war."[23] Others were thinking in terms of a very small tax, beginning at the nominal rate of one-tenth of 1 per cent on incomes of $100 per annum.[24] One of the questions debated was whether corporations should be taxed 1 per cent or 2 per

---

[23]*Congressional Record*, Vol. 44, Part 4, pp. 4390-4391.
[24]*Ibid.*, Vol. 44, Part 4, pp. 4414-4415.

cent of their net profits.[25] Since those early, naive days we have had individual income taxes during peace time that soared as high as 91 per cent in the upper brackets, and in war time practically reached 100 per cent. Also, corporations with incomes of over $25,000, instead of being taxed a mere 2 per cent, have until recently been taxed 52 per cent.

II.   Usurpation of Power by Supreme Court

The second trend is what I choose to call the invalid usurpation of power by the judges of our "modern" Supreme Court—a trend so great that the Court has literally become a second unfettered legislative body, for its members are appointed for life. Up until the 1930's, consistent and long-respected interpretations of the Constitution made by that Court would have forbidden much of the so-called welfare legislation which has been enacted in the last 30 years.

But since that time, the judges of our Supreme Court (some of whom were appointed, not in my opinion because of judicial experience or ability or desire to interpret the Constitution, but because of their advocacy of social theories aimed at actually rewriting our Constitution) reversed approximately 150 prior decisions.[26] Many of these reckless steps were taken by five-to-four decisions. It is amazing to realize how powerful a single judge can become in a five-to-four decision on a major public issue dealing with our Constitution!

You may be shocked to learn that as of 1962 the total aggregate judicial experience of the nine Supreme Court justices at the time of their appointments was less than the years of experience of a single judge on the Arizona Supreme Court.[27] And yet the Supreme Court within the week has overruled this state court, holding that a state may not require a loyalty oath of its employees. From now on in order to work for the government, five

---

[25]*Ibid.*, Vol. 44, Part 5, Appendix, p. 70.

[26]Constitution of the U.S.A., Annotated, Senate Document 39, 88th Congress, 1st Session. pp. 1544-1547.

[27]*The Fact Finder*, Vol. 22, No. 15, Chicago, Illinois.

of the nine judges of the Supreme Court say it is no longer necessary to even profess to be loyal to the government.[28]

You may also be shocked to know that as of 1962, Mr. Justice Black, in 102 cases coming before that Court involving communism, or communists, or communist related sympathizers, voted in favor of the communist or communist sympathizer side on 102 occasions—a 100 per cent record.[29] Mr. Justice Black at one time admitted he had been a member of the Ku Klux Klan. Chief Justice Warren and Justices Douglas and Brennen each had a record of above 90 per cent in voting for decisions which favored communists or communist sympathizers.[30]

In fairness I should add that this does not mean the Supreme Court is in favor of communism, but it does mean that that Court (frequently by a divided vote) has gone a long way in protecting those who favor or sympathize with a philosophy of government which would destroy our own nation.

It may further interest you to know that on August 23, 1958, the chief justices of 36 state supreme courts, in a conference at Pasadena, California, in an unprecedented action, adopted a formal resolution, accusing the judges of the U.S. Supreme Court of abusing their Constitutional powers. The Honorable M. T. Phelps, Senior Justice of the Arizona Supreme Court, said:

> It is the design and purpose of the U.S. Supreme Court to usurp the policy-making powers of the nation. . . . By its own unconstitutional pronouncements, it would create an all-powerful, centralized government in Washington and subsequent destruction of every vestige of States Rights expressly and clearly reserved to the States under the Tenth Amendment of the Constitution.
>
> I honestly view the Supreme Court with its present membership and predilection, a greater danger to our democratic form of government and the American way of life than all forces aligned against us outside our boundaries.[31]

---

[28]Supreme Court Decision of April 18, 1966, *Elfbrandt v. Arizona.*
[29]*The Fact Finder*, Vol. 22, No. 15, Chicago, Illinois.
[30]*Ibid.*
[31]*Ibid.*

Since that time the Supreme Court, in my judgment, has become even more arrogant in setting itself up as the god of our political life.

Now I can understand why a distinguished Court would make a wrong or improper decision occasionally which would have to be revised. I can even understand why in certain limited situations, changing social and economic conditions may justify a reversal of prior decisions. But I submit to you that any group of judges who, over a period of 30 years, have revised 150 long-respected decisions (some of which had stood the test of a century) cannot claim to be validly interpreting the Constitution as originally conceived by our Founding Fathers. Rather, I submit many of its decisions strike at the very heart of our Constitution which was "established by the hands of wise men" whom a kind and wise Providence raised up for that very purpose. When the future history of this nation is written, I predict that scholars will tell us that our republican form of government was critically weakened by the "modern" judges of the U.S. Supreme Court. The result of these 150 unfortunate reversals is that the advocates of the all-powerful state have erected such a heavy structure of controls, subsidies and punitive taxation that, in the language of Admiral Ben Moreell, they

. . . have impaired the liberties of the individual to such an extent that many true liberals believe the cause for which the American Revolution was fought has already been lost.[32]

III. Deficit Financing and National Debt

The third trend which places our Constitution and country in great danger is that of deficit financing, which reversed a century and one-half of sound government practices based on the theory that we should pay as we go.

During the last 33 years the annual budget of our country has increased from less than $5 billion to well over

---

[32]Ben Moreell on "Moral Responsibility and Liberty" (Address to National Tax Association, Dallas, Texas, November 26, 1951), p. 8.

$100 billion. Actually the cash budget for next year will be over $140 billion.

Not only has our federal budget increased 20 times over, but, of more concern, our national debt has increased from $16 billion to an admitted $324 billion during this same period. This is the amount presently owed by the United States to creditors. If to this be added accrued liabilities payable in the future, our real indebtedness exceeds $1 trillion. I repeat, $1 trillion![33] That represents a terrible and tragic average indebtedness of $5,200 for every man, woman and child in the United States, or of over $25,000 for a family of five.

Now I know there are some who advocate the principle of deficit financing, saying that, after all, the government is different from an individual. All I have time to say in refutation is that, like individual debt, it may be all right until your creditors close in on you, and then for the individual, bankruptcy is inevitable; and for the government, either a repudiation of its debts, or the confiscation by taxation of individual property to pay the debts. And ex-Senator Byrd of Virginia, who was the Democratic Chairman for many years of the Senate Finance Committee, is authority for the statement that "The national debt is equivalent to the assessed value of all the land, all the machinery, all the livestock—everything of tangible value in the United States." (Verified by a letter from Byrd to Craig W. Christensen, July 20, 1961.)

In commenting on the huge federal debt, Congressman Charles Raper Jonas of North Carolina told the story of the new father who was looking through the window in a maternity ward in the hospital and saw all the newborn babies bawling. He turned to the nurse and said, "Why are all of the babies bawling?"

---

[33]I give this figure of $1 trillion on the authority of The Honorable Maurice Stans, Director of the Budget during the Eisenhower Administration. While it has been scoffed at by some, no serious attempt has been made to contradict it. On the contrary, it has been confirmed by The Honorable Otto E. Passman, Democratic Member of the House and Chairman of the subcommittee in charge of foreign appropriations. Furthermore, this figure does not even include additional billions of dollars in federal guarantees of home mortgage loans, bank deposits, savings and loan accounts, or the full amount payable under Social Security, etc.

"Mister," she replied, "if you were just one day old, wet and hungry, and already owed your part of the national debt, you'd be bawling too."[34]

There are others who say that our national indebtedness is increasing no faster than our Gross National Product since the latter part of the 1940's, so why worry. This is tantamount to saying that we shouldn't be concerned about our present crime wave as long as percentage-wise it doesn't increase any more. Furthermore, since the late 1940's the Gross National Product has been greatly increased by the factors of inflation, huge outlays of government expenditures for goods and services, and large expenditures for social benefits of many varieties, all of which are included in the Gross National Product.

In any event, if you think our present national indebtedness represents no danger, I merely ask whether you are prepared to pay your share of it, or whether you want it to increase further so your children and children's children will inherit an even larger mortgage to pay off.

IV. Loss of Basic Freedoms

The fourth suicidal trend resulting from the first three—confiscatory taxation, judicial usurpation, and fiscal insanity—is the loss of our basic freedoms in this country —past, present, and, ominously, the future.

The sad fact is that nearly every law being passed today is aimed actually at an *enlargement* of governmental power and a *curtailment* of individual liberties. However, because each separate law usually pertains only to a certain group, there is seldom any organized opposition. Obviously, the government wins by "dividing and conquering."

Summarily stated, a rough measure of eroded individual freedom consists of the amount of money that is taken away from citizens by our political authorities, and today the grim fact is that 40 cents out of each of our dollars is seized by local, state, and federal governments through the taxing power.

---

[34]Quoting Maxwell Droke, *The Speaker's Handbook of Humor* (New York: Harper & Brothers, 1956), p. 338.

We who have had the blessings of liberty given to us and who have never had to fight for them (even though we may have assisted other countries in defending their freedom) take liberty itself, I fear, for granted. We are now tolerating an entirely different concept of political power than that vouchsafed to us by our Constitutional Fathers. The form of republican government they originally established already stands in serious jeopardy. Oh, of course, the outward forms are the same—we still have a President, a Supreme Court, and a Congress—but in many areas of our life we now proceed on entirely different premises from those our fathers intended. In the words of Dean Inge:

> History seems to show that the powers of evil have won their greatest triumphs by capturing the organizations which were formed to defeat them, and that when the devil has thus changed the contents of the bottles, he never alters the labels. The fort may have been captured by the enemy but it still flies the flag of its defenders."[35]

In an address given at a general conference of the Church in 1941, the late Bishop Joseph L. Wirthlin stated that ". . . there has been an apostasy from those divinely given principles of government which have been transmitted to us by the inspired men who founded this great nation."[36] President Grant immediately endorsed every word of what he said, "with all my heart."[37]

Consequences of Government Programs

Now, after having summarily treated four major trends of the welfare state, let us note some of the alarming consequences and the obvious failure of some of its programs. Time will permit only a sampling of these.

Governmental Employment

Let's look first at governmental employment. During the first half of this century, federal employment increased ten times while our population only doubled. And between 1955 and 1965, total governmental employment (federal, state and local) increased two and one half

---

[35]As quoted by Admiral Ben Moreell, November 22, 1963. Found in Jerreld L. Newquist, *Prophets, Principles, and National Survival*, p. 339.

[36]Bishop Joseph L. Wirthlin, *Conference Report 10*, 41:70.

[37]*Ibid.*, p. 143.

times faster than the population. In 1955 there was one person on the public payroll to every eight in private employment; by 1965 the ratio was down to one to six.[38]

Federal Spending

Next let's consider federal spending. Whereas it required 160 years—from 1789 to 1949—for federal expenditures for *civilian purposes* to reach a level of $10 billion, it took only another 17 years—to fiscal 1966—to lift them from $10 billion to over $54 billion.[39]

Cost of Government

Now I come to the cost of government, which is one of the most alarming developments in our present culture. As a preface to this, may I point out that Colin Clark, a celebrated Australian economist, has claimed that socialism is inevitable in any country which, over a substantial period of time, takes 25 per cent or more of the national income. Well, does our government take that much? The answer, according to Roger Freeman of the Hoover Institution on War, Revolution, and Peace, is that:

> Governmental expenditures in the United States in 1964 equalled 32 per cent of the Gross National Product and 39 per cent of the national income, with most of those huge funds collected in the form of taxes.[40]

Public Welfare Programs

Now let's look at our public welfare programs. Some years ago the Federal Congress and state legislatures were promised that if we had an increased number of social workers we would "get people off the welfare rolls." So we appropriated huge sums for additional staff members. But since then, although the number of families with a cash income under $3,000 (in constant 1964 dollars) fell from 27 per cent to 18 per cent, the number of children on the Aid to Dependent Children rolls doubled.[41] Admittedly this was

---

[38]Roger A. Freeman, "Big Government—Friend or Foe?" Address at San Diego Open Forum, January 9, 1966, p. 5. Senior Staff Member, The Hoover Institution on War, Revolution and Peace, Stanford University.

[39]*Ibid.,* p. 6.

[40]*Ibid.*

[41]*Ibid.,* p. 10.

in part due to our liberalizing the eligibility requirements, but nevertheless, those on the rolls doubled. Actually in some cases our welfare programs have given encouragement to infidelity and illegitimacy, because such vices have been financially profitable.

Agricultural Policies

Now, what about our agricultural policies? Roger Freeman says,

At the rate at which we are going, the U.S. government will, within a few years, have poured the astronomical sum of $100 billion into farm price supports. But we are farther from a solution than ever and, in spite of all attempts at control, had another record farm crop last year. Suggestions by the country's largest farm organization that government prepare to get out of the program and ease into a free market are being cold shouldered.[42]

The primary reason for the present increase in cost of living is the increase in price of food; yet we still pursue our irresponsible farm policy.

Social Security

Let's go next to Social Security.

When the Social Security Act was proposed 30 years ago, Congress and the public were told that old age and survivors and unemployment insurance would slowly but surely reduce crime and juvenile delinquency, illegitimacy, family breakup and numerous other social ills. Coverage and benefits were later expanded several times, disability insurance was added, but public assistance rolls kept growing at a rapid rate through periods of rising income—as did the rates of crime, juvenile delinquency, illegitimacy, desertion and the other evils which the welfare programs were supposed to cure or at least improve.[43]

Urban Renewal Program

The Urban Renewal Program is, many claim, another example of misdirected governmental action. In a speech on May 27, 1962, New York Mayor Robert F. Wagner, one of America's leading liberal proponents of federal spending, made this public confession:

[42]*Ibid.*, p. 13.
[43]*Ibid.*

Once upon a time, we thought that if could just bulldoze the slums and build shiny new public housing for low-income people, all social problems involving these people would virtually disappear. This has turned out to be not so.

Once we thought that if we built enough playground and other recreational facilities, juvenile delinquency would disappear. This turned out to be not so.

Once we thought that having discovered a magic bullet to kill the micro-organisms that cause venereal disease, we had conquered venereal disease. That turned out to be not so.

In these and many other instances, we solved one problem and uncovered two others.[44]

In commenting on this, Roger Freeman says, "Too often, well-intentioned governmental action did not just uncover two new problems for one old one. It created them."[45]

Slum Clearance Program

Let's now notice the Slum Clearance Program. "In its 13 years it destroyed more than four times as many dwellings as it constructed. Moreover, nine out of every ten of the new apartments were beyond the reach of the poverty families whose housing had been torn down. . . . But does anybody believe that the urban renewal program will go anywhere but up—now that a newly created cabinet department can more effectively promote it?"[46]

Anti-Poverty Programs

Now let's look at the anti-poverty programs. Again I quote Freeman:

To abolish poverty is a noble idea but certainly no new idea. The American people have long been engaged in the most effective anti-poverty program the world has ever seen. . . . Between 1929 and 1963 the number of families with an income under $2,000 a year (1963 dollars) declined from 30 per cent to 11 per cent; of those under $4,000 income, from 68 per cent to 29 per cent.

. . . The theory that underlies the present federal programs is that poverty is a deficiency which is bound to perpetuate itself through generations unless eradicated by governmental action of the type now being initiated. If that hypothesis were true, most of

---

[44]*Ibid.*, p. 14.
[45]*Ibid.*
[46]*Ibid.*

America's 194 million residents would still be poor, ignorant and unemployed as their ancestors were when they landed on these shores. . . .
The American record suggests that . . . poverty . . . can best be
remedied . . . by the individual."[47]

Now why is it that these huge governmental spending
programs are not successful? The reason is so simple that
it generally escapes our notice. The reason, is, in the words
of Freeman, that "there is no limit to human wants or
desires." But in a private economy we can only have what
we pay for, and so the demand is kept within reasonable
limits.

In a governmental economy, on the other hand, we
live under the delusion that public service and goods "come
'for free' with the cost borne by somebody else, or by that
distant abstraction 'the government.' And as long as services or goods can be had gratis or below cost, demand will
always exceed supply," and the government will never
be able to keep up with the demand.

The sad part, also, is that any huge spending program
can seldom be terminated.

Its protagonists or recipients will deny that it has failed and
explain results which did not come up to promises as the consequence
of insufficient funding and inadequate time. According to its
spokesmen, there is nothing ever wrong with a public program that
could not be corrected by doubling appropriation and staff, extending
coverage and territory, or boosting salaries.[48]

Unfortunately, however, the extension and enlargement of many of these programs only aggravates and
compounds the evils of the wrong approach.

Now, I would not have you think from my hurried
denunciation of the welfare programs to which I have
referred that no good of any kind will come from them.
But I do say that in the long run the benefits will be only
transitory and fleeting, and that in the long run, as ap-
praised by our prophets, and as confirmed by the history of
past civilizations, they will be destructive of the character
of our people and, unless terminated, cause the collapse of

[47]*Ibid.*, p. 16.
[48]*Ibid.*, pp. 12-13.

our government. The danger is that our people will look more and more to government, and less and less to their own efforts, which, when carried far enough, will inevitably mean the downfall of our Republic.

Nor would I have you think that I am unsympathetic to the poor, or those in the lower income bracket. As one who was raised in a poor family, I am very sympathetic to their needs. But the solution to their problem is not to have them live off the government. Rather, it is to teach individuals the proper concepts of industry and Christian living which will make them self-supporting and productive members of our society.

I realize and understand that there are plausible theories behind much of our social legislation, but similar theories which were advanced in other civilizations did not stand the test of actual practice. I also realize that many who advocate the current social legislation are as sincere in their advocacy of it as I am in my opposition. While I respect their sincerity, it has little to do with the validity of either position.

While we face some very real social problems, we can solve them only, in the words of Joseph Smith, by teaching "correct principles," in which event the people "will govern themselves." Reliance upon the government to solve these problems only aggravates and spawns more problems and at the same time destroys free agency and private initiative, and in some cases the self-respect of those receiving governmental help.

There are many things which can be done which I regret I do not have time to discuss, but let me briefly mention three things which, as students, you can do in defense of our liberty and constitutional Republic:

First, study diligently and become well informed both with respect to the founding of our Republic and the teachings of our prophets, both ancient and modern. Keep abreast of current affairs.

Second, live a righteous life. Develop a concern for those less fortunate than yourself. Give help to them through the welfare program of the Church, and also through other private endeavors, which help them to help themselves. Never underestimate the power of a righteous example. Theological history is replete with examples of the tremendous power of a righteous minority on a society or nation. Our Church will be blessed by your righteous involvement in its programs and activities and by your witness of its divine origin and that the Church is the veritable kingdom of God on earth which will bless the entire world (D&C 45:9). It is the Lord's divine instrument for spreading His Gospel, which includes the preservation of freedom throughout the world.

Third, go to work in promoting and advocating the cause of freedom in our constitutional Republic, and in electing good and wise men to public office on the local and national level, who understand these principles and who will both defend and advance them. Always remember that, in the words of an anonymous writer:

1. You cannot bring about prosperity by discouraging thrift.
2. You cannot strengthen the weak by weakening the strong.
3. You cannot help small men by tearing down big men.
4. You cannot help the poor by destroying the rich.
5. You cannot lift the wage-earner by pulling down the wage-payer.
6. You cannot keep out of trouble by spending more than your income.
7. You cannot further the brotherhood of man by inciting class hatred.
8. You cannot establish sound security on borrowed money.
9. You cannot build character and courage by taking away man's initiative.
10. You cannot really help men by having government tax them to do for them what they can and should do for themselves.

On a national scale, the only remedy for mounting socialism is that of "political repentance" and the assumption of individual responsibility. And the latter involves personal repentance by the indolent and the uncharitable alike.

As to the real need for political repentance, I summon as my witnesses the first and the last great leaders of the

Democratic Party, Thomas Jefferson and Woodrow Wilson. Of course, others since Wilson's day have claimed to be Democrats, but Wilson was the last to really follow the philosophy of Jefferson—the others have in large part proclaimed the welfare state philosophy.

Thomas Jefferson gave us the great political concept that that nation governs best which governs least. He went further and stated that if he had to choose between a government and a free press, he would choose the press because he had more faith in the *voluntary action* of the people than compulsory action required by the state.

Woodrow Wilson, a half century ago, pointed out that the history of liberty is "the history of limitations of governmental power, not the increases of it." He further stated:

> When we resist the concentration of power, we are resisting the powers of death because concentration of power is what always precedes the destruction of human liberties.[49]

Abraham Lincoln posed the question of whether we could survive half slave and half free. I pose the question of whether we can survive when practically all drink at the public trough and thereby become slaves of the state. After all, the government never produces wealth; it merely consumes it. It can exist only by taxing and seizing wealth of individuals. I submit that by the verdict of history, the limit to this taxing has already been passed.

Alexis de Tocqueville, the observant French writer who studied the noble American "experiment" over 130 years ago, made this acute and penetrating statement:

> I sought for the greatness and genius of America in her commodious harbors and her ample rivers, and it was not there; in her fertile fields and boundless prairies, and it was not there; in her rich mines and her vast world commerce, and it was not there. Not until I went to the churches of America and heard her pulpits aflame with righteousness did I understand the secret of her genius and power. America is great because she is good, and if America ever ceases to be good, America will cease to be great.[50]

---

[49]Woodrow Wilson, Address to New York Press Club, May 19, 1912. Found in George Seldes, *Great Quotations*, p. 750.

[50]Alexis de Tocqueville, *Democracy in America*, 1835; also Newquist, p. 60.

Unfortunately, today too few of our churches are "Aflame with righteousness." Altogether too many of them and other organizations are talking of "co-existence with communism," or "the new morality," or preaching the nonsense that "God is dead." I am happy that on this campus, at least, we still believe in industry, hard work, virtue, honesty, clean lives and that there is a God in the heavens. I am proud that we have no one burning draft cards and that, in the words of Daniel Webster, we are aware that "God grants liberty only to those who love it, and are always ready to guard and defend it."

I am aware that there will be some who will attempt to characterize this address as politically partisan. Admittedly, my address has to do with probably our most important current political problem, but it is not partisan, for I have relied largely on great leaders of the Democratic Party for my quotations. The vice of the welfare state is that it is supported by many in both parties. Fortunately, it is also opposed by statesmen in both parties. I am concerned, not with parties, but with principles. While the party in power must take the responsibility and blame for the welfare programs it has enacted, there are some Democrats for whom I would prefer to vote than some Republicans, because they have not sold out to the welfare state. It is the duty of those of us who believe in the Constitution of our fathers to resist the welfare state at every turn in both parties. My only concern, as I said at the outset of my talk, is to make sure that what I say is in accord with the views of our living Prophet, and of this I am sure. I would sooner follow him than any political leader.

Some of you young men here today may be called upon to pay the supreme sacrifice in defense of Vietnamese liberty, and to protect our own United States from the ever encroaching menace of communism. In the name of Jesus Christ, I pray that the rest of us will have the intelligence, the foresight and the courage to reverse the tragic welfare trend in our country so that when our fighting men return from having fought for the freedom of others, they will find that their own country is still the land of the free and the home of the brave. Amen.

THE FOUNDING, FRUITION, AND FUTURE OF FREE ENTERPRISE

(*This address was given at the first general session of the U.S. Chamber of Commerce, May 1, 1961. For this dynamic speech, Dr. Wilkinson was awarded the George Washington Medal of the Freedoms Foundation at Valley Forge.*)

Each generation of free men has its rendezvous with destiny, for freedom can never be vouchsafed from one generation to another. One generation, as did our Revolutionary Fathers, may win it on the battlefield. Another generation, as we are now doing, may allow their government to wrest their freedom from them.

Our rendezvous today will determine whether we shall continue to live in a "land of the free and home of the brave." or whether we shall go worship the false god of paternalistic government, that in due time we shall join 20 recorded civilizations which have come and have gone —not by conquest from without, but because of the surrender of individual freedom and responsibility to a central, all-powerful government.

Everywhere we hear the hue and cry of Soviet accomplishments in education, science and space technology. To face this challenge the President of the United States, with statesmanlike vision, summons us to duty with these words:

"And so, my fellow Americans: ask not what your

country can do for you—ask what you can do for your country."

This has the ring of our Revolutionary Fathers who pledged, on the altar of freedom, their lives, their fortunes and their sacred honour.

On the other hand, the same President, in derogation of his inaugural address, has now proposed 16 governmental programs which confer special privileges or grant governmental bounties to various segments of our society; such as federal aid to teachers, increased subsidies to farmers, higher minimum wages and increased unemployment benefits to laborers, medical care to the aged, increased federal housing for urban dwellers, etc., etc., etc.

In which of these two directions shall we go? Shall we proceed in the direction of Soviet Russia, where all power and one's position, status, and support emanate from the state? Or shall we revert to the philosophy of our founding fathers who believed that while it is our duty to *support our country,* it is never the duty of our *country to support us.*

In the few moments I have this morning, I propose to analyze these alternatives by briefly tracing the founding, fruition, and challenging future of free enterprise in this country, in contrast to a regimented or collectivist economy.

The essence of the free enterprise system is the freedom to initiate, venture, develop, and produce without interference or restraint, except for *safeguards* to protect *similar rights* of others; and the incentives which come from the right to enjoy the fruits of one's own labor.

I. *The Founding of Free Enterprise*

Free enterprise in this country began with Jamestown. Originally plagued by communal ownership of property, and by a stronger desire to demand *equal shares* than to contribute *equal* labor, this colonizing effort almost ended in disaster. It was saved only by new pioneers who were willing to labor long and hard, with the realization that they would enjoy the fruits of *individual* ownership of their lands and crops.

The Pilgrim fathers had the same experience. Originally agreeing that they would own everything in common, they so lost their initiative that they nearly died of starvation. As Governor Bradford wrote in his diary, they had thought they were "wiser than God," who gave every man his freedom. And so, they turned away from communal ownership and gave each family a parcel of land. And when the harvest was gathered, instead of famine they had plenty.

This experience was repeated 150 years later. During the early part of the Revolutionary War, the Continental Congress took over the economic control of all 13 colonies and its people. However, so disastrous were the consequences that one year before Cornwallis's surrender to Washington, that Congress, in a forthright reversal of policy, repealed all economic control. Freed of this restraint our forefathers proceeded to win their freedom. Then, under the inspiration of God, our Founding Fathers gave birth to our Constitution, described by Gladstone as "the greatest document ever struck off by the hands of men." In this document they gave to the world a new nation, conceived in liberty, and dedicated to the hope that all succeeding generations by following its God-given precepts would remain forever free.

Their dislike of government domination was expressed by none other than George Washington, the father of our country, in these words:

"Government is not reason, it is not eloquence—it is a force. Like fire, it is a dangerous servant and a fearful master."

James Madison, a democrat oft referred to as the father of our Constitution, in explaining its safeguards against the loss of liberty, warned us of the *perils of our own time,* in these words:

"I believe there are more instances of the abridgment of the freedom of the people by gradual and silent encroachment of those in power than by violent and sudden usurpations."

Thomas Jefferson, founder of the Democratic party, advised us not only that that government governs best which governs least, but warned against the *dangerous situation* which *haunts* us today. Said he:

"I place economy among the first and most important virtues, and public debt as the greatest of dangers to be feared . . . To preserve our independence, we must not let our rulers load us with perpetual debt. . . . We must make our choice between *economy* and *liberty,* or *profusion* and *servitude.* . . . If we can prevent the government from *wasting* the *labors* of *the people,* under the *pretense* of *caring for them,* they will be happy."

In line with these utterances, none of our early presidents ever proposed any governmental policy which would interfere with or regulate private control of agriculture and industry. Andrew Jackson objected to the Bank of the United States because he felt that it was an unfair monopoly, aided and abetted by government. He also raised serious questions about government-sponsored monopolies in the building of canals, bridges and turnpikes.

And while we generally think of Lincoln as the preserver of the Union, he was also a strong apostle of the American free enterprise system. In emphasizing the dangers that free men always face, he pointed out that "Capital is only the fruit of labor," and that "capital" is as "worthy of protection as any other rights." (*First Annual Message to Congress,* December 3, 1861). He further warned his fellow citizens against "surrendering a political power" which would "close the door of advancement against" them and "fix new disabilities and burdens upon them, till all of liberty shall be lost."

Grover Cleveland, when he was presented with a legislative bill providing for a very modest federal gift of seeds to farmers, vetoed it on the ground "that though the people should support the government, the government should not support the people."

Woodrow Wilson warned us that "the history of liberty is the history of limitations of governmental power, not the increases of it." He therefore never wanted to see the little red schoolhouse subordinated to the political thinking of Washington; nor did he, in his own language, "want a group of experts sitting behind closed doors in Washington, trying to pray Providence to" the American people.

The same philosophy was expressed by Herbert Hoover when he said:

> Freedom conceives that the mind and spirit of man can be free only if he be free to pattern his own life, to develop his own talents, free to earn, to spend, to save, to acquire property as the security of his old age and his family.

Even Franklin Delano Roosevelt, before he became President, recognized and applauded the limitations on our federal government that our Constitutional Fathers intended. As governor of New York he publicly declared:

> The Constitution of the United States gives Congress no power to legislate in the matter of a great number of vital problems of government, such as the conduct of public utilities, of banks, of insurance, of business, of agriculture, of education, of social welfare, and of a dozen other important features. Washington must never be permitted to interfere in these avenues of our affairs.

And more recently, Dwight D. Eisenhower in somewhat the language of George Washington concluded:

> Every step we take toward making the State the caretaker of our lives, by that much we move toward making the State our master.

Finally, as late as 1950 a Senator from Massachusetts by the name of John F. Kennedy (*Boston Post*, April 23, 1950), expressed the American ideal in these words:

> The scarlet thread running through the thoughts and actions of people all over the world is the delegation of great problems to the all-absorbing leviathan—the state. . . . Every time that we try to lift a problem to the government, to the same extent we are sacrificing the liberties of the people.

Until the advent of the New Deal in 1932 the political philosophy of free enterprise of our Founding Fathers was uniformly followed by all presidents regardless of party. The one great exception was the enactment of the *graduated* income tax law in 1913, which is the most signif-

icant legislation of this century. It came into being only
by virtue of a constitutional amendment, the Supreme
Court having held that such a concept was alien to the
organic law as framed by our Constitutional Fathers. And
even then the proponents of the measure were laboring
under the honest delusion that in peace time the tax would
not exceed 2 per cent, but in times of war it might "soar"
to 5 per cent. Instead it has now pyramided to extremes
beyond the wildest dreams ever envisioned by Karl Marx
in his Communist Manifesto. While this statute did not
in itself change the functions and scope of our government,
it nevertheless gave Congress a new vast and dangerous
taxing power, under which Congress now finances programs which do change the original scope and purposes
of our government.

II.   *The Fruition of Free Enterprise*

With the American philosophy of free enterprise as
the basis of our economic system, until at least the 1930's,
America plunged ahead into her dynamic future. By
the turn of the 20th Century, she had become a tremendous and colorful example of the free enterprise system at
work and had attained preeminence in the entire world.
The steel furnaces in Pittsburgh alone outproduced those
in England and Germany combined. New manufacturing
marvels of every sort had been invented and were already
in production. These were giving Americans the highest
standard of living known to the entire world. By the 1920's
our country was recognized as the world's greatest economic power.

With the advent of the great depression, however, in
the 1930's, we began to accept the philosophy that we
could no longer rely on the sweat of our own brows, on
our own ingenuity and resourcefulness as God's children,
but that instead we had to rely upon the paternalism and
largesse of government. In the intervening 30 years we
have fast lapsed into a welfare state (more correctly, the
"illfare state"). For it is based on the theory that as a people
we are seriously ill and have to call in the government as
our physician.

Up until that time we had been protected from the evils of socialism in this country by the uniform decisions of the Supreme Court which consistently followed the political and economic philosophy of our Constitutional Fathers, and forbade the government from unduly regulating our lives. But this judicial protection of 150 years was ended by the appointment of new justices to the Supreme Court, who, right or wrong, did not confine themselves to interpreting the Constitution in the light of its history and language, but imported into the Constitution external social concepts, which were theretofore alien to our philosophy. Congress became the last bastion for the defense of freedom against governmental encroachment. But instead of adhering to the political faith of our Constitutional Fathers, Congress seized upon the relaxations of the Supreme Court as a field day for curtailment of free enterprise, and the enlargement of governmental powers.

As a result, we now have, among others, the following practices:

1. Annual federal aid to states, localities, and individuals, which amounted to less than $150 million in 1930, has now soared to over $9 billion—more than the total budget of the federal government in any one year prior to World War II. This has to a large extent undermined the sovereignty of the states.

2. Whereas in 1920 government-owned electric utilities accounted for only 5% of the electric power generated in this country, they now account for 25%.

3. One in every six employed Americans is now on a government payroll (national, state, or local). Today over 17 million people are receiving checks from the federal government.

4. Since our entry in World War II, our economy has been under some form of price or wage controls for eight different years. Agricultural price-support programs actually commenced with the New Deal and still exist to this very day!

5. The housing industry is financed or guaranteed largely with government money.
6. The shipping industry is heavily subsidized by the government.
7. Through TVA, and similar huge government projects, whole areas of the nation are in large part dependent on the government.
8. In actual practice the government now fixes hours and conditions of employment, and is intimately involved in wage bargaining.
9. Old and disabled people have become the wards of government. Furthermore, Congress is now in the process of seducing "young men" of 62 to retire and live off the federal treasury. For they will not be drawing out monies paid in for social security. That money was never set aside for its intended use, and has long since been spent on innumerable government projects, and current social security payments already exceed current social security tax collections (1958, 1959 and 1960).
10. The federal debt when FDR came to power was $22.5 billion. It is now around $300 billion. But this is only a part of the story. When you add to the present indebtedness, *accrued* liabilities for services already rendered or goods already delivered, the total federal debt is $750 billion, a sum which represents an indebtedness of $4,100 for every man, woman and child in the United States! The interest we pay on our national debt alone is now twice the amount of the entire federal budget when FDR came to power, and no substantial effort is being made to pay it off.

With these situations in mind, one speaker, in addressing a farm audience, referred to this as the status quo of our times. One of his listeners promptly quipped that that was Latin for "the hell of a mess we are in."

III. *The Future of Free Enterprise*

And now with the Marxist political platform of Los Angeles, which *profanely invokes* the name of Jefferson, and the tendency of many so-called conservatives not to oppose but to merely offer milder socialistic alternatives, it is proposed that we be launched on a new and greatly enlarged extension of governmental paternalism.

We are now to be given medical care by the federal government while we are yet unborn. We are to be educated by the federal government regardless of whether our local or state governments are able to pay the bill. If in agriculture, we are to be further seduced and subsidized by the government. If in industry, we are to be paid a subsistence out of the taxes of our employers while we strike against them. When we get old we are to be hospitalized and kept by the state. And because, when we die, there will be millions to be buried, we can expect a federal aid program to encourage the states to assume the cost of burial and perpetual tomb-stone care. For any other method would not satisfy our sense of democratic social justice nor conform to the prevailing liberal interpretation of the "general welfare" clause of the Constitution!

I ask you, ladies and gentlemen, whether with this kind of paternalism Americans can long remain fearless and free; whether we really believe that to meet the communist challenge we must continue to more and more adopt the regimented economy of the Soviet State; or whether we want again to rely upon the voluntary action and free economy of a God-fearing people. Woodrow Wilson once gave utterance to the last alternative when he said the thing that had made America great is not what it has done under compulsion of law, but what is has done of its own volition.

The tragedy of our time is that during the last 30 years we have fast adopted the ornaments and shackles of an illfare state. On the other hand, the Soviet Union has been adopting certain principles of free enterprise. Thus, in one of his recent conferences, Khrushchev ridiculed the confiscatory nature of our taxes which ascend to 91% of a man's income, pointing out that in Russia the limit is 16%. In recent years, Khrushchev has also introduced wage incentives and other capitalistic reforms.

If we accept the alternative of the free historical American economy, the question then becomes that of how our country can be cured from its present malady—lest the greatest country in the world will conduct a funeral for free enterprise, which means to bury itself.

It my humble judgment there are six ways or programs by which our country can be brought back to normal health and such a funeral avoided.

1. Do Something for Your Country

The first way is that of accepting the philosophy of the President's Inaugural Address rather than his legislative program. We can have no double standard in this country of stating at one time that our survival as a free nation depends on what we can do for our country and at the same time proposing a legislative program founded primarily on governmental handouts to its people.

The only way to compete with the zeal of the Russians for their system is to re-acquire the self-sacrificing patriotism of our fathers, and to rely upon the sweat of our own brows. If we abandon the false god of governmental paternalism and re-enthrone individual integrity, genius, responsibility, and economic rewards, we will widen, and not narrow, the gap between our productive capacity and that produced by Soviet slave labor. At the same time we will start paying off our national debt and not continue, as Lenin said we would do, to spend ourselves into bankruptcy.

2. Avoid Double Standards

The second method by which we can avoid the funeral of free America is by a revived and rededicated devotion of our own to the cause of freedom and our system of free enterprise. If we really believe in it, we must ourselves practice it. We must not be guilty of any double standards ourselves. We must not ourselves give lip service to competition and at the same time violate the anti-trust laws which are designed to foster free enterprise by competition.

If we are going to criticize government handouts for the other fellow, we must not ourselves sup at the public trough. If the payment of subsidies to farmers is morally and economically wrong, by what right does the government subsidize the shipping industry? If the guarantee of loans to veterans and others for housing is wrong, by what right are businessmen entitled to loans on preferred terms to keep their businesses going? If the educator is right in deploring the lowering of the moral standards of the nation resulting from government handouts, by what right does he ask the government to subsidize his university? If we in the West are critical of the federal government using our taxes for slum clearance in New York City, by what right do we ask the federal government to build federal electric power lines to our farms and cities and give us preferential rates over those taxpayers who pay for these power lines?

3. Support Development Organizations

My third program for the preservation of our free enterprise is that we ought to be willing to pay the price of its preservation by properly financing those who fight its battles. American business is often penny wise and pound foolish in its expenditure of both time and funds for the defense of the free enterprise system upon which its survival depends. For the most part, chambers of commerce, taxpayers and citizen research agencies, even trade organization, are starved for funds. Particularly is this apparent when comparisons are made with the millions poured by labor into union and political action treasuries, much of which is spent for promoting the regimentation of our economy.

Even more basic is the unwillingness of top flight businessmen to accept, or if they do accept, to devote the necessary time and energy to civic and trade group appointments, which are established to study and to formulate policies and procedures pertaining to local, state, or national problems. If businessmen refuse to take any leadership in local civic affairs, by what right can they blame local citizens from seeking government counsel and leadership in local affairs?

4. Demand Fair Treatment

My fourth program for preventing the liquidation of our system of free enterprise is that the government be fair and consistent in its dealings with all segments of our economy—it must observe the Golden rule of doing unto one group what it does unto another. It must not have a double standard whereby it imprisons businessmen for conspiring to fix prices and at the same time promotes and encourages unions to conspire to fix wages. And if you think it is impossible to correct the present double standard, let me quote from none other than Franklin Delano Roosevelt:

> It will never be possible for any length of time for any group of the American people, either by reason of wealth or learning or inheritance or economic power, to retain any mandate, any permanent authority to arrogate to itself the political control of American public life.

On the authority of his statement I give you the challenge, without respect to party, to correct the present one-sided political control of our public life.

5. Push for Economic Progress

My fifth proposal deals with legislation needed for the immediate present, of which you will hear more throughout this conference—all of which is designed for America to make progress through voluntary action and to achieve better jobs for more people. This legislation is not in the direction of stifling but of freeing the economy.

First of all we must increase our rate of new investment. As I understand the situation, Russia at the present time is putting 25% of its productive capacity into capital goods. In our country we are putting only 10% into capital goods. We can increase the percentage if we have *intelligent* tax reforms, promote judicious utilization of savings, promote the availability of credit for plant investment, and obtain the right to faster and more realistic depreciation write-offs. Programs of this kind will do more to alleviate the anxiety and misery of those who are out of work than any amount of government subsidies. I congratulate the President on making a proposal of this kind in his tax message to the Congress.

Next, there must be *increased mobility of labor and resources.* This can be best achieved by more widespread information regarding job opportunities and by breaking down local and state barriers to the free movement of persons and goods. Furthermore, we must rid ourselves of un-American union restrictions on freedom of occupation, and vigorously oppose all forms of payments for work not actually performed.

In addition, there must be an *increase in the flexibility in both directions of wages and prices.* In the interest of further opportunity for the free American workman we must not put men in straight jackets by adopting rigid rates and prices. For similar reasons we must question industrywide collective bargaining and long-term contracts which provide for annual wage cost increases, regardless of productivity or prosperity.

Next, legislation should *increase the flow of invention and innovation!* This is one of the unique advantages of the American system—it permits genius and labor to enjoy the fruits of their talents and every laborer to climb as high as he can on the ladder of economic success. To that end we must oppose any increase in government-held or controlled patents. Furthermore, we must always seek better means of increasing effective and legitimate competition. Monopoly stultifies, but competition energizes, our economy!

Finally, we must *increase our exports in international trade.* Brisk trade in great volume is important to our economic health and welfare. American "know-how" is still a very precious ingredient of our free enterprise system. We should not hesitate to use it with great vigor and great purpose.

6. Educate for Free Enterprise

My sixth and last proposal for the preservation of our economic freedom is to insist that our schools educate our students in the gospel of free enterprise. Here again we must do away with our double standard of giving lip service to and living off our American system of free enterprise while at the same time we either fail to teach its principles, or, in many cases, teach concepts which would destroy it.

Probably fewer than one out of every 20 of all high school students takes even one course in economics, and only about one-fifth of all college students do so. And much of what little is taught is weak, misleading, or even wrong—in many cases it does more to prejudice students against than to convert them to free enterprise.

The reason for this is not hard to find. The best estimate available is that fewer than one-tenth of all elementary and fewer than one-fourth of all secondary school teachers (majoring in social sciences) *take even one course* in economics while at college. In fact, it is estimated that nine out of every ten teachers colleges fail to have a single economist on their faculties. Over three-fourths of our states do not demand a course in economics as a requirement for certification. The remedying of this dangerous situation is a program worthy of this great organization.

I submit that businessmen themselves are largely to blame for the dearth of economic literacy in the country. The boards of trustees of most institutions of higher learning and the boards of education of most secondary and elementary schools are largely officered by businessmen. What have they done to become acquainted with the curricula of their various institutions? What have they done to make sure that teachers basically trained in the principles of free enterprise system are employed? In many cases not only have they done nothing but they have recommended to their various business corporations that they contribute to educational institutions whose economic philosophy is alien to free enterprise. In these days in which business *is asked to and should make substantial contributions* to institutions of higher learning, I submit there is a duty on the part of the donors to see that the recipients of their gifts not betray the hand which feeds them.

In summary, my six proposals merely envisage that we shall do away with the hypocrisy of our civilization. There must be no double standard for the president, for government, for business, for education, or for individuals. We must renew and dedicate ourselves to the cause of freedom which is more important than life itself. If we achieve that goal and shoulder our own responsibility, we need not worry about our economic growth. For it is the history of all civilizations that free and responsible God-serving people are always prosperous. We need to worry about our economic growth only when we have a regimented and controlled economy. That is the reason we are worrying now. Should we engage in further regimentation we will have grave cause to worry about the continuation of our Republic, for in the wise and prophetic words of Somerset Maugham:

A nation that wants anything more than freedom will lose its freedom, and the irony of it is, if it is comfort and security it wants, it will lose them, too.

THE VIETNAM WAR

(Address given to the Headquarters Company of the 259th Petroleum Quarter-masters Battalion of the United States Army Reserve, composed largely of BYU students, on May 18, 1968, as they were leaving for active service.)

What has happened to you as members of the 259th Battalion is precisely what happened on other historic occasions at this University. In World War I, although our enrollment consisted of only 353 college students, some 514 University and BYU High students were enlisted in the service of their country. Most of them volunteered. The BYU was closed. Sixteen of them gave their lives. I had the privilege of being one of those who was in the infantry company on this campus.

The story was repeated on a larger scale in World War II, during which 2,540 students of BYU served in the armed forces and 117 made the supreme sacrifice.

Unfortunately, figures are not available for the Korean conflict, but in that war also BYU was represented by students, faculty and staff. Percentage-wise, there were not as many serving as in World Wars I and II but that is because the Korean War was on a smaller scale, and because in my judgment, the Congress made no declaration of war. That conflict did not end as satisfactorily as hoped because, in the belief of many, political considerations and pressures from the United Nations did not permit General MacArthur and others to achieve the total victory which the ideal of freedom deserved.

If you will go to Memorial Hall in the Wilkinson Center on this campus you will see engraved in permanent bronze the names of the former students who gave their lives in World Wars I and II. To this group we will soon be adding the names of former students of this institution who have maintained the integrity of our country by giving their lives in the Korean and Vietnamese conflicts.

Present Criticism and Defeatism not Different from other Wars

I know there is criticism of the present war and that in some areas and among certain opportunist politicians, the American people are being urged to discontinue the present war. Many of you who are not acquainted with the history of the past may get the impression that this is something that has not happened in previous wars. As you go into active duty you should know that in every war in which we have been engaged in this country there have been some who, not realizing that eternal vigilance and even warfare is the price of freedom, have been defeatists and did not want us either to engage in or to continue the conflict then existing. There have been periods of great discouragement in all of our past eight wars, much more so than in the present one.

When the Continental Army under Washington was at Valley Forge in the winter of 1777-78, living conditions were bad, morale was very low, hundreds of enlisted men deserted and even commissioned officers threatened to abandon their posts. Provisions had to be commandeered by the Army because farmers in the neighborhood refused to sell food for the depreciated Continental currency. At the same time, members of Congress were talking about replacing Washington himself.

Every winter during the Revolutionary War morale problems and desertions were serious and as late as January, 1781 there were actual mutinies among the troops from Pennsylvania and New Jersey that had to be put down by threats of force. It was in this situation that Tom Paine's pamphlet "The Crisis" gave great heart to Americans with these eloquent words:

These are the times that try men's souls; the summer soldier and the sunshine patriot will, in this crisis, shrink from the service of his country; but he that stands it *now* deserves the love and thanks of man and woman.

He condemned those whose loyalty faded with the first frost.

The War of 1812 was so unpopular that the states in New England threatened to secede.

The Civil War was not without great moments of discouragement. Resistance to the draft was constant. This resistance resulted in the New York City draft riots of 1863, which produced wholesale destruction of property. As many as 74 people were killed. These riots had to be suppressed by the use of federal troops. Criticism of President Lincoln for his conduct of the war became so great and he became so unpopular that shortly prior to the election when he was running for his second term as President, he called his cabinet together, admitted that he expected the administration to be ousted, but urged them to be loyal to the administration which would succeed them. A short time afterward came news of the great victory at Atlanta in which Sherman defeated the Confederate forces. With this news a wave of patriotism swept the country and, contrary to his own belief, Lincoln was again elected President and was permitted to continue the war which saved the Union and abolished slavery. As happened at that time, victory today, either by negotiations or on the battlefield, could immediately change the mood of our people, even those who are discouraged.

In any event, none of you should for one moment think that the present criticism of the war in Vietnam is unique. As a matter of fact, it is not nearly as serious as it was at the time of the Revolutionary War because had we lost that war we would never ourselves have enjoyed freedom. Had we lost the Civil War we would not have preserved the Union. There is no such threat hanging over our heads as far as the Vietnam War is concerned.

Student and Political Dissenters

I was shocked a couple of weeks ago to find a 4-page advertisement in the New York Times purportedly signed by either the presidents of the student body or the editors of the school papers of approximately 500 universities in this country, declaring that the Vietnamese War is "immoral and unjust." To the casual observer it might appear that that represented most of the colleges and universities in the country. The fact is that there are 1700 universities and colleges not represented in that particular ad and, furthermore, even with respect to the 500, many of them were represented only by the editor or student body president (not by both), showing that such officers were not united in their sentiments even on the 500 campuses.

I propose today in my limited time to prove the fallacy of the charge that the Vietnamese War is "immoral and unjust."

The War in Vietnam Is Both Just and Moral

The facts are that this war is as "moral and just" as any war in which we have been engaged—in many respects much more so. The Revolutionary War began because we felt we were unjustly taxed without representation. No enemy was bombarding our shores and there was no planned killing of our people as in the case of the communists against the South Vietnamese.

The Civil War, when it finally broke forth, was a war to preserve the Union, for the Southern States had seceded. They were not attacking our people or infiltrating our country. True, an ultimate purpose of the Civil War was to free the slaves, but even the slaves were not subjected to the torture and destruction of life as were the people of South Vietnam.

We entered World War I to save the Allied Powers from losing their freedom, and to make the world safe for democracy. We did save Europe, although no war can ever make the world permanently safe for democracy. Each generation has to safeguard its own freedom. According to Mussolini, a major war generally occurs every 25 years, and that has been the history of our own country. You soldiers should always remember that.

We entered World War II to protect our own freedom as well as that of our Allies. Admittedly, we were attacked at Pearl Harbor but the Japanese had no intention of invading this country. In all probability we could have negotiated a peace at that time by turning over the Hawaiian Islands and our other possessions in the Pacific to the Japanese, just as today we could negotiate a peace by giving Ho Chi Minh complete access to South Vietnam. Thank God we did not do so!

We are at war in Vietnam at the present time to insure the same freedom—this time freedom for the South Vietnamese people—to protect them against a ruthless communistic enemy who would subject them to godless communism and deprive them of the dignity of free people, and also to safeguard our national interest by stopping an aggression which could eventually spread to our own shores. Prior to World War II, France controlled practically all of Indochina, including Vietnam, and at the conclusion of World War II, the French again returned to reduce that land to a colonial possession. Except for the fact that the French had lately been in control of the Vietnamese, it was the same as if the British had returned to again make us a colonial possession.

In 1945 Ho Chi Minh declared the independence of North Vietnam and formed a government at Hanoi. After the failure of the French and Ho Chi Minh to negotiate a political settlement, war broke out. By 1954, the French were defeated, more politically than in the battlefield. Even before their defeat at Dien Bien Phu, the French had decided they could no longer continue the war. Paris was busily trying to extricate France from its predicament through a "negotiated settlement" which came with the Geneva Accord.[1] This agreement partitioned

---

[1]"Vietnam: Some Neglected Aspects of the Historical Record," issued by the Republican Conference's Committee on Planning and Research of House of Representatives; reprinted from Congressional Record, August 25, 1965.

Vietnam at the 17th parallel, the territory above that to be in North Vietnam; the territory south of that to belong to South Vietnam. While the United States did not support many of the provisions of the Geneva agreement and was not a party to it, it did issue a declaration stating that it would abide by this accord as long as the signatories refrained from the use of force.

But Ho Chi Minh, as has been true in practically all communist international relations, never intended to abide by the Geneva Accord. That Accord was a part of the communist plan to deceive the enemy while at the same time proceeding with a plan of world domination, either by peaceful or belligerent means. So, immediately after the signing of the Geneva Accord, Ho Chi Minh proceeded with his plan to bring again the people of South Vietnam under communist control and either to dominate or destroy his old nationalist allies. Within days he advocated a continuation of the struggle, in his words, "to democratize South Vietnam," which in communist jargon means "communizing" that country. "The struggle," he said, "will be long and difficult. All the soldiers of the North and the South must unite to conquer victory."

Some five years later he again confirmed their plans to conquer all of South Vietnam, when he said:

... we (the Lao Dong/Communist Party) are building socialism (meaning communism) in Vietnam. We are building it, however, only in half of the country, while in the other half we must still bring to a conclusion the democratic-bourgeois and anti-imperialist revolution. Actually, our party must now accomplish, contemporaneously, two different revolutions, in the North and in the South. This is one of the most characteristic traits of our struggle.[2]

The Geneva Accord also provided for withdrawals of military forces into their respective areas, North and South of the 17th parallel. Instead, however, Ho Chi Minh was careful to leave guerilla cadres scattered throughout the South, and in four of the provinces he actually left communist administrators in power. Arms dumps were

---

[2]"The Faceless Viet Cong," reprinted in *Foreign Affairs Quarterly Review*, April, 1966. Originally from a Hanoi interview by two correspondents of the Italian Communist Party Journal *Unita*, published July 1, 1959, in *Unita* and published in Belgian Communist paper *LeDrapeau Rouge* July 10, 1959.

secretly established for later use and secret agents were left behind to penetrate the police, armed forces and administration of the Saigon government.

True, Ho Chi Minh took tens of thousands of his sympathizers North, but they were there trained for the purpose of infiltrating back into the South to engage in the subversion and overthrow of the Saigon government. Before, however, they were used for this purpose, they were used to put down counter-revolution in the North. "A Documentary Study of Communism in Vietnam" by the American Bar Association, which is just off the press, estimates that between 1954 and 1956, the blood bath which Ho Chi Minh inflicted on his own North Vietnamese in connection with his land reform movement, took the lives of more than one hundred thousand people.

After this chapter of murder and destruction, Ho Chi Minh turned his attention to the South. Initially the movement was non-violent. But after only limited success through non-violent means, the "Viet Cong," as they became known, turned to kidnapping, assassination and terror which took many forms. Sometimes it was the ambush of a group of farmers; sometimes the burning down of a whole village; other times the kidnapping and torturing of village chieftains or their children. Indeed, for the most part they attempted to kill anyone identified with the established order, such as the hamlet chief, teacher, tax collector or the police. The report of the American Bar Association referred to above states that since 1957 it is estimated that 16,000 South Vietnamese officials have been assassinated, and an additional 10,000 kidnapped. Indeed, the study concludes that for all practical purposes, the communists had either recruited for themselves or literally wiped out the entire class of natural leaders in the villages and hamlets of South Vietnam.[3]

As illustrative of the way that Ho Chi Minh and the Viet Cong ravaged the South Vietnamese, I quote from

---

[3]Roger Swearingen and Hammond Rolph, *Communism in Vietnam, a Documentary Study*, published by American Bar Association, 1967, p. 118-121.

Dr. Stephen T. Possony, director of the Hoover Institute
on War, Revolution and Peace:

If the United States had been experiencing equivalent losses to
terrorism (comparable to what South Vietnam has experienced) we
would have suffered about óne million fatalities and abductions. If
the United States were to equal the combat losses of the South
Vietnamese so far, this would amount to at least 600,000 men.[4]

Dr. Possony points out also that in the process the South
Vietnamese inherited 2 million refugees, half of whom were
unsettled, which equated in terms of our population, would
mean our inheriting 24 million refugees, half of whom
would be unsettled. These facts, I think, should give
pause to the idle criticism that the South Vietnamese have
not helped bear the brunt of the war.

There can no longer be any question that the North
Vietnamese government has supported the Viet Cong in
this attempted devastation of South Vietnam. This was
the conclusion of the International Control Commission
Report in 1962, a commission composed of representatives
of many countries appointed to investigate what was going
on in Vietnam. It is not any propaganda issued by our
State Department. Even today, communist action is
conducted at every level with assassinations, guerilla
attacks, Viet Cong battalion-like units, and the engagement
of North Vietnamese regiments in South Vietnam, despite
the refusal of the North Vietnamese negotiators in Paris
to admit it.

Commitment of U.S.

It was because of these gross violations of the Geneva
Accord, which Ho Chi Minh never intended to observe,
that President Eisenhower, in a letter to the President of
South Vietnam, offered to "assist the government of
Vietnam in developing and maintaining a strong, viable
state, capable of resisting the attempted subversion through
military means."[5] Later, President Kennedy went further

[4]Stefan Possony, *Twin Circle*—The National Catholic Press, May 5, 1968, page 12.

[5]*Background Information Relating to Southeast Asia and Vietnam* (Revised Edition,
June 16, 1965), compilation of speeches and documents prepared by Senate Committee
on Foreign Relations.

and declared: "The United States is determined that the Republic of Vietnam shall not be lost to the communists through lack of any support which the United States can render."[6]

In July of 1965 President Johnson declared:

We are in Vietnam to fulfill one of the most solemn pledges of the American Nation. Three presidents—President Eisenhower, President Kennedy, and your present President—over eleven years, have committed themselves and have promised to help defend this small and valiant nation.

Strengthened by that promise, the people of South Vietnam have fought for many long years. Thousands of them have died. Thousands more have been crippled and scarred by war. We cannot now dishonor our word or abandon our commitment or leave those who believed us and who trusted us to the terror and repression and murder that would follow. This, then, my fellow Americans, is why we are in Vietnam.[7]

In the light of this history which I have given and the pledges made by three Presidents, I think it must be plain to you that the South Vietnamese and the United States are in South Vietnam to fight the cause of liberty. I admit that the cause for which we are fighting would have been better understood and we would be more united as a nation had we had an open declaration of war, as contemplated by the Constitution, instead of edging into the war step by step. This should be a lesson to us for the future.

I recognize also that the question of whether we should attempt to police the world is one on which honest minds of free men may differ. But for anyone to say that our war in Vietnam is "immoral and unjust" is to show a startling lack of knowledge of the ideals which gave birth to this country and which have sustained us as a nation. I do not think that any college editor or student body president making such a statement shows sufficient comprehension of our American heritage as to be qualified for

[6]Joint Communique issued by President Kennedy and Vice President Chen Cheng of the Republic of China, *The Department of State Bulletin*, August 28, 1961, p. 372.

[7]Press Conference Statement by President Lyndon B. Johnson, The White House, July 28, 1965, published in the booklet *Why Vietnam*, by U.S. Government Printing Office, Washington, D.C.

graduation from an American university. I am informed that when students in Singapore were demonstrating against the Vietnamese War, the government granted the students visas and offered to ship them to North Vietnam. The result was that the demonstrations immediately ceased. Perhaps we should give our dissenters the same choice.

As I see it, there are at this time only three alternatives:

One would be unilateral withdrawal from Vietnam, which no responsible leader has suggested.

The second is a negotiated peace, which we are attempting. God grant that out of our honorable attempts we shall not surrender by negotiation.

The third is that of continuing the war and stopping the spread of communism in South Vietnam. If by negotiation we can do that, our efforts will be glorified; but if by negotiation we surrender the rights of the people of South Vietnam to their own liberty and their own security, we shall have compromised our ideals and desecrated our word of honor. If by negotiation we cannot win our objective, we should then pursue this war with a vigor and determination to win, the like of which has not yet characterized our efforts. If our cause is just, as this is, we ought to do everything short of atomic warfare to accomplish our ends, for the cause of freedom is much more important than the cause of peace. Further, mankind will never enjoy lasting peace without first having endured freedom.

I recognize also that for ultimate victory it may be necessary for us to aid in political and economic reconstruction in South Vietnam.

Your Duty and Opportunity

This brings me, members of the 259th Battalion, to your duty and opportunity.

Practically all of you are members of a Church which believes that the Constitution of the United States came into being under divine inspiration and that it is our duty to honor and protect it. This means honoring our commitments and international obligations. The First Presidency of the Church, in a statement issued on April 6, 1942,[8] declared that when the "manhood of the Church" is called "into the armed services" of their country, "their highest civic duty requires that they meet that call." To those who have any scruples about the murderous nature of warfare, the First Presidency continued:

> If, harkening to that call and obeying those in command over them, they shall take the lives of those who fight against them, that will not make of them murderers, nor subject them to the penalty that God has prescribed for those who kill. . . .[9]

As late as 1955 President McKay said:

> We love peace, but not peace at any price. There is a peace more destructive of the manhood of living man than war is destructive of the body. Chains are worse than bayonets.[10]

Unfortunately, the world has not learned to do away with war and we know from the Prophets that wars will continue to the millennium.

I had the experience in 1914 of sitting in the Salt Lake Tabernacle, when David Starr Jordan, president of Stanford University, a recognized leader of education in the country, was concluding a nationwide speaking tour. His theme throughout the country had been that at long last nations, like individuals, could conciliate and arbitrate their differences and that there would be war no more. At the conclusion of his address, Dr. James E. Talmage, who was a friend, approached Dr. Jordan and stated: "Since you omitted from consideration the main knowledge that we have in this world, you have arrived at the wrong answer." Dr. Jordan wanted to know what information he had failed to consider, and Dr. Talmage said he had failed to consider the revelations of the Lord from Old Testament times on down through and including the present dispensation—namely, that wars will continue until the millennium. In August of that year David Starr Jordan was proven wrong, and James E. Talmage was proven right, because World War I broke on the horizon.

---

[8]*112th Annual Conference of The Church of Jesus Christ of Latter-day Saints*, April, 1942, p. 94 [hereafter referred to as Conference Report].

[9]*Ibid.*

[10]*Conference Reports*, April, 1955, p. 24.

Let me urge you not to be discouraged by false political prophets who, by their utterances, would discourage us from honoring our sacred obligations. I understand that the morale of our fighting soldiers in Vietnam is high; unfortunately, it is low among some politicians and others who have forgotten the reason why this country was born and the reasons for its continued existence. Aside from our moral and legal commitments to South Vietnam, we have the great opportunity to deny Southeast Asia to the communists. "The loss of South Vietnam," said Eisenhower, "would set in motion a crumbling process that could, as it progressed, have grave consequences for us and for freeom."[11] Vietnam is a test case for "wars of national liberation" upon which Hanoi, Peking and Moscow hope to change the balance of power in Asia.

I challenge all of you to meet the test. Indeed, any argument as to why we are in Vietnam is now moot. We have half a million men in Vietnam and are presently spending in excess of 30 billion dollars a year. More than 20,000 Americans (the size of our studentbody) have lost their lives. It is our duty to see that they have not died in vain.

I hope and pray that we will be successful in our negotiations for freedom at Paris, but if we are not, I pray you will realize that we are in this war to win, and that we will all carry our nation's responsibility with honor and integrity.

You go with our blessings and prayers. If you cheerfully accept this call as an opportunity it will be very profitable to you. You will learn much and magnify your calling. If you merely go because you are required to, you will destroy your own morale and not be a good soldier. I trust you will all be good soldiers.

My last admonition is that you keep yourselves clean, and the Lord will not only assist you in doing your duty, but will protect you. We are proud of you as you leave and will be proud of you as you return.

---

[11]Quoted by Foreign Policy Association in "Vietnam: Vital Issues in the Great Debate," 1966, page 5.

(The following also deals with the Vietnam War and is the latter part of the address given by Dr. Wilkinson at the 95th Annual Commencement Exercises of the Brigham Young University on May 29, 1970.)

I would not have you think from what I have said I agree with the way in which the Vietnamese War has been prosecuted. The sad aspect of the conflict, which is corroborated by speeches of the Presidents and by briefings I have personally had by General Abrams and Ambassador Bunker, is that we never had the intention of really winning this war in the traditional sense—we only intended to effect a stalemate. In my view, we should never enter any war unless we have the resolve and determination and fortitude to win. Had we had these virtues in Vietnam, my judgment is that this war would have ended years ago, and ended in victory. But again these views do not detract from the morality of our cause to safeguard the freedom of the South Vietnamese.

I come next to the false issue that the tragedy at Kent State is somehow the causal result of the President's decision, in an effort to shorten the war, to drive the enemy from sanctuaries across the Cambodian border. That conclusion can come only from frenzied students and vote-seeking politicians bent on achieving their own ends.

Much as we regret the fatal shooting of four students, we are in no position to judge where the responsibility for those deaths lies, and in no event can they be reasonably attributed to the transitory military operations in Cambodia. Prior to the unfortunate shooting there had been three nights of violent student demonstrations, the ROTC building had been burned and 26 campus security police had been overwhelmed, the city was under curfew, the governor had warned the students against violence, still they had assembled in defiance of an order for them to disperse.

Whether, under these circumstances, a small contingent of 50 national guardsmen who were showered with rocks, cement, and stones, taunted by obscene language, surrounded by hundreds of rioting students, and whose supply of tear gas was running out were

justified in retaliating with rifle fire is not for us to determine. Rather, I suggest that until the presidential commission to be appointed by the President makes its report, we
should withhold our judgment.

I congratulate the students of BYU for exercising that
restraint and for not clamoring for a holiday in premature
protest against the action of the Ohio National Guard. For
even if the youthful guardsmen were to blame, this would
not be a cause for continued disturbances at Kent State
or any other campus, for in the words of Abraham Lincoln,
"There is no grievance which is a fit subject of redress
by mob action."

One of the most disheartening, and embarrassing,
results of student disorder on college campuses has been the
lugubrious explanations which administrative officers have
resorted to in order to make their retreat seem less abject.
I am not unmindful of the difficult position my counter-
parts at many universities have had forced upon them by
militant, amoral faculty and revolutionary students. I
suggest, however, that many educators have provided a fa-
cade of plausibility for assaults upon their institutions by
attempts to explain, and even justify, those who have attacked them. For administrators to explain that shouted
obscenities are just a plea for a hearing is to destroy any
possibility of meaningful dialogue. The militants who are
throwing the rocks and lighting the bombs are under no
such attractive illusions about themselves. Basically, they
resent being indulged and have nothing but contempt for
those who do the indulging. I am deeply grateful for the
support I can count on from BYU faculty and students—
whether we always agree fully or not.

May I suggest again that the phenomena now occurring on our campuses, while more violent and more far
reaching, is not entirely new to America. As one who had
the privilege and honor to participate in World War I, I
recall that we had dissenters and pacifists at that time—
idealists who thought war was unnecessary and immoral
per se. That has happened in every way. Unfortunately
the history of civilization is to the contrary. Man's free-

dom has to be protected and preserved by each generation, and those of you in this class who are members of The Church of Jesus Christ of Latter-day Saints have certain knowledge, available to all but not generally accepted, that while we must continually strive for peace and brotherhood, the sure word of prophecy is that wars will continue to the millennium.

This does not of course mean that we should be fatalists. We should continuously pray for peace and strive with all our might for it, but abject retreat from principle has never provided the basis for lasting peace. If this is an unpopular position, and if we at BYU stand relatively alone among major universities in taking it, we do so with full recognition of what we uphold. For our Twelfth Article of Faith provides: "We believe in being subject to kings, presidents, rulers, and magistrates, in obeying, honoring and sustaining the law." Further, the official statement of the Prophet Joseph Smith, incorporated as the 134th Section of the Doctrine and Covenants, provides: "We believe that all men are bound to sustain and uphold the respective governments in which they reside . . . and that sedition and rebellion are unbecoming every citizen thus protected, and should be punished accordingly: . . ."

Our President is dedicated to winding up this unpopular war as fast as is consistent with a just and honorable peace. He deserves our support. Unreasoned dissension not only gives aid and comfort to our enemy but strains the unity and support of our own government. When a delegation called on President Lincoln to criticize him for our reverses in the Civil War, he answered by this appropriate analogy:

Suppose, he said, all you owned was in gold, and the gold had been put into the hands of an acrobat to carry across the Niagara River on a rope, would you shake the rope and keep shouting contradictory advice; or would you hold your breath and your tongue, and keep hands off until he was safely over? The government is carrying an immense load and doing the best it can. Don't badger us. We'll get you safely across.[12]

[12]Brant House, ed., *Lincoln's Wit* (New York: Ace Books, 1958), p. 204.

As we see the world around us, seething with discontent and disruption, pessimism and hate—a world literally aflame—it would not be difficult for some to believe that all is lost and give up even trying. But we must never abandon our faith and hope for the future, for the doctrine of faith underlies everything we have tried to teach you here at the University. I would challenge each one of you that despite the conflict and turmoil on every side, you arm yourself with the armor of faith and wherever you go carry with you the message of the Master to love the Lord with all our hearts and our neighbors as we would ourselves. Ours is the responsibility to teach this doctrine to all the world. If you do that, the world about you can be in turmoil but you can have within you that inner peace which "surpasseth all understanding."

As you go forth to serve mankind, I pray for the Lord's choicest blessings to continuously abide with each of you, which I do in the name of the Lord Jesus Christ. Amen.

ACADEMIC ANARCHY vs. MANAGEMENT OF UNIVERSITIES

(Address delivered to the Rotary Club, Oakland, California, on September 3, 1970. For this address Dr. Wilkinson was awarded his second George Washington Honor Medal of the Freedoms Foundation at Valley Forge.)

Introduction

I want it understood that what I have to say will be said on my own responsibility as an individual, and not as president of Brigham Young University, for it has not been cleared with my Board of Trustees.

Since my time is necessarily limited, I may have to sound somewhat dogmatic. If I had more time I might make some mild, but only mild, reservations on what I say to you. I find myself in somewhat the same position as a federal judge before whom I practiced law at one time. He would generally announce a decision at the end of a trial and always preface his remarks with the comment that "this court may be wrong but it is never in doubt."

Extent of Disturbances and Riots

I need not go into detail as to what has been happening on the campuses of America, but as a preface for suggestions I intend to make I will quickly summarize the extent of the student disturbances and riots and the demands and objectives of the militants. The problem is not one of normal academic unrest, but of academic disruption, violence, and anarchy.

According to the report of J. Edgar Hoover on campus disturbances for the year ending in June 1970, there were 1785 demonstrations on the 2300 college campuses. On some campuses there were many. On many other campuses, as at Brigham Young University, which now in terms of full-time students is the largest private university in the country, there were none. We don't claim to be entirely unique. We are probably, however, the only large campus which has been free from trouble.

The closing months of the last school year brought more riots, demonstrations, boycotts, protests, open warfare, vandalism and other disorders in American colleges and universities than at any other time in the history of the nation. These resulted in student deaths from shooting, the wounding and injury of scores of persons, and the arrest of hundreds. Damage ran into the millions of dollars, while the loss of time and work in education is inestimable. Let me give you just a few examples of these riots as reported in the newspapers:

At Santa Barbara, the students completely burned a Bank of America branch.

At Cornell fire gutted the black studies center.

At Rice, fire which was started with kerosene, did extensive damage to the ROTC Building.

At Berkeley police fought a pitched battle for three days with radicals who hurled rocks, smashed windows, ripped down the American flag, attacked a faculty club, destroyed the furniture and smashed down the doors.

At Kansas a fire bomb destroyed much of the Union Building. Damage was estimated at $2 million.

At Stanford fire from arson destroyed the *life's work of several scholars* at Stanford's Center for Advanced Study in the Behavioral Sciences. Total property destruction at Stanford was estimated at $580,000 in six weeks.

At Fresno State College fire bombs destroyed a $1 million computer.

After President Nixon announced our entry into Cambodia there were scores of disorders. The most serious of these riots were at Kent State and Jackson State resulting in the tragic deaths of several students. On May 8 a new "Strike Information Center" at Brandeis University reported there were 356 schools striking with faculty and administrative support. These were accompanied by a rash of attacks on the ROTC. Records kept by the Army, Navy, and Air Force show more than 400 anti-ROTC incidents at many of the 364 schools where ROTC units function. There were 73 attempts to blow up ROTC buildings.

Fire bombs were thrown into ROTC buildings at Oregon State, Princeton, Hobart College and Washington University at St. Louis. Shots were fired into the home of the Stanford ROTC commander. At Southern Illinois students threw fire bombs out of windows. About 300 students went on a fire-setting spree at Michigan State. The National Guard was called in as 1500 rampaging students sacked the ROTC building at Maryland.

There were 67 instances of vandalism in which ROTC offices were entered, records were destroyed, weapons and ammunition stolen and property defaced. One hundred forty-five assaults involving personal injury and damage to property were launched.

At the University of Michigan on May 7, a group of students occupied the ROTC building for nearly 24 hours. A fire was started in the basement. No one was punished —university authorities said none of the vandals could be identified. If during a 24-hour period no method could be found to identify at least part of these students, those responsible for identification either did not want to find out or were overly naive.

ROTC enrollment has dropped from 298,952 in 1961-62 to 157,830 in 1969-70, or nearly 50%.

Since April 30 nine schools have voted to discontinue ROTC including Harvard, Dartmouth, Yale and Columbia, despite the fact that in the past decade 63% of all newly commissioned officers in the Army came from ROTC units. This to my mind shows the schools which closed out ROTC have little regard for duty to their country.

One reason for the zeroing in on Kent State University by so many radicals is that it houses the Liquid Crystal Institute, home of research projects with military potential.

With this background of student disturbances and riots (1785 during the last fiscal year) you will appreciate the story that is going the rounds of academic circles that a college president died and was consigned to Hell. But he was there for six months before he knew where he was. The current joke among college presidents themselves is that becoming an administrator in higher education today is comparable to buying a ticket on *The Titanic!*

Objectives of the Revolutionary Leaders

The tragic aspect of most of these destructive riots is that the leaders openly admit they are intent upon the "destruction of our existing social order." Their heroes are the leaders of the most ruthless dictatorships—Lenin, Mao-tse-tung, Castro, Ho Chi Minh, Che Guevera. During the riots at Columbia, members of "Students for a Democratic Society" wrote on college buildings, "Lenin won, Castro won, and we will too." In some of their rioting they have carried the red flag of the Communist Revolution and the black flag of anarchy.

Michael Klonsky, national secretary of SDS, has written, "The National Liberation Front in Vietnam and the oppressed peoples in the U.S. are fighting the same enemy, American Imperialism . . . Remember Ho, Mao, Fidel, etc."

Eldridge Cleaver expressed the same philosophy in saying, "We're out to destroy the present machinery of the ruling class."

That National Liberation Front, another militant student organization, some time ago published and mailed to citizens of California its "Declaration of Entity and of Purpose," which declared, "The current government of the United States of America to be an unlawful and illegal one," and gave notice of their intent to "conduct a controlled punitive action against United States federal forces and municipal forces on a limited scale from the City of San Francisco on the south, to the Oregon border on the north." It ended by declaring "All citizens are hereby notified that a state of revolution shall begin as of March 15, 1970, ALL POWER TO THE PEOPLE." There is no question but that the hard-core leaders of these student riots were either communists or believe in communism. There is no question either but that some have engaged in treasonable activities, which is that of giving aid and comfort to the enemy even though they have not been legally charged with such activities.

These leaders are willing to seize on any issue that will accomplish their aims. At the beginning of the disturbances in Berkeley, the chief grievance was the racial issue. This permitted them to inflame not only blacks but sympathetic and sometimes gullible whites against the so-called "establishment."

What is not generally known is that the decision to exploit this issue was originally made in Moscow in 1928. Instructions were then given to use the Negro question to incite trouble and revolution in the United States. As has been pointed out by Manning Johnson, (a former ranking Negro communist in the United States, who later broke with the party and became an undercover worker for the FBI), the communists from then on busied themseles with the Negro. They infiltrated Negro churches and social groups in order to prepare the Negroes to be sacrificed in the revolution to come. It is a distinct tribute to most American Negroes that most of them did not fall for the Red blandishments.

Later, as the war in Vietnam became unpopular, the revolutionists emphasized the Vietnam war issue. When, in turn, the administration let it be known that our troops would be withdrawn from Vietnam as soon as practicable and the Vietnam war issue was dying out, they seized upon the Cambodian issue, and now that our troops have been withdrawn from Cambodia, the revolutionists are emphasizing air pollution, the decay of our cities and the athletic programs of our universities. These shifting issues are consistent with the instructions that have been continually issued by the national leaders of the Students for a Democratic Society, which are that its members should make use of any issue which is locally most popular.

While a number of university administrative officers blame the war in Vietnam or the incursion in Cambodia as the cause of student unrest, this claim is patently false. The foreboding of campus disturbances occurred long before today's activists even knew where to find Vietnam on the map. Nearly all unbiased authorities agree that the termination of the Vietnam war will only shift the emphasis of the campus militants. To me, attempts to blame President Nixon's decisions for campus unrest represent nothing but an attempt by university administrators to cover up their own failure to govern their universities. If Vietnam and Cambodia were the cause of campus disorders, why is it that there are scores of universities and colleges in this country which have had no real disturbances or riots and which have consequently received no publicity?

I admit that the decision to go into Cambodia gave the student revolutionists a much needed opportunity to further inflame their fellow students, but this was because the fuse of revolution had already been lighted and because somehow our universities had failed to teach our students the lofty concept of freedom which gave us birth and has sustained us as a nation and to which the Vietnamese are entitled as much as are we. Our students have not been inspired with Douglas MacArthur's hallowed words of "duty, honor, country."

Suggestions for Better Management of Universities

I now come to what should be the constructive part of my talk—my suggestions for better control of the University—in other words, *Proper University Management* vs. *Academic Anarchy*.

At the outset may I make it plain that the universities themselves are not primarily to blame for the attitude and lack of proper motivation on the part of students who come to their campuses. We will not entirely reform our universities in this country until we reform our society. We are failing as a nation because parents are not fulfilling their roles as parents but are excessively concerned with their occupations or social life and pay too little attention to the proper training of their sons and daughters. They have not taught adequate standards to their children, or assumed responsibility for their proper spiritual, cultural and patriotic motivation.

We are failing as a nation because too many teachers are less concerned with effective teaching than they are with "research grants," the number of hours they teach, the class load they carry, their rate of pay, their retirement benefits, and in general "what's in it for me." Many have lost the sense of dedication which is the hallmark of every good teacher.

We are failing as a nation because too many men of the cloth have forgotten to minister to their flocks and have discontinued preaching the word of God. They have turned into politicians and preach that which is the uncertain opinion of man rather than the sure word of God.

Nevertheless, I do think that the universities themselves must plead guilty to having permitted and in many cases encouraged destructive disturbances and riots on their various campuses. What suggestions I have today will be in this area.

My first suggestion is that we must abandon the idea that the university is a law unto itself and that a campus is an asylum for those who would spawn seditious ideas and otherwise violate the law. The medieval custom or tradition which permitted sinners and violators of the law to flee from civil justice by gaining sanctuary in a monastery or university, where they could do penance for their misdeeds, has no vestige of justification in our modern civilization. The only sound concept was enunciated by the late Theodore Roosevelt who declared that, "No man is above or below the law." This should apply with special force to university students for they are the ones who ought to set an example to society.

I suspect that up until recently, the preponderant feeling of university presidents has been that universities ought to govern themselves and be essentially free from any civil or criminal restraint. Admitting that it would be better if the universities did govern themselves, the fact is that many have not properly done so. I suggest that the moment an unlawful disturbance occurs, or other laws are violated, police, with or without invitation from school authorities, should enter the campus and see that the laws are enforced. I think the first duty of any citizen, especially a university president, is to assist in the enforcement of the law.

Second, a reappraisal needs to be made of the philosophy of many academicians that legislatures should not interfere either with the governance of universities or what is being taught there—that education is not the business of the legislature. My answer is that since the taxpayers put up the money for the creation and maintenance of the universities, their representatives, namely our legislators, should be very much concerned with what is going on in our universities. The discipline of many universities in recent years does not indicate to me that they have a celestial glory deserving to be free from close scrutiny. I submit also that there have been instances of seditious teachings and pornographic performances on our campuses, where legislators, in the absence of responsible action by university administrators, have been justified in stepping into the breach and taking action. Admittedly legislators are not above criticism, but they are on the whole responsible men, and I am willing to trust their combined judgment. With a clear recognition of their own limitations, they should nevertheless supervise education more, not less.

My third suggestion is that boards of trustees throughout the country ought to reassert their duties and prerogatives as trustees. In too many instances, over a long period of years, they have known relatively little of what transpires in their universities and have failed to set the policy of the institutions over which they presumably, but in some cases perfunctorily, preside. It has become the custom in many instances for trustees to delegate policymaking powers to faculties of the institutions, who often have a conflict of interest in resolving policy questions. While, of course, boards of trustees should use proper restraint in passing on the minutia of purely academic matters, that should not preclude them from overall decisions as to the propriety of courses to be offered or discontinued, in particular to pass on courses which would truly be in the public interest and not in the interest of pressure groups —courses which would lift and improve the quality of our civilization rather than destroy the established morals of a great civilization.

I read recently of a new course proposed by students in which the class was to photograph and reveal undercover police activity. This course is entitled, "Repression and the Movement." The description of the course reads as follows: "We will publish leaflets and pamphlets, sponsor rallies, photograph and reveal undercover pigs and anything else we can search our minds for. The course shall be run and controlled by those of us who participate." While this is not contained in the university catalog, I am informed certain departments will give credit for it under the heading of "research." To assert, as in this situation, that the board of trustees should have no authority to step in and either initiate or veto courses is tantamount to saying that we should do away with our trustees and give academic anarchy full sway.

As in the case of legislatures, there ought to be more and not less supervision of our universities by boards of trustees.

My fourth suggestion is that boards of trustees should give almost exclusive power to the presidents of institutions to carry out decisions of the boards and to administer the affairs of the institutions. Unfortunately, in many institutions the boards have delegated so many administrative functions to the faculty that when a crisis arises the president is often powerless to act.

The often impossible situation of a university president

is described in a short parody entitled, "The Lament of a University President."

> I'm not allowed to run the train,
> The whistle, I can't blow.
> I'm not the one who designates
> How far the train will go.
> The students rant and rave and scream
> For this privilege or that.
> The faculty is wont to change
> Curriculum format.
> I'm not allowed to blow off steam,
> Or even ring the bell.
> But let the damn thing jump the track,
> And see who catches hell.

The fact of the matter is that faculty members usually are not hired as administrators, and many of them have little competence in that respect. While, of course, the stature of a university is directly correlated with the quality of its faculty, we must remember that administrative decisions often cannot wait on the slow, deliberative process of faculty analysis. Imagine Dr. Hayakawa having to wait for a faculty senate to tell him whether he could jerk the wires off an unauthorized sound truck.

My own view is that (1) the trustees should determine the policies of the university, (2) the president should have the authority and responsibility to carry out those policies, and (3) the teachers should focus their activities on teaching and related activities. This division of duties has been tragically ignored in many institutions. Obviously the president should obtain the advice of faculty members on academic matters. I can't imagine that a responsible president would not welcome, and depend on suggestions from his faculty on many matters, for faculty expertise is the great resource of any university. But there is no way that the faculty can possibly share the perspective or respond to the responsibility that a president must assume. When it comes to overall discipline on the campus, the president must be the commander-in-chief. Consequently, when a new president takes charge, he should have the right to choose his entire administrative staff. Otherwise he runs the risk of failure in carrying out his policies.

The power to nominate faculty members should be restored to him also. They should not be chosen exclusively by their friendly peers on the faculty without a careful, independent investigation by the president. When faculty members, department heads, or even deans have complete freedom in selecting fellow faculty members, it is only natural that they select people of their own kind, including their own academic and political preferences and biases. This makes for an imbalanced faculty which can hardly be objective in searching for the truth. Admittedly the president may also make mistakes in suggesting faculty appointments, but surely he is as concerned as any dean or department chairman and is less likely to be governed by departmental friendship and traditions. Furthermore, he is directly accountable to his trustees whereas faculty members are not. When he has to "face the music" he is more likely to play a responsible tune.

My fifth suggestion is that there should be much more emphasis on teaching on the part of faculties. I do not believe in the prevailing philosophy of "publish or perish." While of course research should be encouraged, I would rather have an undergraduate child of mine in a classroom under a teacher of limited scholastic reputation who had the ability to inspire, than under a Nobel Prize winner, who either never had the ability to teach or has lost the zest for it because of his being absorbed in research. While research is indispensable for the university as a whole, it is not necessary for all teachers to be engaged preponderantly in research—indeed some ought to be required to do very little. I understand that in certain leading institutions of higher learning in this country most undergraduate classes are taught by student assistants. That is a tragedy and a serious indictment of an administration which permits it. Indeed, freshmen should be taught by the most experienced and inspirational teachers. Many teachers do not want to teach these classes. They therefore prevail upon their friend (the department chairman) to free them from these classes. That is why there needs to be a strong president with supporting officers—who can help see that proper assignments are made.

In the sixth place universities should not condone any encouragement of riots or revolution by faculty members. Any teacher who either *encourages or participates* in such conduct should be discharged forthwith.

A staff report of the Florida House of Representatives (1/16/70) Select Joint Committee on Campus Unrest and Drug Abuse reported in part: "In nearly every instance of campus unrest problems which could be documented, we find that the leaders were for the most part being counseled, guided and occasionally directed by faculty members."

Robert Nisbet, University of California professor of sociology, writes in the British magazine *Encounter:* "Without faculty stimulus, financial contributions and other forms of assistance, the student revolt could never really have got off the ground.

"Not obviously, all of the faculty . . . But it was . . . a powerful minority, often contained within its Nobel Prize winners and others of equal stature . . ."

Dr. S. I. Hayakawa, president of San Francisco State College, has said: "The worst enemies of American higher education are professors, or a minority of professors within it. They've got an awful lot of routine undergraduate teaching to do, and they are bored stiff. The only way they can get a little excitement . . . is to appeal to their students for admiration and they appeal therefore to the most radical and most immature of their students."

My seventh suggestion is to eliminate our loose ideas of permissive education and lack of discipline and restore to the campus the rigorous discipline which made our institutions great centers of learning—not of revolution.

In order to gain immunity for the unlawful acts which they have already committed and still threaten to commit, many of the rioters such as those at Columbia demanded amnesty for all of their violations of law; others, such as students at the University of Colorado, would remove from college administrators all rights to discipline any student and would have the discipline in each case administered by the courts; and to cap it all, students at the State University of New York at Onconta demanded that agitating students be given a weekly allowance of twenty-five dollars for spending money so they could continue their agitation.

In my judgment students who would destroy either the government which gives them more opportunities than any other nation in the world for both their material and educational advancement, or who would destroy the educational institutions created by our government or made possible by our system of free enterprise, should be expelled forthwith. There should never be appeasement or capitulation of amnesty for these militant students, for any show of weakness will only result in further academic anarchy.

My eighth suggestion is that boards of trustees and/or presidents, and/or faculties should not be permitted to close schools early and give academic credit for courses not completed or without the requisite examinations. *Higher Education & National Affairs* reported on May 22 that fourteen universities and colleges had closed for the year. The total was probably much higher than that.

I understand that at one of our leading state universities this year the student assistants who taught 60% of the undergraduate students struck for an entire month, in the middle of the semester, during which time there were no classes. Also when trouble arose near the end of the year they dismissed classes at least a month early. Yet the students received full credit. This is academic anarchy. This is a violation of the contractual obligation of the university, a fraud on its students and the employers who subsequently employ them.

In a letter published in the *New York Times,* five students took the Harvard faculty to task for its vote on May 6 to allow students not to complete their academic year but get credit for their courses anyway.

This action, the students said, constituted "a complete abandonment of academic standards by a university faculty, previously considered among the world's greatest." I agree with these students. Indeed, to my mind, and I say

this as a Harvard man, it will not long continue to be
among the world's greatest unless, instead of abandoning,
it improves its standards of conduct and requirements of
scholarship.

It is gratifying that the viewpoint of these Harvard
students has been vindicated by the Court of Appeals for
the State of New York (the highest court in that state).
In a recent ruling that court, in an action filed by the
New York and Rurgers Universities Schools of Law, unani-
mously held that law school students who (1) had not taken
the number of classroom periods specified for any particular course in the catalogs of their respective approved law
schools, and (2) who had not taken final course examinations to test their understanding of the context of the
course, were not eligible to take the bar examinations in
New York State, even though they had been given credit
for those courses and had been graduated by their respective institutions. This of course applied not only to New
York and Rutgers Universities, but to other universities as
well. The tragedy is that students who had paid tuition
for full courses, but were not given them, are now being
denied the right to take bar examinations. Thanks to the
Court of Appeals, the integrity of legal education was preserved despite the lack of integrity of educational administrators.

Nor is there any excuse for the suggestion that colleges
should close down so students may take a week or more to
engage in politics just before the elections. With their
meager knowledge of what makes our country "tick" and
without having yet made any major contribution to our
country, there is ground for the argument that they have
done too much politicking already.

My ninth suggestion is that our laws ought to be more
vigorously enforced and our judges ought to be more severe
in their judgments. It is shocking to me as a lawyer to note
that although hundreds of students have been arrested
around the country, few have been brought to trial. Those
who have faced a judge have escaped, for the most part,
with small fines for misdemeanors.

There have been only three arrests on federal charges of sabotage and destruction of government property.

More information should be given by universities to their students as to federal laws. College students and faculty are shocked when they learn how tough these laws are:

A 1917 law making any attempt to interfere with and obstruct the United States in preparing for and carrying on defense activities an act of criminal sabotage. This carries a penalty of 30 years in prison and a $10,000 fine.

The destruction of government property is punishable by 10 years in jail. It also carries a $10,000 fine.

Law enforcement officials complain they have trouble getting students or school authorities to identify anyone involved in the anti-ROTC incidents. No wonder that the revolutionaries on campus repeat the same acts time and time again on the same and different campuses.

My tenth suggestion is that there ought to be better business management among institutions of higher learning. If business men, who pay the taxes, ran their businesses with the profligacy as many institutions of higher learning they would go broke overnight. I have time for only one example. In 1958 the Educational Facilities Laboratories conducted a survey of the utilization of buildings of sixty-four-year, degree granting liberal arts colleges in the North Central region of the United States. Of the 53 colleges reporting, there was an average utilization of only 40 percent of classrooms and 25 percent of laboratories. Yet most of them planned new buildings or the renovation of old buildings, and many were clamoring for federal funds for this purpose. This to my mind indicates an extravagance which should not be condoned either by the tax payer or private benefactors.

My eleventh and final suggestion (you will note I have one more than the Ten Commandments given to Moses) is that instead of our states giving fixed appropriations to our state institutions of higher learning, they should give a certain sum to each student which he can use for his tuition or educational expenses in any accredited university of his choice, public or private, church-related or otherwise. When most of us were in college three-fourths of the students attended private colleges; now three-fourths of them attend public institutions. Some of these state institutions have become so large they have lost the intimate touch indispensable for proper education, which is one of the genuine causes for dissatisfaction on our campuses.

This change in appropriations would permit a student, if he desired, to attend some well-recognized private institution where there have been no riots or disturbances and where there is the proper climate for obtaining an education. This would bring about a competition in education comparative with competition in business. This would be healthy for education and do away with the monopoly and uniformity that state institutions are fast developing. It would make both state and private institutions responsive to the will of the legislature and to the parents who, after all, are the ones who pay the money for the education of their children. It would also force educational institutions to be more economical in operation, which is badly needed. I do not claim credit for this idea. It is being increasingly asserted by prominent educators, many in state institutions. Stated briefly, the effect of this could be that universities would have to satisfy the students and their parents rather than their own smug selves.

In conclusion may I say just one word with respect to the claim advanced by some extreme militants—that the demonstrations and riots are necessary to preserve the traditional concept of free speech. This is nonsense. A survey of 60,447 faculty members conducted last year under a sponsorship of the Carnegie Commission on Higher Education found more than 80 percent of those who replied agreed that "campus demonstrations by militant students, instead of being necessary to preserve free speech are a threat to academic freedom."

May I also comment with respect to the claim that the disruptions on our campuses are caused by a lack of money. In the words of Sidney Hook that is "noisome hogwash." The universities which have had the most trouble have been those which have had the most money. All the money in the world will not correct the false notion that the purpose of a university is to engage in political reformation rather than education. It will only accelerate and aggravate the present malady. Political reformation should be left to our lawmakers, not the noisy militants on our campuses.

When our university administrators abandon their administrative cowardice and show the courage necessary to conduct sound and sensible educational programs instead of attempting to usurp the functions of our legislatures then, and only then, will there be bright hope for the future of higher education in America, for only then will universities and colleges receive the support of the American public.

ADDRESSES ON
SPECIAL OCCASIONS

Section 3

President Nathan Eldon Tanner, second counselor in the Church First Presidency, left; Paul Harvey, newspaper, radio-television commentator; and BYU President Ernest L. Wilkinson confer at BYU commencement exercises May 29, 1970. Mr. Harvey was awarded the George Washington Honor Medal of the Freedoms Foundation for his address on this occasion, and President Wilkinson won the medal also that year for his address to the Oakland Rotary Club.

BYU President Ernest L. Wilkinson, right, escorts famed poet and author Carl Sandburg at commencement exercises June 5, 1959.

ON THE OCCASION OF THE
OF THE FORMATION OF THE
BRIGHAM YOUNG UNIVERSITY
STAKE

(Address given on January 8, 1956, at the conference in which the Brigham Young University Stake was organized.)

This is an historic occasion for the creation of a stake on this campus.

It is just 150 years since the birth of the Prophet Joseph—a young boy who at the age of 15 in the search for truth knelt in the Sacred Grove. There the heavens opened to him and he saw and heard the Father and the Son. The dispensation of the fullness of time, during which the children of men were to receive and enjoy more spiritual and more scientific knowledge than in all previous dispensations of time, was ushered in.

It was just 125 years ago that Joseph, with his brothers Hyrum and Samuel, Oliver Cowdery, and the two Whitmer brothers, by direct authorization of the Lord, organized His Church—the Church to which you and I belong. Five of the six organizers varied in age from 19 to 24. The other, Hyrum, had just turned 30. In years of age they were no older than many of you students today. But the Prophet Joseph for nine years had gone through a rigorous training under the direct tutelage of the Lord and was the one person in this dispensation to whom revelation for his Church was given.

It was just 111 years ago in June, 1844 that the

Prophet and his brother Hyrum were martyred by a mob, the members of which were determined to put an end to the teachings which they espoused. For the same teachings, the gospel of love and salvation, our Master had surrendered his life at the age of 33; the Prophet Joseph had ended his mortal existence at 38.

The martyrdom of the Prophet no more put an end to the revealed gospel of Jesus Christ than did the martyrdom of the Savior himself. Truth will always persist and in the end will be triumphant.

The news of the Prophet's death was transmitted to Prophet Brigham Young, the president of the Quorum of the Twelve, who was in New Hampshire preaching the gospel and campaigning for the election of Joseph Smith as President of the United States. He hurried back to Nauvoo, and as president of the Twelve presided over the Church until the First Presidency was reorganized. When the mantle of the Prophet Joseph was seen to descend on him there was never any doubt thereafter among the faithful that he was God's chosen apostle to lead the chosen people. From then on for 33 years, equivalent to the entire length of life of the Savior, he stood at the head of this Church on the earth and was its Prophet and leader. Two years before his death he founded this University.

The news of the Prophet Joseph's death, emblazoned as screaming headlines in a newspaper, also attracted the attention in Scotland of a young Scotch boy by the name of William Budge. Although he had never heard of Mormonism, this young boy resolved that if the Prophet Joseph and his brother were willing to die for their beliefs their message was worth investigating. So he sought out Mormon missionaries, became converted to the Church, and was called on a long mission, first to England, then to the continent of Europe.

It was just a hundred years ago last October that this Scotch boy, who had never set foot on American soil, converted a young dynamic German educator by the name of Karl G. Maeser to this Church. Brother Maeser was then in his early twenties, the same age as the Prophet Joseph when, under the inspiration of the Lord, he organized this Church. This was the same man who 20 years later President Brigham Young chose to send to Provo to organize the Brigham Young Academy. When he asked for instructions Brigham Young said, "I have only these: that you should teach not even the alphabet or the multiplication tables without the aid and blessings of our Heavenly Father—that is all—God bless you—goodby."

And without purse or scrip, but with the blessings of our Heavenly Father and the help of a loyal and enterprising and faithful stake president, Brother Abraham Smoot, he founded this University, which for spiritual training is already the greatest university in the world and which, in the not too distant future, for the promulgation even of secular truth will be in the vanguard of educational institutions of the world.

In the early days Brother Maeser, as principal of this school, and Brother Smoot as President of the Utah Stake, which embraced all of Utah County, were spiritual and educational partners. Brother Maeser was the school master. He began with a class of 29. Brother Smoot never hesitated to supply all the funds he could raise. When Brother Smoot died, he was indebted to the banks for over $30,000, the equivalent of over $500,000 today, for monies which he had personally borrowed and used to finance the educational venture of Brother Maeser.

There were times when Brother Maeser and his faculty went a little hungry, but they did not have as many heart failures or stomach ulcers as we have today. One time Brother Maeser, in a period of discouragement, as we all have, decided to resign and accept a position in Salt Lake City at what was then a fat salary. His family got partly packed, ready to move, and then waited impatiently for the signal to go. After some waiting and when he was in a good mood they asked how many days before they should set out for Salt Lake. He replied solemnly that he had had a vision in which he saw a temple hill where the University is now located dotted with buildings of the Lord's great educational institution and that he had decided to stay in Provo and contribute his part in the growth of that institution.

As we organize this stake, I suspect that Joseph Smith, through whom the gospel of life and salvation was again restored to the world, Brigham Young, the founder of this school, and Karl G. Maeser, its spiritual architect, might be looking in upon us. That requires no more faith or imagination to believe than it did in the days of Columbus for people to believe that the earth was round. Sometime man will understand how the Lord can answer our prayers and know what we are doing just as readily as today we can understand television or atomic radiation. We still cannot understand the unexplainable fact of life or the manner of creation; yet we know there is life and that we exist.

I imagine that the Prophet Joseph is comparing the 6,000 students in attendance with the six young men who organized this Church 125 years ago. I think Brother Maeser must be pleased that his 29 students of 80 years ago have grown to such a large number. I sense that Brother Brigham is recalling that when he died, there were only 20 stakes in the entire Church and that today there is being created the 225th stake of the Church composed entirely of students of the academy he founded. I am sure that each of them is pleased with this sight and with the marvelous work and a wonder that are being accomplished.

And if they could talk to us what would they say?

I can answer only be telling of what they did while they were in mortality and what they urged members of the Church to do.

I am sure that all three would place main emphasis upon our acquiring a proper education, both as a part of our school and as a part of our stake activities.

It was through the Prophet Joseph Smith that the Lord revealed the indispensable part that education must play in our salvation. As found in Section 130 of the Doctrine and Covenants it reads:

Whatever principle of intelligence we attain unto in this life, it will rise with us in the resurrection. And if a person gains more knowledge and intelligence in this life through his diligence and obedience than another, he will have so much the advantage in the world to come." (D&C 130:18-19.)

The Prophet Joseph took this literally. He determined that Latter-day Saints should have all the education available.

. . . One of the first things he did in the first year of the history of the Church was to organize in the community the common schools of the Church. He called Oliver Cowdery and W. W. Phelps to be the first two "school masters" of the Church educational system. Then, in Kirtland, Ohio, in 1832, he established a unique mechanism in the field of formal education when he called the brethren together and established the School of the Prophets.[1]

What did they study? About the same things you study. First, religion; the Bible and the Book of Mormon were the paramount texts. They studied the three R's; they studied history and geography. We have a record of a few of the books that they used: the Bible, the Book of Mormon, Whelpley's Compendium of History, *Kirkham's* Grammar *(which I found to be merely a high school grammar book), Olney's* Geography, *and Jacob's* Latin Grammar. *They studied law; they studied everything that man should know. . . When the Kirtland Temple was built, the upper floor was divided into classrooms and numbers were placed on the doors. And the men and women of the Church went "back to school."*[2]

When the Saints moved to Nauvoo he founded the University of Nauvoo. As if that were not enough, the Prophet studied law at night in the office of Judge Higbee, a non-Mormon lawyer. "He studied Latin. He employed a professor to teach him Greek and Hebrew and at the time of his death he was in the process of mastering the German language."[3]

---

[1]Dix W. Price, "Joseph Smith, Ph.D.," from series of *Selected Speeches* (Provo, Utah: Extension Publications, Adult Education and Extension Services, Brigham Young University, April 5, 1955), pp. 2-3.

[2]*Ibid.,* p. 3.

[3]*Ibid.,* p. 5.

In the words of Elder Dix Price who spoke to us a year ago:

. . . The best example of the educational progress of the Prophet. . . is this: When he translated the Book of Mormon, [you know, of course, that] by the aid of the Urim and Thummim and the power of God (as he stated in the Wentworth letter), he was able to envision the meaning of the characters on the plates. He was then left to the task of recording the story in *his own* language. Thus, the first edition of the Book of Mormon could be expected to be only as perfect in grammar and composition as was the Prophet's education at that time. It is a well-known fact that he made some three thousand grammatical mistakes in the first edition of the Book of Mormon. He later corrected most of these mistakes in subsequent editions. But six years later, when he translated the Book of Abraham, he did a perfect literary job. Not one single correction has been made in that part of the Pearl of Great Price. Here is a Prophet of God improving his grammar, improving his English, improving, yes, perfecting his mastery of composition.[4]

The religious premise for this abiding faith in education is recorded in Section 88 of the Doctrine and Covenants:

And I give unto you a commandment that you shall teach one another the doctrine of the kingdom.

Teach ye diligently and my grace shall attend you, that you may be instructed more perfectly in theory, in principle, in doctrine, in the law of the Gospel, in all things that pertain unto the kingdom of God, that are expedient for you to understand;

Of things both in heaven and in the earth, and under the earth; things which have been, things which are, things which must shortly come to pass; things which are at home, things which are abroad; the wars and the perplexities of the nations, and the judgments which are on the land; and a knowledge also of countries and of kingdoms.[5]

Having been thus taught of the Lord the Prophet gave utterance to these glorious truths:

Man was created to dress the earth, to cultivate his mind, and to glorify God.

We consider that God has created man with a mind capable of instruction and a faculty which may be enlarged in proportion to the heed and diligence given to the light communicated from heaven

---

[4]*Ibid.*
[5]D&C 88:77-79

to the intellect; and that the nearer man approaches perfection, the clearer are his views, and the greater his enjoyments.[6]

One of the grand fundamental principles of "Mormonism" is to receive truth, let it come from whence it may.[7]

The principle of knowledge is the principle of salvation.[8]

The Prophet Brigham Young, even though he had only 11 days of formal schooling in his entire life, had the same abiding faith in education. In instructions which he gave to the Saints before leaving Winter Quarters on the heroic trek across the plains, he said:

It is very desirable that all the Saints should improve every opportunity of securing at least a copy of every valuable treatise on education—every book, map, chart or diagram that may contain interesting, useful and attractive matter, to gain the attention of children and cause them to love to learn to read; and also every historical, mathematical, philosophical, geographical, geological, astronomical, scientific, practical, and all other variety of useful and interesting writings, maps, etc., to present to the general church recorder, when they shall arrive at their destination, from which important and interesting matter may be gleaned to compile the most valuable works on every science and subject, for the benefit of the rising generation.[9]

Under his leadership one of the first acts of the pioneers when they arrived in the valley was to found the University of Deseret.

At a World Fair held in San Francisco near the turn of this century his definition of education was used as a classic statement of its purpose and function. That definition is:

Education is the power to think clearly, the power to act well in the world's work, and the power to appreciate life.[10]

No better statement has been composed by anyone. Listen to other utterances of the founder of this institution:

---

[6]Joseph Smith, *History of The Church of Jesus Christ of Latter-day Saints,* ed. B. H. Roberts (Salt Lake City: Deseret Book Co., 1904), Vol. 2, p. 8 [commonly called *Documentary History of the Church;* hereafter referred to as *DHC.*]

[7]*DHC,* Vol. 5, p. 499.

[8]Joseph Smith, *Teachings of the Prophet Joseph Smith,* ed. Joseph Fielding Smith, 2nd ed. (Salt Lake City: Deseret News Press, 1940), p. 297.

[9]Reference unavailable.

[10]*Improvement Era,* Vol. 23 (July, 1920), p. 831.

114 EARNESTLY YOURS

We might ask when shall we cease to learn? I will give you my opinion about it; never, never.[11]

Not only does the religion of Jesus Christ make the people acquainted with the things of God, and develop within them moral excellence and purity, but it holds out every encouragement and inducement possible, for them to increase in knowledge and intelligence, in every branch of mechanism, or in the arts and sciences, for all wisdom, and all the arts and sciences in the world are from God, and are designed for the good of his people.[12]

Brother Maeser had the same philosophy:

I should be ungrateful if I did not place myself on record as being conscious that the Brigham Young Academy has been a chosen instrument in the hands of the Lord God of Israel, to plant the seed for an educational system that will spread its ramifications throughout the borders of Zion, penetrating with its benign influence every fireside of the Saints, and open to our youth the avenues to all intelligence, knowledge, and power.[13]

I have traced the educational views of Joseph Smith, Brigham Young, and Karl G. Maeser because I want you to note they do not separate education from the gospel. It is a part of it. I am aware that in discussions of the new stake there has been much speculation as to whether it will be run by the University or by the Church. I should like to suggest to you that there are no such alternatives. For the University does not exist apart from the Church and operates only as an arm of the Church. The instructions that are given to me as President of the university from day to day are the same instructions as will be given to President Romney as President of the Stake. We have both been instructed by the First Presidency that the primary purpose of any student at this institution is that of obtaining a true education. This includes both revealed and unrevealed knowledge. A student will not accomplish his purpose here if he is active in the stake but fails in his intellectual pursuits in the University. Likewise, he will not accomplish his purpose here if he excels in intellectual pursuits but ignores his spiritual growth and becomes inactive in the stake.

[11]*Journal of Discourses,* Vol. 3, p. 202.
[12]*Journal of Discourses,* Vol. 13, p. 147.
[13]Reinhard Maeser, *Karl G. Maeser* (Provo, Utah: Brigham Young University, 1928), pp. 125-126.

The Lord gives us revealed knowledge as to matters which we cannot learn for ourselves. As to other matters, he expects us to learn for ourselves and to work out our own destiny. There must therefore, in this University and this stake, be a fusion of spiritual and what is thought of as secular knowledge. More accurately stated, all knowledge is spiritual—all is a part of the Gospel.

In the words of President George H. Brimhall,

> Revelation and Science are complements of each other, sources of truth; they both belong to God. Through one is emphasized a knowledge of His will, and through the other, stress is placed upon His works.[14]

> It ill becomes the theologian to fight physical truth revealed by science, nor is it consistent for the scientist to scorn truth revealed by Deity. Revelation and Science at variance is like the two hands of the same person seeking to disable each other.[15]

We therefore invite you to participate fully in both the University and this great stake of Zion. You are the best student body in the world. We love you. We admire you. We are happy you come from some 31 countries. We know some of you are having your problems. So did we of the older generation. Solving these problems will develop your character. Following the path of least resistance makes both trees and men crooked. Don't follow that path.

You will find President Romney and me traveling down the path of eternal truth and activity together. We ask your full cooperation and we are sure we will have it.

---

[14]George H. Brimhall, *Long and Short Vange Arrows* (Provo, Utah: Brigham Young University Press, 1934), p. 30.
[15]*Ibid.*

WOMAN, MOTHER'S DAY, MOTHERS

(From address given to the Kiwanis Club, Provo, Utah, on May 10, 1951.)

Before I get to the serious part of my talk, I think that a few comments about women in general might be appropriate. Woman's first home, according to history, was in the Garden of Eden. There man first married woman. It is strange that the incident should have suggested to Milton "Paradise Lost."

Man was put in a profound sleep, a rib was taken from his side, a woman was created, and she has been his affliction ever since. Thus man's first sleep became his last repose. But the rib apparently contained very dynamic material. In my youth I recall my father always urged that I consider the parentage of those of the opposite sex who seemed to appeal to me. He often said, "I know you don't know it, but goodness is bred in their bones." And history bears him out. The versatility of that rib passeth all human understanding. The wonder is that there are so many women of proper demeanor when, in fact, they were made out of the crookedest part of man.

In the book of Genesis we read of one called the "First lady on the land." The Creator first "saw everything that he had made and believed that it was good,"

and then rested. Then he made man and said he was
good; and rested. Then he made woman out of the rib
of a man, but he said nothing—and there has been no
rest for man since. The "First lady" was called woman
"because she was taken out of man." We now realize
that in the long process of history she has taken out
of man plenty. As the poet says, "Disguise our bondage as
we will, 'Tis woman, and woman rules us still."

Because of woman's predisposition and tendency to
marry, an early Connecticut statute provided: "No gospel
minister shall unite people in marriage. The civil mag-
istrate shall unite people in marriage; they may do it
with less scandal to the Church." And, much as the
Pilgrim fathers were comforted by the women, they had
their full share of matrimonial troubles. One of the old
tombstones in the graveyard of the Pilgrims at Plymouth
Rock reads "Obediah and Sarah Wilkinson—their
warfare is accomplished."

Also, before I get too serious with respect to our
mothers, let me read a choice description of how many
of us celebrate Mother's Day:

HOW WE KEPT MOTHER'S DAY[1]

One year our family decided to have a special celebration of
Mother's Day, as a token of appreciation for all the sacrifices
that Mother had made for us. After breakfast we had arranged, as
a surprise, to hire a car and take her for a beautiful drive in the
country. Mother was rarely able to have a treat like that, because
she was busy in the house nearly all the time.

But on the very morning of the day, we changed the plan a
little, because it occurred to Father that it would be even better to
take Mother fishing. As the car was hired and paid for, and we might
just as well use it to drive up into the hills where the streams are. As
Father said, if you just go out driving, you have a sense of aimless-
ness, but if you are going to fish, there is a definite purpose that
heightens the enjoyment.

So we all felt it would be nicer for Mother to have a definite
purpose; and anyway, Father had just got a new rod the day before, which he said Mother could use if she wanted to; only Mother
said she would much rather watch him fish than try to fish herself.

[1]Condensed from "The Leacock Roundabout" by Stephen Leacock, *Reader's
Digest*, May 1950, p. 83.

So we got her to make up a sandwich lunch in case we got hungry, though of course we were to come home again to a big festive dinner.

Well, when the car came to the door, it turned out that there wasn't as much room in it as we had supposed, because we hadn't reckoned on Father's fishing gear and the lunch, and it was plain that we couldn't all get in.

Father said not to mind him, that he could just as well stay home and put in the time working in the garden. He said that we were not to let the fact that he had not had a real holiday for three years stand in our way; he wanted us to go right ahead and have a big day, and not to mind him.

But of course we all felt that it would never do to let Father stay home, especially as we knew he would make trouble if he did. The two girls, Anna and Mary, would have stayed and gotten dinner, only it seemed such a pity to, on a lovely day like this, having their new hats. But they said that Mother had only to say the word and they'd gladly stay home and work. Will and I would have dropped out, but we wouldn't have been any use in getting the dinner.

So in the end it was decided that Mother would stay home and just have a lovely restful day around the house, and get the dinner. Also it turned out to be just a bit raw out-of-doors, and Father said he would never forgive himself if he dragged Mother round the country and let her take a severe cold. He said it was our duty to let Mother get all the rest and quiet she could, after all she had done for all of us, and that young people seldom realize how much quiet means to people who are getting old. He could still stand the racket, but he was glad to shelter Mother from it.

Well, we had the loveliest day up among the hills, and Father caught such big specimens that he felt sure that Mother couldn't have landed them anyway, if she had been fishing for them. Will and I fished too, and the two girls met some young men friends along the stream, and so we all had a splendid time.

It was quite late when we got back, but Mother had guessed that we would be late, so she had kept back the dinner to have it hot for us.

We sat down to a big roast turkey. Mother had to get up and down a good bit during the meal fetching things, but at the end Father noticed it and said she simply mustn't do it, that he wanted her to spare herself, and he got up and fetched the walnuts from the sideboard himself.

The dinner was great fun, and when it was over all of us wanted to help clear the things up and wash the dishes, only Mother said that she would really much rather do it, and so we let her, because we wanted to humor her.

It was late when it was all over, and when we kissed Mother before going to bed, she said it had been the most wonderful day in her life, and I think there were tears in her eyes.

Mother's Day originated in 1914 when President Woodrow Wilson established the day as a time for "public expression of our love and reverence for the mothers of our country."

So much is written about the great men of our country and their accomplishments we often forget that except for their mothers, they would never have become great; they would have had no real accomplishments. This was certainly true from the beginning of our great country.

Historians and poets, statesmen and orators, have ever accorded to the mother of Washington a signal influence in determining his character and career. So universal is this sentiment, that the American people consider the noblest tribute to her memory is the inscription upon her monument, "MARY, THE MOTHER OF WASHINGTON."

His school days closed a month before his sixteenth birthday. His vacations, and such other times as he could command, were spent with his brother Lawrence at his home. Lawrence was a military officer, and his residence was the temporary home of other military men. George enjoyed their company, and became somewhat fascinated with military life, for which Lawrence thought he was especially adapted. For this reason he proposed that George should become a midshipman on a British man-of-war. The proposition fired the soul of our young hero, and he besought his brother to obtain the consent of his mother. After much conversation, explanation, and pleading, Lawrence obtained the consent of his mother; and, soon after, a British man-of-war moved up the Potomac, and cast anchor in full sight of Mount Vernon. On board this vessel a midshipman's warrant was obtained for George, who was more elated over this bit of fortune than over any previous experience of his life. What had been a sort of dream to him had suddenly become reality. His preparation for departure was soon made. His trunk was packed and carried on board the ship that would bear him away from his native land. He was arrayed in the gay uniform of a midshipman, and nothing remained but to bid his mother and other relatives farewell.

But when he stood before his mother in his naval costume, so tall and robust in figure, so handsome and graceful, so noble in appearance, the thought that she might never behold him again completely overcame her usual firmness and self-control, and she burst into tears. "I cannot let you go!" she exclaimed: "It will break my heart, George.' The son was taken by surprise, and well-nigh unmanned at the sight of his mother in tears. "But how can I refuse to go now that I have enlisted, and my trunk is on board?" he said. "Order your trunk ashore, and return your uniform, my son, if you do not wish to crush your mother's heart," nervously and feelingly answered Mrs. Washington, "I cannot bear the thought."

It was a trying ordeal for George; a sudden and sharp turn to make in his life, if he yielded to her request. But fortunately for him and the American republic, he made it in the manliness of his soul. "Mother, I can never go and cause you so much grief. I will stay at home," he answered. Then it was that "Washington the Father of his Country," was assured, and the Declaration of American Independence promised! We are not competent to say exactly what might have been the result to this country had George persisted to be a midshipman in the service of the king; but we are certainly justified in saying there would have been no Brandywine and Valley Forge, no Monmouth and Yorktown. The mother's tears blasted the hopes of the delighted midshipman, but made it possible for freedom to rear its temple on these shores.[2]

Great mothers have generally left their imprint upon their children, sometimes despite indolent and even worthless fathers. Dickens, for instance, wrote: "I think it is sometimes written that the virtues of the mothers shall be visited on their children, as well as the sins of their fathers."

The simple story of Lincoln, as told by Ida M. Tarbell, is completely convincing on this point:

Abraham Lincoln, born in Kentucky, was descended from New England ancestry, from which he inherited an intense love of liberty, thoroughness of character and perfect integrity. As often happens, these qualities did not appear in his father who was poor, improvident and ignorant. His mother was an energetic Christian woman of much refinement whose devotion to her domestic and maternal duties soon wore out her frail body, but imprinted her image indelibly on the heart of her son. Many times he said that all he was he owed to her. Then it must be assumed that to her he owed his rugged honesty, which became part of his name, and that thoroughness which led him to commit much of the Bible to memory, and which lay at the foundation of his success.

---

[2]William M. Thayer, "The Mother of Washington," from "Turning Points in Successful Careers," *Mothers' Day*, ed. R. H. Schauffler (New York: Moffat, Yard & Co., 1917), pp. 265-267.

Tradition has it that Mrs. Lincoln took great pains to teach her children what she knew, and that at her knee they heard all the Bible lore, fairy tales, and country legends that she had been able to gather in her poor life.

Lincoln's life had its tragedies as well as its touch of romance— tragedies so real and profound that they gave dignity to all the crudeness and poverty which surrounded him, and quickened and intensified the melancholy temperament which he inherited from his mother. Away back in 1816 when Thomas Lincoln had started to find a farm in Indiana, bidding his wife be ready to go into the wilderness on his return, Nancy Lincoln had taken her boy and her girl to a tiny grave, that of her youngest child: and the three had there said goodby to a little one whom the children had scarcely known, but for whom the mother's grief was so keen that the boy never forgot the scene.

Two years later he saw his father make a green pine box and put his dead mother into it, and he saw her buried not far from their cabin, without a prayer. Young as he was, it was his efforts, it is said, which brought a parson from Kentucky, three months later, to preach a sermon and conduct the service which seemed to the child a necessary honor to the dead.[3]

You will recall that in later life the Civil War President often said: "All that I am or hope to be, I owe to my angel mother."

I suppose that one of the really great tragic things of our individual lives is that we never see all that our mothers have done for us until it is too late to let them know that we see it.

Although my mother passed to the Beyond some years ago, I want to take this belated occasion to express my gratitude for what she meant to me, although at the time I never realized it.

All her life she was busy with the rearing of her children and with Church responsibilities. My earliest memory of her is when she was president of the Primary Association of her ward, in a ward which had no meeting house, and all the children of our ward used to come to our home to Primary. Later, she was president of the Relief Society of our ward, and I recall she used to take

[3]Ida M. Tarbell, "The Mother of Abraham Lincoln," from the Publications of the Lincoln History Society, *Mother's Day,* ed. R. H. Schauffler (New York: Moffat, Yard & Co., 1917), pp. 227-228.

me, as a boy, along with her in a horse and buggy to gather contributions and gifts for the poor of our ward.

Always she was intent that I should obtain an education, and she was willing to make any sacrifice that all of her children should obtain all of the educational training that was available to them. This at times, and I say it frankly, led to some conflict in our home. In those days my father, who himself had had but probably two years of elementary schooling in his life, was not quite sure that too much education was the proper thing for his children. In my early life I recall that he had quite an obsession against education. In later years that obsession has been directed largely against doctors. At the age of eighty-five, it became necessary for him to have three operations, all within a period of twelve months, medical attention that, except for his distrust of doctors, he would have had many years previously. Those operations have enabled him to live additional years and will perhaps enable him to live much longer. Yet, because you can't very well change the thinking of one his age, he still insists that each operation took ten years off his life.

My mother, on the other hand, was always willing to accept new ideas, to learn new things. While my father has been pretty much set in his ways all his life and in his ideas, my mother, like most mothers, was always looking for some stimulating thought, some new ideal, some better concept of living. Indeed, she was so ready at all times to accept something new that, much to the disgust of my father, she was never able to turn down a book agent and very seldom a solicitor or peddler who ever came to her door.

Before she married my father, she had only one year of college, and I assume that in those days that was pretty much the same as high school training today. She was so busy rearing her family that we never knew that during that one year of college she had taken great pleasure in doing some charcoal sketches. If she ever aspired to be an artist, none of us ever knew about it.

In her middle sixties, because of a serious heart condition, she was required to leave the Rocky Mountains and live at sea level in California. At the age of sixty-five, practically an invalid, she wrote me in New York that she had begun to paint, and while she was painting she wanted, at the same time, to take a few lessons. It was suggested that she would be very happy if her son would send her some money to take some painting lessons. In the same way that my father often became impatient at what he thought were the impractical things she wanted to do, my Scotch instinct rebelled at spending good American coin for what I thought were probably worthless painting lessons for a woman sixty-five years of age. Nevertheless, I sent her the money, but with the comment that she should not take her painting too seriously.

Imagine my surprise when in less than a month's time she sent me one of her paintings, and imagine my further surprise when, over the period of the next five years before she passed to her reward, she completed over 100 paintings.

I have said that sometimes we do not take the time to really appreciate what our mothers have done for us until it is too late. I had that experience, for in 1945, when I was giving all my energies to the prosecution of some large lawsuits, and heard that my mother was ill, I just didn't feel that I could get away for a few days, and by the time I did leave, it was too late; my mother had passed to her reward.

And while we are expressing our regrets at not having let our mothers know of our gratitude, I think it would be well also to express our gratitude to our wives and mothers of our children.

I acknowledge in my case that I have been anything but an ideal husband. The result has been that my wife started graying at 30 while I still do not have any gray hairs.

To the extent that our children have demeaned themselves properly and made good citizens, nearly all of the credit must go to their mother, for I have to admit that during the period of my law practice, I didn't pay anywhere near the attention to them that they should have been paid. I suspect that I was almost in the same category as Mr. Justice Pierce Butler of the United States Supreme Court. As a young lawyer he also devoted himself unremittingly to the practice of the law. Because of the pressure of his cases, he generally shunned any social engagements and his wife generally had to go alone. On this particular night he also declined to go and so his wife asked him if, in addition to working on legal matters, he would see that the children got to bed properly. When she came home around midnight, Pierce was still at his desk working over some law case. His wife asked him how the children were. He said that one of the "little brats" didn't want to go to bed, so he had to give her some corporal punishment and force her into bed.

Mrs. Butler, on going to the bedroom to find out what the situation was, found that her husband had forced one of the neighbor children into bed.

May I conclude this informal talk by quoting the words of Napoleon: "The future of the child is always the work of the mother. Let France have good mothers and she will have good sons."

May we by our conduct honor our mothers, and may we also treat them properly on Mother's Day and not compel them to stay home and cook dinner for us.

ADDRESS AT THE FUNERAL
OF MRS. VERA SJODAHL KING
ON JULY 30, 1955

May I begin by expressing to the sons and daughters of Vera Sjodahl King my gratitude for being asked to participate in this service. I am honored because my life has been made richer and fuller by the religious and statesman-like philosophy and integrity of your courageous father. From him I have learned that it more important to be right in one's own mind and at peace with one's own conscience than to follow every whim of fickle public opinion.

I am honored because Sister Wilkinson and I have prized as one of our choicest blessings the association we have had with your affectionate, understanding, and deeply religious mother.

We are met to pay tribute to your mother, a noble woman who came from a noble lineage, to render such comfort as we may to you, as sons and daughters and friends, and in so doing to again reflect upon the purpose of life and the progress that we ourselves have made upon the roadway of eternal progress.

Death of the material body must come to all of us. One of the most familiar aphorisms of the law is that nothing is as certain as death, yet nothing is as uncertain as the time of death. In the words of Andrew Jackson, "When death comes he respects neither age nor merit; he sweeps from this earthly existence the sick and the strong, the rich and the poor, and should teach us to live to be prepared for death."

Sister Vera Sjodahl King was the daughter of a very distinguished father and a very understanding and loyal mother. Her father, John Mattson Sjodahl, was born in Sweden in 1853. After studying in the common schools he entered Bethel Seminary in Stockholm and later Regent's Park College in London. He was raised a Lutheran but joined the Baptist Church at 13 years of age. After his schooling he became a Baptist minister; later, early in his life, he became general secretary of the Norwegian Baptist Union with headquarters in Trondhjem, Norway. Tragedy struck early in his marital life, for his first wife and their two children all died after a relatively few years of marriage.

It may have been the meditations caused by their deaths that caused him to sympathetically investigate the gospel. In any event, in his early 30's he heard the message of some Mormon elders and was immediately impressed with the dynamic message of the restored gospel. Sincerely, earnestly and eager in his desire for the truth, but yet wanting to make sure he was not pursuing any illusory trail, he left his native land, emigrated to Utah where he resolved to study the gospel in its native habitat—where he could study it, not only in philosophical terms but where he could witness its effect on the lives of other members. His investigation satisfied both his scholastic background and his spiritual yearnings. He settled in Manti and joined the Church on October 7, 1886. There in 1888 he married your grandmother, Christine Christofferson, a daughter of Danish converts to the Church. They were the first couple to be married in the Manti Temple.

He was then called on a mission to Palestine and Switzerland. On returning to Salt Lake City he was named to preside over the Scandinavian meetings of the

Church in Salt Lake City. A product of the classical European education, Brother Sjodahl was a gifted linguist, being able to speak in six different languages, among them Hebrew, Greek and Latin. He became a gifted and learned speaker and writer for the Church. His broad scholastic background enabled him to become one of our fine theological scholars, and he pursued his fine talents and his training in writing for all Church publications. A gentleman and a scholar, Brother Sjodahl became an outstanding authority on the Book of Mormon. He was editor of the Deseret News in 1898-99 and again from 1906 to 1910, and continued to write for its editorial columns thereafter.

He was called on another Church mission to Great Britain in 1914 about the time World War I broke out, and remained there for $4\frac{1}{2}$ years, doing much of the editing of the *Millenial Star*.

At one time, on appointment of the First Presidency, he travelled to Sweden to present a Book of Mormon to King Oscar II. Upon his return, Brother Sjodahl became associate editor of the *Improvement Era*. During this time he wrote "The Doctrine and Covenants Commentary," "Introduction to the Study of the Book of Mormon," "Joseph Smith—Was He a Prophet of God?" and "The Reign of the Anti-Christ". I should like to suggest to you children that it would be a fitting tribute to your mother and her father, if you have not already done so, for you to read these books.

Vera's mother, like Vera, was a loving, affectionate mother who taught her children to have a deep and abiding love for the gospel which was reflected in their lives.

Vera was born in Manti in 1891 but lived practically all of her childhood in Salt Lake City. A deeply religious girl, she often during her womanhood spoke of the rich and spiritual experiences in her home. I have heard her tell of a patriarch who visited her parents as a friend of the family. Suddenly, under inspiration, he placed his hands on Vera's head and gave her a blessing. Among other things he told her she would pass from mortality to immortality . . . without tasting the sting of death, and that she would travel throughout the world and be received by kings, rulers and magistrates. In her childish mind she could not understand how this could happen, but she nevertheless believed it would happen.

Both of these prophetic utterances were fulfilled. She slipped away in her sleep. The opportunity to be received by kings, rulers and magistrates was made possible when in 1912 she married William Henry King, one of the most brilliant public servants Utah has ever produced. At that time her husband already enjoyed a great reputation in his profession of the law, and in public life. At the age of 21 he had been president of the Utah Territorial Senate. Before he was 30 he had been associate justice of the Utah Supreme Court. Before the turn of the century he had been a member of our National House of Representatives for a term, but declined re-nomination. He had been a law partner of George Sutherland, later U.S. senator, president of the American Bar Association and justice of the U.S. Supreme Court.

Four years after his marriage to Vera, William Henry King was himself elected to the United States Senate, defeating his former law partner, George Sutherland. As such he served the State of Utah in the Senate with distinction and with integrity from 1917 to 1941, a period of 24 years.

From the beginning of his period of service in the Senate he was one of its recognized leaders. As such he was invited on a number of occasions to many foreign countries by kings and others where Vera was royally entertained as foretold by the humble patriarch who had visited her parents' home.

Because of his brilliance, his knowledge of history, including his love for ancient Greece and his befriending of the rights of minorities and the liberty of individuals as opposed to State domination, there stands in Athens, erected by the Greek government, a monument in his honor. Other countries including the Philippines have named streets in his honor. Very few Americans have thus been honored by foreign governments.

And may I, as one who was once honored by the Senator inviting me to be his secretary, say for the benefit of his children today that their father throughout his long public life was a great defender of the American Constitution and the American way of life as it was known to our Constitutional Fathers and to the Mormon Pioneers. He prized above all his freedom and liberties of the American people, and he never wanted the American citizens to become subjects of a bureaucratic government. He never allowed his political allegiance to turn him from his duty as a senator representing all of the people, and when the leader of his own party, the President of the United States proposed to subvert the Constitution by packing the Supreme Court, it was Senator King who wrote a majority report for the Senate Judiciary Committee in which he said:

We recommend the rejection of this bill as a needless, futile, and utterly dangerous abandonment of constitutional principle.

It would subjugate the Courts to the will of Congress and the President and thereby destroy the independence of the judiciary, the only certain shield of individual rights.

Its ultimate operation would be to make this Government one of men rather than one of law, and its practical operation would be to make the Constitution what the executive or legislative branches of the Government choose to say it is—an interpretation to be changed with each change of administration.

It is a measure which should be so emphatically rejected that its parallel will never again be presented to the free representative of the free people of America.

This report, written by Senator King, is one of the greatest documents in support of the Constitution ever to emanate from the Congress of the United States. It is not too much to say that your father's leadership in that day saved the Constitution of our country. I wish we had men in the Senate of equal vision and courage to save it today.

I mention this at this funeral to let you children know that few men in the Senate of the United States possessed his integrity and courage. Had our representatives in Congress all respected their oath of office to honor

and uphold the Constitution of the United States as did
he, we would not today be in the danger we are of losing
our liberties and our possessions and becoming, like
many other countries of the world, a socialistic state. I
am sure your mother would like at her funeral that this
be said about her distinguished husband and your great
father.

It was my privilege to first meet your mother when
Sister Wilkinson and I went to Washington, D.C., 32 years
ago. Prior to that time meetings of our Church had
generally been held at the home of Senator Reed Smoot.
By that time we had grown in numbers so that we met
in a very humble hall at 1731 Eye Street. For the first
time in Washington a Relief Society was organized. Sister
Don B. Colton, wife of our Republican Congressman,
was nominated and sustained as president of that Relief
Society. In the democratic and humble pattern of our
Church, where faith in God and belief in Jesus Christ
transcends all political beliefs and overrides all social
barriers, Sister Colton proposed your mother, wife of
the Democratic Senator, as her first counselor. From
that time on Sister King was a devoted leader of the
Relief Society of our Church in the nation's capital.

I talked to Sister Colton about your mother this
morning. She said your mother was a wonderful counselor.
The first Relief Society meetings in Washington were held
in her home, which became a center of religious and
social life for the Saints in Washington.

Sister Colton commented that they soon found out
she had a marvelous testimony of the gospel—she was
therefore called upon to give the theology lessons as well
as being a counselor in the presidency. In this capacity
she often related the spiritual experiences in her home as
a girl—presided over by a Swedish father and a Danish
mother.

She had a remarkable gift of understanding. Those
of all walks of life, both in and out of the Church, sought
her understanding and advice, and she never turned away
anyone who wanted her time and her sympathy and her
understanding and her counsel and advice.

From that time until her death Sister King was almost continuously serving her Church in one capacity or another. An exceptional teacher and one possessed of great faith, both gifts which she obtained undoubtedly from her distinguished parents, she was generally teaching some class or another. This interest and activity in the Church continued after she returned to Salt Lake City, and I understand that prior to her last illness she was again a counselor in the Relief Society in this North 13th Ward.

I had the pleasure and privilege of spending an evening with her about a year ago. She told me of having again been called to work in the Relief Society by the young bishop of this ward. She was grateful beyond measure for that opportunity for service. She told me that she spent most of her time in that work and in keeping in communication with her children. She spoke tenderly and affectionately of all of them. She spoke only briefly of the social and other recognitions that had come to her in her lifetime, for to her the important thing was continuing to be active in the Church. She was more interested in matters of the spirit and in her children.

I am happy that her son, John, a graduate of West Point, now a major in the Air Force, was able with his three children to visit his mother shortly before she passed on. I am happy that Kathleen, her oldest daughter, David, her eldest son, Eleanor, her other daughter, are able to be at this funeral today. I know that their mother loved them, and that she was always thinking of their welfare and hoping that they too would find in the Church the same inspiration, solace and satisfaction that she did.

I can pay your mother no greater tribute than this— that with all of the public acclaim which came to her husband and herself she always maintained a modest sweetness and spiritual calm. The glamour of her position never disturbed her spiritual equilibrium. She was

a noble woman who gave cheer and good will and determination to live a useful life to the scores of her friends
and admirers. She was a loyal wife and a devoted, intelligent, affectionate mother.

ADDRESS AT THE FUNERAL JOHN C. SWENSON ON SEPTEMBER 2, 1953

J. Golden Kimball once began a funeral sermon by saying it is difficult to speak at a funeral, because it's inappropriate to say anything against a dead man. That difficulty is obviated in the present case because John C's life was in the open, and he would not want me to represent him other than he was.

What I have to say, therefore, will not be an orthodox funeral sermon. I shall not talk of salvation, for John C's sake, because if John C. has not earned it, my talk won't help him. I shall not talk of the hereafter for his children's sake, for if the example of their father will not guide them, what I say will be of no help.

I merely want to speak of John C. Swenson, the man—one who was the teacher of many of us and the friend of all, one who always had a sense of balance, who always made his friends feel that they were important and yet who never permitted any of them to become puffed up in pride or inflated with too much wisdom. He always brought all of us back to the reality of life.

He was essentially a philosopher, especially as defined by one Braston, who has said that "philosophy is common sense in a dress suit." Brother Swenson was always giving

us generous doses of common sense, keyed to the experiences of the listener, but dressed up in the rich
language of John C. and made delightful by his
Scandinavian—Stanford—Oxford brogue. No one has
been able properly to describe it, or determine just where
and how much of that dialect he acquired. I know of no
one who has been able to imitate it, but it was always
stimulating.

Thoreau has told us that "To be a philosopher is
not merely to have subtle thoughts, nor even to found a
school, but so to love wisdom as to live according to
his dictates, a life of simplicity, independence, magnanimity and trust."

John C. Swenson had all these attributes. He lived
simple all his life. He died in the same home in which
he had lived for 54 years. To him material things were
of little consequence. He much preferred the meditation
and exhilaration of the human mind.

John C. always preserved an independence of
thinking. He lived in the present and was always
analyzing current problems. He never accepted at face
value the promises of either political party. No political
party ever had a life tenancy on his vote. He even recognized that Church leaders, when left to their individual predilections, could be wrong. He had a penetrating
mind which permitted him to size up an individual or
situation without the disintegrating erosion caused by
too much study. His greatest intellectual strength was that
of good balance.

Amused and entertained by the fact that in a political campaign two important Church men were talking
heatedly to each other under a pine tree at Aspen Grove,
he quipped that he didn't think they were discussing the
nature of Joseph's vision.

When a prominent member of the faculty took himself too seriously in a faculty meeting and announced
what he really was going to do, Brother Swenson commented that he had some doubt as to whether this man's
"rudder was strong enough for his sail."

When a speaker would become too vociferous he would comment that he was generating more "heat than light." When a speaker gave evidence of not having any strength of conclusions, he would comment that he was shooting moth balls rather than buck shot.

At one time someone was extolling to John C. the Word of Wisdom virtues of a man whose character was known to have some very serious defects. The expositor told John C. that this man lived the Word of Wisdom so perfectly he never lost a tooth. John C's ready answer was "I would sooner lose my teeth than lose my soul."

At another time, in commenting on a prominent woman who in her early life had also been a strict disciple of the Word of Wisdom, but who had been a little free with her affections, Brother Swenson remarked:

"She observed the Marquis of Queensbury rules much more with respect to the Word of Wisdom than with respect to her own boy friends."

In commenting on an individual noted for his "straddling of the fence" on every issue of the day, he commented,

"You know the Lord has blessed this man with a high degree of protective coloration."

Never taking himself too seriously, he recently climbed the stairs to Herald R. Clark's office, which, with his heart condition, he should never have done. On mounting the top and gasping for his breath he explained to Brother Clark that on coming up the stairs he had had palpitations of the heart, that he was just trying to determine whether it was physical or spiritual palpitation.

I repeat, he was always original in his thinking. He had a classic way of reducing men to their proper stature and of placing situations in proper perspective. He always cherished and gloried in his independence of expression.

Thoreau's third requisite of a philosopher was that he should live a life of magnanimity. Stated another way, his life should be generous, unselfish, lofty, high-minded, exalted in purpose. Brother Swenson had that quality to a rare degree. In his evaluation of others, he was never mean, vindictive, selfish, or ignoble. In disagreeing with one he never became disagreeable. While there are times when some of us thought he should have been more positive, and would have liked him to reveal his inner spirituality more often, he had that balance which always restrained him from questioning another's motives or destroying another's faith. He loved and believed in people and they loved and believed in him. Everything he said was in a spirit of humor and kindness. He never slandered anyone.

Thoreau's final attribute of a philosopher was that he should live a life of trust. Brother Swenson did that all of his life. Beginning as a member of the faculty of BYU in 1898, when salaries were irregular and pay checks far between, he had to trust others. But he trusted more than the presidents and trustees of the BYU. He trusted life. He obtained great exhilaration from it. He trusted the Lord. Never blessed with the materialistic goods of this world, he and his trusting wife had 10 children, 9 of whom survive. These 9 are all graduates of the BYU. We are honored with two of them, Albert and Margaret, being on our faculty today.

I don't want any of you to get the impression John C. was not religious. He had deep spiritual convictions. Recently when he was confined to the hospital, I had the pleasure of calling on him. The visit, as always, was pleasant, although he was gasping for breath. He good-naturedly chided me over the progress of the University. He wanted to know whether the brethren had received a new revelation for financing the school. But he paid a great tribute to them as leaders and to Karl G. Maeser. He told of first coming to Provo as a homesick boy; and how Brother Maeser had stopped him on the street and spoken a word of encouragement. He said he immediately resolved to stay and "stick it out."

If I were tense when I arrived to visit him, I was relaxed when I was ready to leave. As I started to shake his hand to bid him good-night, he asked me if I would administer to him. He then produced a bottle of holy consecrated oil and I was privileged to anoint his head and to ask the Lord's blessing upon him. He rallied that night, and the next day sent his word of appreciation to me for my visit and blessing. He was always generous in praise of others, and grateful for small favors. I never promised him recovery, but many were surprised he ever got out of the hospital.

During the last few weeks, the BYU has lost three of its greatest men: E. L. "Gene" Roberts, also a great philosopher, an idealist, who applied the same standards to athletics as he did to any other activity of life; Amos N. Merrill, a great educational enthusiast and promoter of faith; and now John Canute Swenson, a philosopher and realist—one of my stimulating teachers, my debating coach, my devoted friend and supporter when I returned to the BYU as president. Their going is a personal loss to me.

Fortunately, I had an opportunity to seek counsel from each of these three giants before they passed on; I hope that in the immediate days ahead, I may, in the interest of the BYU, have the wisdom and courage to follow their advice.

In closing I merely want to pay this tribute to Brother Swenson. Not only was he a great teacher, he was a good citizen. He was no hypocrite. The Prophet Joseph when he was asked for an evaluation of himself said this:

> I do not think there have been many good men on the earth since the days of Adam; but there was one good man, and his name was Jesus. Many persons think a prophet must be a great deal better than any one else. Suppose I would condescend—yes, I will call it condescend!—to be a great deal better than any one of you, I would be raised up to the highest heaven; and who should I have to accompany me? I love that man better who swears a stream as long as my arm yet deals justice to his neighbors, and mercifully deals his substance to the poor, than the long smooth-faced hypocrite. I do not want you to think that I am very righteous for I am not.

Brother Swenson, while he seldom swore, always dealt justly with his friends and neighbors. He always gave of his talents to others. He never thought of himself, nor was he accepted as a Pharisee, but according to the standard set by Joseph, he would be loved by him more.

To the family may I now say:

Your husband and father lived the kind of life to which we should all aspire. His entire life was devoted to the service of his fellow men. And because of his magnanimity, he was always happy. Some people seem to derive their happiness out of being unhappy. Not your father. I am sure he enjoyed every waking day, every sleeping night, and every person he met. His service and unselfishness brought to him their own reward. Not the least of that reward has been his devoted wife and loyal family, nearly all of whom, as though it were providential, visited him just a few days before he passed on to a new experience. I give it to you as my solemn conviction that his happiness and reward will continue in the eternities.

And in behalf of the University may I express to you the gratitude of that institution for his 54 years of unselfish service. If we thought it would produce results we would probably place a large banner at the entrance to the Campus reading: "Wanted: another John C. Swenson."

May the Lord bless you as members of his family to treasure his memory and follow his example—to respond to your great heritage! May the Lord bless all of us to preserve our balance and thrill to the many facets of life, as did Brother Swenson, I ask in the name of the Lord Jesus Christ, Amen.

RELIGIOUS SERMONS

Section 4

Accompanied by Sam Brewster, left, BYU Physical Plant Department director, and Dr. Ernest L. Wilkinson, Brigham Young University president, President David O. McKay snips ribbon to open new campus road.

President Ernest L. Wilkinson, right, welcomes Church President Joseph Fielding Smith to a Devotional Assembly in George Albert Smith Fieldhouse at BYU, January 12, 1971.

"MAN SHALL NOT LIVE BY BREAD ALONE"

(*Address given on the CBS Radio "Church of the Air" in the Tabernacle, Temple Square, Salt Lake City, Utah, June 17, 1956.*)

In the year 1923 nine of the world's wealthiest men attended a meeting at Chicago's Edgewater Beach Hotel, built on the beautiful shores of Lake Michigan, luxurious and elegant in its accommodations. These men represented nine of the largest financial enterprises in the world.

Those present were:

The president of one of the world's largest banks;

The world's largest wheat speculator;

The president of the world's largest utility company;

The president of the world's largest gas company;

The president of the New York Stock Exchange;

A distinguished member of the President's Cabinet;

The greatest "bear" in Wall Street;

The president of the Bank of International Settlement; and

The head of the world's greatest monopoly.

At few meetings, if any, in the world's history, has there been more private wealth and material success represented. Judged by contemporary circumstances, here were nine men each of whom had achieved the pinnacle of success.

But twenty-five years later history recorded a different story.

The president of one of the world's largest banks- had been forced to resign his position because of income tax irregularities which resulted in the government obtaining a judgment against him for over one million dollars.

The world's largest wheat speculator had lost twenty-nine million dollars in a stock market crash.

The president of the largest utility company had been a fugitive from justice in a foreign land.

The president of the largest gas company had served time in prison for mail frauds and was then in a mental institution.

The president of the New York Stock Exchange had recently been released from Sing-Sing Penitentiary.

The member of the President's Cabinet, convicted of accepting a $100,000 bribe as a government officer, had been pardoned from prison so he could die at his home.

The greatest "bear" on Wall Street had quietly put a bullet through his own head.

The president of the Bank of International Settlement had taken his own life on his beautiful summer estate.

The head of the world's greatest monopoly, a Swedish financier, had ended his life with a revolver in his Paris apartment.

In contrast to their earlier records of fabulous material success most of these men had now been weighed in the balance and found wanting.

Some two thousand years earlier Jesus of Nazareth had been led by the spirit into the wilderness to be tempted of the devil. There, in an arid and rugged country, amidst wild beasts he fasted for forty days. Weak, exhausted, the pangs of hunger gnawing at his very vitals, Satan tempted him by saying "If thou be the Son of God, command that these stones be made bread." But the Savior endured his pangs of hunger, withstood the temptation, and replied: "It is written: that man shall not live by bread alone, but by every word that proceedeth out of the mouth of God."

Later Satan took him up into an exceeding high mountain and showed him all the kingdoms of the world, and their glory, and said unto him:

"All these things will I give thee, if thou wilt fall down and worship me."

But Jesus answered: "Get thee hence Satan; for it is written, Thou shalt worship the Lord thy God, and him only shalt thou serve." (Matthew 4:5-11)

Unmindful of the Master who made it plain that worldly wealth and power were merely means to an end, history is replete with prominent men who have made the mistake of exclusively devoting their talents and life to worldly pursuits, or to worldly matters—only to realize too late that they had travelled the wrong road.

Cardinal Wolsey, as the King's principal minister, had given all the energies and abilities of his life to King Henry VIII. But when the King, against the traditions and standards of his church, sought to divorce Catherine of Aragon and to marry Ann Bolyne, the Cardinal did not support him. Wolsey was thereupon accused by the King of high treason and ordered to London for trial. Overtaken on the way by illness, he remarked to the constable in whose custody he was: "had I but served God as diligently as I have served my King, he would not have given me over in my grey hairs."

The Savior recognized this truth from the beginning. He knew that when the final test came he could rely on the riches of Heaven, for had he not told his followers: "Lay not up for yourselves treasure upon earth where moth and rust doth corrupt, and where thieves break through and steal; but lay up for yourselves treasures in heaven, where neither moth nor rust doth corrupt, and where thieves do not break through, nor steal. *For where your treasure is, there will your heart be also.*" (Matthew 6:19-21)

The treasure of the nine rich men had been their material possessions. When Caesar took from them the things which belonged to Caesar, they lost their interest in living, and had not the spiritual reserve necessary to further carry on.

Contrast their lives with the life of the Russian novelist, Count Leo Tolstoi, who forsook his royal title and wealth to live as Christ lived; or with the service of Albert

Schweitzer, German musician, philosopher, physician, and philanthropist, who went as a missionary-doctor to French Equatorial Africa to give medical and philosophical assistance to needy natives.

My friends, for what are you living? If you are accumulating earthly treasures what do you intend to do with them? Think not for one moment that there is anything inherently wrong in acquiring worldly possessions, provided you acquire them honestly and not at the expense of your fellow men. It is not money that is the root of evil, but the love of money to the exclusion of the more real and enduring values of life. This country has been the beneficiary of large fortunes of great men. We owe our extensive library system in large part to Andrew Carnegie. Many educational institutions have profited greatly from the wealth of John D. Rockefeller. This year has witnessed the greatest philanthropic gift of all times—that of $210 million by the Ford Foundation to private institutions of higher learning and hospitals. In this day when we have the misguided idea that the government can solve most of our problems for us, we need more industrial leaders of vision, not fewer.

But the acquisition of temporal wealth must be based on honest Christian practices—both by capital and by labor; and should proceed from a desire to use that wealth for spiritual purposes—in the service of one's fellow men. Further, in the gaining of wealth one should also cultivate and enjoy the riches of the spirit which are the realities that will withstand trial and tribulation. Such riches can be enjoyed in the days of prosperity as well as in the days of adversity. They belong neither to the rich nor to the poor but to him who keeps himself in tune with the eternal spirit of our Eternal Father. The Lord, speaking through the ancient prophet, Jeremiah, has said: "I the Lord search the heart. I try the reins, even to give every man according to his ways, and according to the fruits of his doings." (Jeremiah, 17:10)

To a modern-day prophet, the same God has said:

Wo unto you rich men that will not give your substance to the poor, for your riches will canker your souls . . .

Wo unto you poor men, whose hearts are not broken, whose
spirits are not contrite, and whose bellies are not satisfied, and whose
hands are not stayed from laying hold upon other men's goods, whose
eyes are full of greediness, and who will not labor with your own
hands!

But blessed are the poor who are pure in heart, whose hearts
are broken, and whose spirits are contrite, for they shall see the kingdom of God coming in power and great glory unto their deliverance;
for the fatness of the earth shall be theirs. (Doctrine & Covenants
56:16-18.)

The enduring truth that is missed by many people in
our civilization is that nothing belongs to us in perpetuity
except the opportunity to do good, and that in doing good
we obtain not only eternal rewards, but the spiritual
strength necessary to sustain and enjoy this life. For in the
words of Jesus, "whosoever will save his life shall lose it
and whosoever will lose his life for my sake, shall find it."
(Matthew 16:25.)

As president of a university, I have had the opportunity to study the lives of men and women who have been
out of college twenty-five, forty, and fifty years, and to
speak to many college students who are at the threshold of
their careers. Invariably, I am impressed by the fact that
they who have placed their reliance upon selfish desires
have lived empty and unsatisfactory lives. And when the
course of life is once run, it is impossible to retrace and
relive it. "For of all sad words of tongue or pen, the saddest
are these, it might have been." (From "Maud Muller," by
John Greenleaf Whittier.)

Four years ago a young student came to my office and
said he had to quit school because he did not have enough
money to continue. On inquiry I found that he was paying $100 per month on an automobile which he had with
him at school. At the institution with which I am associated, this is sufficient for most students to pay their tuition, room and board and all other educational expenses.
I therefore suggested he sell his automobile and with the
money he was paying thereon each month, he acquire an
education. To anyone with unclouded vision, the choice

would have been obvious. But this boy chose the automobile and quit school. I heard from him the other day. His automobile was worn out and he had lost his job because he was not prepared to handle it. Recalling that his fellow classmates had now graduated, he inquired if he could get a janitorial job so that he might take a part-time course. Well, he might be able to salvage the four years of wasted time by now going part-time for about eight years, but he may also have formed habits of mental indolence so that he may never complete his college education.

How much more meaningful is the story of the young couple who live next to our campus. Less than a month ago their young son, five years of age, was riding a small bicycle down a steep hill from the university. Getting out of control, his bicycle crashed into a passing automobile driven by one of our students and he was killed. In a collision of this kind there is always a question of who is to blame. Admitting the five year old was going too fast on his bicycle, still might his life have been saved if the passing motorist had been driving more carefully? What should these bereaved parents do to compensate themselves for the loss of their child? Complain to the university about an unsafe hill? Sue the driver of the automobile for damages? Or become bitter and let this misfortune corrode and canker their souls? Well, here is what they did. Two weeks after their son's death, the university received the following letter:

Dear Sirs: This letter is to kindly request permission to set up a scholarship fund of $440 each year to run indefinitely, perhaps to be used by students who are widows or children of widows (or widowers). This fund would be in honor of our five-year-old son, Roy, who died two weeks ago on a street next to the campus after completing a visit to your great university.

Let us add that this proposed gift is not insurance money, as we had no insurance on him. Before his death, Roy sold garden seeds and did odd chores, saving every penny he ever earned. Then after his death, his friends gave (*to him,* we are sure) hundreds of dollars in donations. We, his parents, desire that his name should be kept alive and we know of no worthier way.

(signed) Edwin and Glenna Klein, parents of Roy Klein.

By thus commemorating the life of their five-year-old youngster, this young father and mother have achieved victory over death—they have turned tragedy into sweet and lasting memories. Not rich in earthly goods, but willing to share what they have in memory of their lost child by helping others, they have become rich in the things of the spirit. Not living by bread alone, they belong to those of whom Coleridge wrote:

> He prayeth best who loveth best
> All things both great and small.
> For the dear God who loveth us,
> He made and loveth all.
> The Ancient Mariner

In the words and life of our Saviour are found the living water and bread of life. "Blessed are they who do hunger and thirst after righteousness, for they shall be filled."

I add my own testimony that whosoever believeth and liveth in Him shall never die but shall spring up into everlasting life. I do it in the name of Jesus Christ. Amen.

THE TREE THAT PRODUCES
THE FRUIT

(Address given November 12, 1951)

Many observers of Mormonism have marveled at its fruits—few have attempted to carefully examine the tree that produces it; yet this latter is the more important field of inquiry, for the fruit is the product of a single season and varies in perfection according to the circumstance of wind and water and care, whereas the tree is capable of producing over and over again in abundance.

To understand the fruit one must understand three things pertaining to the tree: the spirit of testimony which gives it impetus; the philosophy that gives it purpose; and the priesthood organization which lends it direction and power.

Observers of Jesus, as he preached in ancient Palestine, said of him, "He taught them as one having authority and not as the scribes." (Matthew 7:29.) In their comment they unwittingly touched upon the crux of the whole matter. Jesus and those who are truly his followers know whereof they speak. Their faith is not a product of reasoning; it does not arise from observation—although both may make it usable—it emanates from the Spirit of God and sets them apart from those who lack that spirit.

In the year 1839, Joseph Smith, the Prophet of The

Church of Jesus Christ in those latter days, sat across the room from James K. Polk, President of the United States of America, in the White House at Washington, D. C. In answer to the President's question, "What is the difference between you Mormons and the rest of us Christians?" Joseph Smith replied, "We have the Holy Ghost."

The tree of Mormonism has spirit in its branches. It is not a dead tree. Mormonism is based, not upon a mere belief in God, but on a real knowledge that he is. Listen to the certainty in these words of Joseph Smith in relating his first vision:

> However, it was nevertheless a fact that I had beheld a vision. I have thought since, that I felt much like Paul, when he made his defense before King Agrippa, and related the account of the vision he had when he saw a light, and heard a voice; but still there were but few who believed him; some said he was dishonest, others said he was mad; and he was ridiculed and reviled. But all this did not destroy the reality of his vision. He had seen a vision, he knew he had, and all the persecution under heaven could not make it otherwise; and though they should persecute him unto death, yet he knew, and would know to his latest breath, that he had both seen a light, and heard a voice speaking unto him, and all the world could not make him think or believe otherwise. So it was with me. I had actually seen a light, and in the midst of that light I saw two Personages, and they did in reality speak to me, and though I was hated and persecuted for saying that I had seen a vision, yet it was true; and while they were persecuting me, reviling me and speaking all manner of evil against me falsely for so saying, I was led to say in my heart, Why persecute me for telling the truth? I have actually seen a vision; I knew it, and I knew that God knew it, and I could not deny it, neither dared I do it, at least I knew that by so doing I would offend God, and come under condemnation.[1]

This certainty is had by tens of thousands in the Church, from the time of Joseph Smith until now. Certainty concerning God and his church has been the outcome of personal revelation. It is not the study of Joseph Smith and his visions which brings final conviction to us. It is the personal experience with the Holy Ghost which may be had, and is had by those who seek it in faith.

---

[1]Joseph Smith, *History of The Church of Jesus Christ of Latter-day Saints,* ed. B. H. Roberts (Salt Lake City: Deseret Book Co., 1927), Vol. I, pp. 7-8.

It was the spirit of testimony which enabled the Mormon pioneers to sing, "And though we die before this journey's through, all is well." It was the spirit of testimony in the early Latter-day Saint colonies of the West, which caused families to hang on despite bitter hunger and other privations. It was the spirit of testimony that caused missionaries to leave their Rocky Mountain homes and draw their handcarts a thousand miles over the plains in order to make new converts.

It is the spirit of testimony today that causes Church members to attend meetings; to devote long hours in voluntary service; to pay a tithe of their income; to produce for the Church Welfare program.

To understand "Mormonism" as a force one must understand the philosophy of life that permeates all that the Church is and does.

Human happiness is the aim of the Church. In the words of the Book of Mormon, "Man is that he might have joy." And the Prophet Joseph proclaimed, "A religion that does not make a man happier here and now is not worth having."

All Mormon philosophy stems from these following fundamental propositions:

1. Man is co-eternal with God. He existed before the world was, and will live again beyond the grave.

2. Man is the literal spiritual offspring of God and like his parents may become a God.

3. All blessings are predicated upon obedience to law.

4. God does not leave his children helpless but reveals himself to them.

5. Jesus Christ has revealed the way to happiness, made possible the resurrection from the grave and the overcoming of sin, and through the delegation of his power officiates in saving ordinances for the living and the dead.

Unlike man-made philosophies, which develop from pure reasoning and logic, those fundamental concepts were revealed to man by God. Yet these and the entire philosophy that has developed from them are rational. They are in harmony one with another, and with all truth.

When we look upon man as an eternal being, a God in embryo, he becomes important in our eyes. Certainly "the worth of souls is great in the sight of the Lord." To Latter-day Saints the individual is more important than the State or any earthly organization. He existed before they came into being and will survive when they have returned to the dust. Thus, the care of the body is important, and also the cultivation of the intellect, and the development of love.

With eternity in mind marriage and children assume new importance and meaning; our dead return to life and claim our love and the whole of existence becomes beautiful and meaningful.

With an understanding of blessings and punishments as the results of the operation of law and order we gain incentive to learn what those laws are and gain the desire to obey them that we might have happiness.

In a world of law and order the gods of whim and intrigue are replaced and superstitions disappear. Through the ordinances of the priesthood the power of God is continually manifest among us. The influence of the Holy Ghost is felt. The sick are healed. New tongues are spoken.

We are not worshiping at dead shrines and grasping at the meanings of ancient prophets. We are living in the present. This is the Church of Christ with his present direction and power.

A man with a testimony of God and a great philosophy of life is still weak when standing alone. It is organization that brings power and lends direction for the movement of that power. The Church of Jesus Christ of Latter-day Saints has been productive because it has harnessed the latent power of its members, and in keeping with the principles of a great philosophy given direction and purpose to that power.

Spiritual emotion must find expression or it will die. Even selfishness will die if it is not exercised. The love of man is born, will only perish if we do not find expression for it in service. The love of God, which on occasion strikes deep into the heart, only perishes if we do not enter into his labors.

The Church offers a fellowship with others who are seeking to obtain happiness according to spiritual law.

The Church offers opportunity for growth through service. No one who is willing sits on the sidelines. The work of the Church is divided and sub-divided so as to bring every person into activity.

The Church offers to every member to take part in helping those who are hungry or destitute. This is done collectively through fast offerings and welfare projects. It offers ownership in beautiful churches, temples, and schools through the payment of tithes and offerings.

The Church provides opportunity to partake of holy ordinances, to participate in sacred music, to both hear and bear testimony, and even to act in God's name.

Try as he might man's will is not always master of his fate, the captain of his soul. Paul cries out in agonized desperation, "The good that I would I do not; but the evil that I would not, that I do . . . O wretched man that I am! Who shall deliver me from the body of this death?" (Romans 7:19, 24.)

The answer follows immediately, "I thank God through Jesus Christ our Lord." Christ made the difference. The Church comes to Paul's rescue and helps him live the better life. And it helps us too.

It is the genius of Mormonism, that the Church makes every member a partner with God. As holders of the priesthood we act in his name, enter into covenants, heal the sick, comfort the afflicted, and teach one another the things of the kingdom.

It is this power to act in God's place, to sense the stirrings of Godhood within us, to feel in part his emotions as we bless mankind in his name, that lifts the members of the Church into the possession of powers they little dreamed of, and gives such a taste of the ultimate joy that may be obtained, that having thus tasted of the fruits of Godliness man prizes that feeling above all earthly things. This is what gives life and power to the tree, and this is what those observers who have not shared this experience cannot understand. For example, men have gone through our Church Welfare centers, they have examined our records, and have observed our people under the Church Welfare Plan—but they have not been able to emulate it. And they cannot. The plan will not work for them. The tree planted by their hands would remain barren. It needs the power of God flowing through the branches to furnish the seed of life. Those engaged in God's work must exercise his power and feel his divine approval if the work is to survive more than a passing enthusiasm.

Most Christian churches sense the need of tithes and fast offerings. They find the scriptures requiring them. But without the priesthood, the power of God which stirs men's souls, they cannot collect them.

Yes, the fruits of Mormonism are only possible from a living tree that has its roots in eternal verities. The fruit for a given season may be scrawny and poor, worms may infest it and hail mar it, but the tree continues to bear, and given proper cultivation, sunshine and rain, its fruits become beautiful and increase from generation to generation.

PAYING TITHING

(*This address was delivered originally at a general meeting of the Brigham Young University faculty at the Preschool Faculty Workshop, September 24, 1957.*)

The theme of my talk today is different from that of any other college president. My justification for this is that this institution is different. Without disparaging in any way the many fine accomplishments of other institutions and their many fine programs which we are copying (and we need to adopt more of them), I am convinced that the genius of this institution consists in its differences from rather than its similarities with other institutions.

The University Handbook of BYU contains the standards by which teachers are engaged and promoted on the faculty of this institution. These standards, I should add, were approved by this faculty a few years ago. One of the qualifications which are standard for that of an instructor, an assistant professor, an associate professor and a full professor is the following: "Belief in, and adherence to the principles and teachings of the gospel as taught by The Church of Jesus Christ of Latter-day Saints." Admittedly, this belief in these principles does not apply to those few who have honored us by becoming members of our faculty and who are not members of our faith, although we expect of them, and I am happy to say that we receive, standards of conduct that are worthy of emulation by our students. What I have to say today will apply to the members of the faculty who are members of our Church.

One of the principles of our Church to which we pledge adherence when we become members of the faculty is that of the payment of tithing. It therefore becomes necessary for me as the administrative officer of this institution, when teachers are employed and when they are advanced, to determine whether or not they are adhering to that particular principle. That is implicit in the standards adopted by the faculty and certainly favored by the Board of Trustees. I consider the performance of this obligation as one of the primary obligations of every member of the Church on our faculty.

I make no apology for this straightforward statement because the future growth of Brigham Young University and the Church School System—and of the Church itself—depends upon the extent to which the members of the Church faithfully comply with this commandment of the Lord.

Apart, however, from the great religious and educational program that could be conducted by the Church if all members paid a faithful tithing, there are more fundamental reasons for each of us paying his tithing.

In the first place, it ought to be sufficient for us that the payment of a tithing is a commandment of the Lord *to us* as well as to those who lived in former dispensations.

Historically tithing is older than Israel. For example, Abraham, a patriarch, paid tithes to Melchizedek, the Priest of the most high God. (Genesis 14:18-20.) Jacob (Israel) covenanted with the Lord to "give the tenth" unto Him. (Genesis 28:20-22.) The same commandment was enjoined upon the children of Israel after they had been brought out of Egypt (Leviticus 27:30, 32.) History records that as long as the Israelites faithfully complied with the law of the tithe they prospered; when they failed, the land was no longer sanctified to their good. Holy prophets admonished, rebuked, and reproved with sharpness as the people time and again fell into transgression. One of the most cryptic admonishments is found in the last book of the Old Testament. There, Malachi, with stern rebuke, said:

> Will a man rob God? Yet ye have robbed me. But ye say, wherein have we robbed thee? In tithes and offerings. (Malachi 3:8; 3 Nephi 24:8.)

Tithing was still practiced at the time of our Lord's personal ministry, approved and commended by him and continued as a church function during the apostolic period and for a considerable time thereafter.

Gradually, however, during the Great Apostasy and the Dark Ages, tithing lost its sacred character and was appropriated by different nations as a means of taxation. In the ninth century, Charlemagne made it a part of the state revenue. In England the tithe was imposed by authority of the civil law, and inured to the benefit of the established church. It then consisted of one-tenth of all rental produced. It thus lost its voluntary church significance and had to a large extent lost its virility when the gospel was restored.

On July 8, 1838, the Prophet Joseph approached the Lord with the question: "Oh, Lord, show unto thy servants how much thou requirest of the properties of thy people for a tithing." The answer was the revelation of tithing comprising the 119th Section of the *Doctrine and Covenants:*

> Verily, thus saith the Lord, I require all their surplus property to be put into the hands of the bishop of my Church in Zion, For the building of mine house, and for the laying of the foundation of Zion and for the priesthood, and for the debts of the Presidency of my Church. And this shall be the beginning of the tithing of my people. And after that, those who have thus been tithed shall pay one-tenth of all their interest annually; and this shall be a standing law unto them forever, for my holy priesthood, saith the Lord. . . . And I say unto you, if my people observe not this law, to keep it holy, and by this law sanctify the land of Zion unto me, that my statutes and my judgments may be kept thereon, that it may be most holy, behold, verily I say unto you, it shall not be a land of Zion unto you. And this shall be an ensample unto all the stakes of Zion. Even so. Amen.

We are not here concerned with the first part—commanding the saints to put all their surplus property in the hands of the bishops. We are concerned with that part which enjoins on each of us the responsibility of paying one-tenth of our interest annually. This has been clearly interpreted to mean one-tenth of one's entire income—not merely one-tenth of the residue which one has left after all expenses, all other Church donations, or even after all taxes have been paid.

Forceful aids in interpreting this language, because of their candor, are the words of the founder of this institution:

> One thing is required at the hands of this people, and to understand which there is no necessity for receiving a commandment every year, viz.: to pay their tithing. I do not suppose for a moment, that there is a person in this Church, who is unacquainted with the duty of paying tithing, neither is it necessary to have revelation every year upon the subject. There is the Law—pay one-tenth.
>
> (*Journal of Discourses*, Vol. I, p. 278)

> I do not own a house, or a single farm of land, a horse, mule, carriage, or wagon, or wife, or child, but what the Lord gave me, and if He wants them, He can take them at His pleasure, whether He speaks for them, or takes them without speaking. (*Journal of Discourses*, Vol. II, p. 307)

The former Presiding Bishop of the Church, Joseph A. Wirthlin, defined a "tithe" as follows:

> How many times the question is asked, "What is a tithe?" The very word itself denotes one-tenth. A tithe is one-tenth of the wage earner's full income. A tithe is one-tenth of the professional man's net income. A tithe is one-tenth of the businessman's net income. A tithe is one-tenth of the farmer's net income, and also one-tenth of the produce used by the farmer to sustain his family which is a just and equitable requirement, as others purchase out of their income such food as is needed to provide for their families. A tithe is one-tenth of the dividends derived from investments. A tithe is one-tenth of net insurance income less premiums if tithing has been paid on the premiums. (*Conference Report*, April 1953, p. 98)

A second reason why we should pay our tithing is that we have been assured by our Church leaders that we will be individually blessed financially if we keep this commandment. I suppose the person in our day who preached this doctrine more than anyone else was the late President Grant. He believed it from the bottom of his heart, and, although born a very poor boy, was sufficiently blessed in this world's goods that he was able to serve the Church for over a half a century without accepting compensation therefor. President Grant's testimony on this is as follows:

> I bear witness—and I know that the witness I bear is true—that the men and women who have been absolutely honest with God, who have paid their one-tenth . . . God has given them wisdom whereby they have been able to utilize the remaining nine-tenths, and it has been of greater value to them, and they have accomplished more with it than they would if they had not been honest with the Lord. (*Conference Report*, April 1912, p. 30.)

Philosophically, I have never felt that I should pay my tithing with the expectation of receiving a *quid pro quo* in the form of monetary reward, but I would be ungrateful here today if I did not acknowledge in your presence that when the payment of tithing on my part has required the greatest sacrifice, I have always received the greatest blessings. I assume that you are acquainted with many of the testimonies of other members of the Church to this effect. For the present, however, let me give you the experience of other men who are not of our particular faith, but who attributed their success to the complete adherence to this and other fundamental Christian commandments.

Let me start out with the story of a great furniture manufacturer of Grand Rapids, Michigan. He was starting over in life. His first attempted business had not been a success. The tiny string of credit which he had to depend upon in his new venture was made up of the faith of a few close friends rather than the calculated mathematical confidence of banks.

One day he walked slowly through the empty rooms of the little factory. He was alone in the building. As yet the machinery was not in place. When he came to a remote corner of one of the upper floors, he knelt, closed his eyes, and prayed.

Then he got up and went out into the world again and began his hard business fight. The machinery came at last, and he started to make furniture. He borrowed and borrowed; his improving business records strengthened his credit.

But there was a mystery about him in the fields of credit. Although he began to look more and more safe to the credit men, he seemed to insist on giving money away. While he was borrowing, he gave. Sometimes he said "no" to those who asked for financial aid for religious or philanthropic purposes. But when he did say "yes," he said it with an alacrity that astonished the recipient. He did not give money to foolish ventures or to unsound enterprises, but it was a puzzling thing to the bankers to have him borrow from them while he was giving money freely to help others who were finding the world a hard place in which to live.

His business grew; within a few years it became well-established; his furniture became known to the trade for its honest quality. At last, there came a time when borrowing was no longer necessary.

His tiny string of credit had become a thousand-stranded cable; he was one of the marked successes in the furniture world.

When he died, after a well-rounded life, the mystery of his gifts was explained. It seemed that during all his business career he had considered that the money which he borrowed, the money which he earned, and the money which he gave away was not his own money at all; it was God's money.

Over his casket, that day of the funeral, the clergyman of the church which he had attended told the story.

"I have carried a secret about our friend," ran the gist of the clergyman's story, "which I have never been able to reveal until now. He asked me never to tell it while he was alive.

"When he was making his second start in life, so he told me, he knelt in an empty room in his new factory; and he told God that he wanted to take him into partnership, that one-tenth of all the earnings should go to him, and that he would use the money in all his business ventures as if it were God's money."

Another example of the benefits of tithepaying is that of Matthias Baldwin, founder of the Baldwin Locomotive

Works. His rigid precept was to set apart one-tenth of all
the earnings of his company for the use of the Lord. In
dark days, when his firm was struggling against terrible
financial difficulties, he continued to do so, pointing out to
his associates that this was their one safe investment.
When his own firm had reached a crisis, he continued the
payment of tithing in the form of notes signed by himself.
All were eventually paid.

Two large manufacturing concerns in the West were
headed by Thomas Kane, one of the most notable tithers
in the United States. During his life he spent many
thousands of dollars in trying to prove to his fellows the
moral and material benefits of tithing. His inquiry, sent
out in the form of a pamphlet, has become famous wherever
it has gone. It runs:

My personal belief is that God honors, both temporally and
spiritually, those who devote one-tenth of their income to his cause.
I have never known an exception. Have you?

It is said that in forty years Mr. Kane, who used the *nom
de plume* "Layman," never received an affirmative answer
to his query.

Jay Cooke, who founded the banking firm of Jay
Cooke and Company in 1861 and was substantially the financier of the Union cause during the Civil War, tithed
in hard times and good, for he held firm to the belief
that what he had achieved was due to his sharing his profits with God.

In the Southwest there is a string of twenty-eight
stores which form a great monument to a business man
who, through his business career, followed the practice of
tithing. He explained once to friends why he tithed.

"Why, you and I tithe each other," he said. "We
would not lend a neighbor money with which to run his
business without interest. Neither would we expect him to
lend us money without paying interest. I found I was using
God's money and the business talents he had given me
without paying him interest. That's all I've done in tithing—just met my interest obligations!"

Take the case of Charles Page of Tulsa, Oklahoma. As a young man he and the late Senator J. H. Lewis of Illinois had completely failed in business. His failure completely demoralized him and in the vernacular of the street he was "going to the dogs." As he emerged from a saloon in Seattle, he was asked for a contribution by a white-haired Salvation Army woman.

"I'm broke," said young Page. "I'm down to my last dollar."

"Well, why don't you tithe?" she asked, still smiling.

"Tithe? What does that mean?" asked the young fellow.

"Why, the Bible says that we ought to give one-tenth of what we have to the Lord," she explained.

"All right!" said the youth. "I've got a dollar and fifteen cents. I'll do better than one-tenth. "I'll give fifteen cents." He tossed the fifteen cents into the tambourine and went his way.

This lasting Bible lesson was the most important thing that ever happened to this young man. From that day, so they tell you in Tulsa, Charles Page "tithed" and more than "tithed." "Charlie" Page has been working with "God's money" ever since. His good fortune at striking oil has been phenomenal; there is a tradition in the oil fields of the country that "Charlie" Page never misses a "hole." Where he drills, oil comes, they say. You cannot get Page to talk about his "partnership"; it is his own private affair. But once he told a friend in speaking of his success at drilling:

> I think I've missed only two holes in my life. You see, I couldn't miss, because I was in partnership with the Big Fellow and he made Geology.[1]

Now I am aware that there are some of you who have certain doubts as to whether monetary reward will be the recompense for your obedience to this law of tithing, and while I philosophically have always had certain doubts of my own, nevertheless the realities have been otherwise,

---

[1] William G. Shepherd, "Men Who Tithe," *The Improvement Era*, Vol. 31 (June 1928), pp. 635-636.

and I would merely like to suggest if there be any of you of little faith on this matter, that I have never known a person in our Church who faithfully paid one-tenth of his income to the Lord, who did not get along just as well on the other nine-tenths of his income. If nothing else, it taught him habits of frugality and of economy.

Those of us who have faith in the promises of the Lord should need no explanations of the financial benefits of the law of tithing. Yet some psychologists have attempted to give them. Professor Robert Sessions Woodworth, one-time head of the Department of Psychology at Columbia University, put the cold yardstick of the science of psychology up against the beliefs and successes of tithers. He stated: "The belief that their money was a loan from God and that they were in partnership with him, would give these men who tithe more confidence and self-reliance, would minimize all difficulties in their eyes, and would, no doubt, go far toward bringing them success . . . their belief, considered by itself, does present an element of mysticism, and this belief was doubtless strengthened by their putting it into action; had they merely entertained it as an abstract conviction it would never have impressed them so deeply."

A third reason for the payment of tithing is that keeping of this commandment pays one a soul satisfaction. Some of you may have known the late Fred G. Taylor of Ogden, a young man very successful in developing a large sugar organization. During the boom which followed World War I, when the price of sugar reached an all-time high, his company started expensive remodeling in one of its plants. Shortly afterward, a general depression hit the country and the bottom fell out of the sugar market. This company, together with many others, found itself in a very precarious financial position. A man of high technical ability and natural leadership, with a limited knowledge of finance, Fred reproached himself for not having foreseen the depression, with its attendant difficulties for his company.

To restore the company to a sound basis, an outsider

put up substantial funds upon condition that his own representative replace Fred Taylor as general manager. Fred declined another position offered him, because he considered the action taken by the new management unwise and lacking in regard for many faithful employees. Though he not only had lost his own financial backlog in the depression but was greatly in debt, he resigned.

When he reported to his sweet wife what had happened, she said, "Fred, I've had an intuition that something like this would happen. We haven't been living close to the Lord. We're going to have to start again from scratch, and this time I want your promise that every cent of money we take in will be properly tithed."

Fred thereupon turned over to his creditors what was then one of the large, handsome homes in Ogden, started a new business, and moved with his family to Harrisville.

Later, when he had re-established himself, he was appointed head of the Sugar Institute, Inc., in New York City, which was the national trade association for all cane sugar companies in the country. While there he became president of New York Stake, a man loved and respected by every member of the Church in that part of the Lord's vineyard. That was some years after his financial debacle, but he was still paying his previous debts.

One day he came to my office on Broadway near Wall Street, where I was practicing law. President Grant was along with him. President Taylor said he was getting together a few of his very close friends that evening to tell them an important story, and I was invited. When we sat down to dinner, he proceeded to recount what I have just related to you. He concluded by saying this was the happiest day of his life: he had just paid off the last of his debts and had also paid tithing on much of the income he had lost in the depression following World War I. He had much more soul satisfaction that night than he could have gained by accumulating millions.

This leads to another question that is frequently asked: "When should I pay my tithing?" The answer is obvious:

"Whenever you receive an increase." Thus wage earners, or school teachers or others who receive their salaries monthly should pay their tithing monthly. Farmers or others who receive increase at varying times should pay their tithing when they receive their increase. No one should expect to spend a large share of this increase before he pays tithing on it. The school teacher, for example, who spends eleven months of his salary before he pays his tithing will find that he can't very well pay one-tenth of his income annually out of one-twelfth of his income. Pay your tithing as you receive your increase.

This advice was also given by President Grant:

> The payment of our tithing in the season thereof—when we get our income—makes it come easy. I find that those who pay tithing every month have very much less difficulty in paying it than those who postpone payment to the end of the year. . . .
>
> The Lord, you know, does not send collectors around once a month to collect bills; He does not send us our account once a month; we are trusted by the Lord; we are agents; we have our free will; and when the battle of life is over, we have had the ability and the power and the capacity to have done those things which the Lord required us to do and we cannot blame anybody else. (*Improvement Era*, January, 1941, pp. 9, 56.)

The danger of delaying in the payment of tithes is strikingly portrayed in another story told by President Grant:

> On the subject of tithing I heard a very splendid illustration given by a teacher in one of our children's classes: She brought with her ten beautiful red apples. She explained that everything we have in the world came to us from the Lord, and she said, "Now, if I give you these ten apples, will you give me one of them back again? Now, any one of you children that will do that, hold up your hand."
>
> Of course, they all held up their hands. Then she said, "That is what the Lord does for us. He gives us the ten apples, but He requests that we return one to Him to show our appreciation of that gift."
>
> The trouble with some people is that when they get the ten apples, they eat up nine of them, and then cut the other in two and give the Lord half of what is left. Some of them cut the apple in two and eat one-half of it and then hold up the other half and ask the Lord to take a bite. That is about as near as they see fit to share properly and show their gratitude to the Lord. (*Conference Report*, April, 1945, p. 6.)

Now I know that varying excuses are made by some people to justify themselves in not paying tithing. Let me take up some of these excuses one by one and point out the fallacies in them. The first is that "I cannot afford to pay tithing." The tragedy of that excuse is that it is usually used by those who can most easily afford to pay. President Brigham Young, for instance, had this to say:

> It is very true that the poor pay their tithing better than the rich do. If the rich would pay their tithing we should have plenty. The poor are faithful and prompt in paying their tithing, but the rich can hardly afford to pay theirs—they have too much. If he has only ten dollars he can pay one; if he has only one dollar he can pay ten cents; it does not hurt him at all. If he has a hundred dollars he can possibly pay ten. If he has a thousand dollars he looks over it a little and says, "I guess I will pay it; it ought to be paid anyhow"; and he manages to pay his hundred dollars. But suppose a man is wealthy enough to pay ten thousand, he looks that over a good many times and says, "I guess I will wait until I get a little more, and then I will pay a good deal." And he waits and waits and waits like an old gentleman in the East; he waited and waited and waited to pay his tithing until he went out of the world, and this is the way with a great many. (J.D. 15:163-164)

Another fallacy of this excuse is that the poor are exactly those who are most in need of the financial blessings of paying tithing.

Mary Smith, the widow of Hyrum Smith, remained faithful to the Church after the death of her husband. Under very adverse conditions she followed the admonition of Brigham Young to come west. After arriving in the Valley of Salt Lake in 1849, she tried to maintain and support her family. Despite a scarcity of food and clothing, she insisted on paying a full tithing. Her son, Joseph F. (who at that time was only ten years of age, but who in later life became an apostle and the sixth President of the Church) tells this story of his mother:

> I recollect most vividly a circumstance that occurred in the days of my childhood. My mother was a widow, with a large family to provide for. One spring when we opened our potato pits, she had her boys get a load of the best potatoes, and she took them to the tithing office; potatoes were scarce that season. I was a little boy at the time, and drove the team. When we drove up to the steps of the

tithing office ready to unload the potatoes, one of the clerks came
out and said to my mother: "Widow Smith, it's a shame that you
should have to pay tithing." . . . he chided my mother for paying her
tithing, called her anything but wise or prudent; and said there were
others who were strong and able to work that were supported from
the tithing office. My mother turned upon him and said: "You ought
to be ashamed of yourself. Would you deny me a blessing? If I did
not pay my tithing, I should expect the Lord to withhold his blessings
from me. I pay my tithing, not only because it is a law of God, but
because I expect a blessing by doing it. By keeping this and other
laws, I expect to prosper, and to be able to provide for my family."
(*Conference Report*, April, 1900, pp. 48-49.)

I remember as a young bishop of thirty in the New
York Stake one of the faithful members of my ward who
came to me with a very substantial payment of tithing.
Knowing that his income was only a small percentage of
some others in the stake, who did not pay as much tithing
as he, I said to him, "Hugh, how can you afford to pay so
much tithing?" The rebuke was electric. He said, "Afford!
In my situation I cannot afford not to pay tithing." I
submit that this is the proper answer.

Another excuse offered by members of the Church for
not paying tithing is the claim that one's faithfulness
should not be measured by what he does with his material
possessions—that to do so is placing a price tag on one's
religion. Most of these persons are known as five per centers,
or as one per centers or token tithe payers. Actually I guess
even the term *token tithe payers* is too generous for them and
is in a way a contradictory term. If anyone pays less than
one-tenth it is not a tithe, for a tithe—by definition—is
one-tenth. Perhaps we should say, then, that these people
make a token payment to the tithing fund. Some of them
are pious persons who move in the best Church-going
circles and would never think of drinking coffee or
saying "Damn." In my mind they are the modern-day
Pharisees. Unless they are willing to render an account
of their substance to their God and impart of their substance to those in need, I don't think that, without full
repentance on their part, there is much chance for their
salvation either in this life or the life to come. Why shouldn't

one be measured by his faithfulness in accounting for his
stewardship to the Lord?

Lest you think I am overemphasizing what I would
say, I recall that the parables of the Master were nearly
all concerned with the poor, caring for the sick, succoring
those in distress. Contrary to the superficial thinking of
many people, Jesus was intensely practical. He talked in
terms of parables which had to do with people's material
welfare. Sixteen of his recorded 38 parables had to do with
money and property. Paying tithing is the best way I know
for one to rid himself of the un-Christian trait of selfishness. I suspect that the excuse of professing not to believe
in tithing is one of those rationalizations not even believed
in by the rationalizer. To those who reason this way, let
me give you the words of one of my predecessors, President George H. Brimhall:

> Tithing is the acid test of Mormonism and the first steps to
> apostasy are: (1) Diminution in payment of tithes, (2) excuse hunting
> that does not satisfy the soul, (3) cessation of tithe paying.

Another excuse for not paying tithing is offered by
some people who claim they have already done enough for
the Church—and for the Lord. For example, there are
some returned missionaries who take the attitude. "I
have given a great deal of my life to the Church, and have
spent a good deal of my money in the service of the Church.
Let that substitute for the tithing others pay." The short
answer to that excuse is that it is not the full truth. For
generally the expenses of a missionary are paid by his
parents and not by him. As to his time, seldom does one
go into the mission field who does not receive more than
he gives. The obligation of tithing rests upon all of us
regardless of our other service to the Church. Even tithe-
payers not of our Church recognize that tithe paying is
separate and apart from other service to the church. A
bishop of another church, which was in need of money,
at one time went to "Charlie" Page, to whom I have
already referred. Page had by that time become impatient
with churches that were in financial need; he couldn't

understand it. The bishop seated himself at Page's invitation, but before the bishop could say a word, Page looked him squarely in the eyes and said, simply: "Bishop, do you tithe?"

"Why, I give my entire time to the Church," was the answer.

"Yes, I know," answered Page. "I understand that, but do you tithe?"

The bishop admitted that he did not. He got no money. By the same reasoning non-tithepayers cannot expect to receive tithe blessings.

We are taught in the *Doctrine and Covenants:*

There is a law, irrevocably decreed in heaven before the foundation of the world, upon which all blessings are predicated—And when we obtain any blessing from God, it is by obedience to that law upon which it is predicated.

(D&C 130:20-21)

This of course applies to the law of tithing as well as to the other laws of the gospel. If we want the blessings of tithe paying, *we must pay a full tithing.* This applies to everyone—a General Authority of the Church, a member of the BYU faculty, a teacher in an LDS seminary or institute, a missionary, a widow, a child, or anyone else.

Another excuse offered by some for not paying tithing is that many tithe payers are poor; therefore the law of tithing does not work. To this, all I can say is that there may be other facts. I am certain that not all those who are poor have been faithful tithe payers of the Church, and I am equally certain that most tithe payers of the Church are not poor. Those who pay seldom boast about their tithe paying nor are they given any publicity. Also, it should be remembered that many of the blessings of the Lord promised to the tithe payer are not monetary in nature.

A final excuse is sometimes given by students. Sometimes you find a student who says: "I am a student. I don't believe I should pay tithing while I am going to school, for my educational expense is merely to permit me to earn more later." I mention this because I have known of some teachers who have acquiesced in this advice. The answer is that it is just as much of a capital investment for a student to go on with his education as it is for a businessman to put money into his business. The law of tithing requires one-tenth of income in the case of both. It is interesting to note that the original BYU Stake, in the first year of its existence, with a membership of 4,800 students, received over one quarter of a million dollars in tithing. Seventy per cent of the students paid a full tithing; 12 per cent paid a partial tithing, and 18 per cent did not attend tithing settlement. Undoubtedly many of those not attending tithing settlement were exempt from the payment of tithing because of having no income.

I am simple enough to believe from many experiences that even in the financial affairs of life it pays one to pay tithing. May I therefore plead with each member of this faculty to make sure that you pay a full tithing, not only for your own blessing but for the blessings that will inevitably be showered on this institution, which needs divine protection and development. And when I say full tithing, I mean *one tenth of all that you make, without any deductions for your personal expenses.* I mean one tenth of your entire salary, not what many call "take-home" pay, for in my opinion the obligation to pay tithing to the Lord exceeds in importance of the obligation to pay taxes to Caesar. If you run into difficulties because of extra expenses for illness or otherwise, I will recommend that the School Teachers' Loan Fund loan you money for the payment of your tithes. I consider that just as sound an investment as the purchase of a home. In one case you get a roof over your head; in the other you develop a home within your soul.

I had a bishop come to me once and say, "You surely must pay low salaries at BYU."

And I said, "Why do you make that conclusion?"

He said, "I have one of your teachers in my ward, and when it came to tithing settlement last year, he paid $150 and stated it was a full tithe." The bishop went on to say, "How do you expect your teachers to live on $1,500 a year?"

All I could tell him was that the representation of this teacher that he paid a full tithe was an academic fable.

Since salaries paid to the faculty of this institution now compare favorably with those paid by the other institutions of higher learning in the Rocky Mountain area and are higher than those paid in many institutions throughout the country, please don't slander the good name and good faith of this university by making a token payment to the tithing fund and reporting it as a full tithing. Such an act only compounds the sin. The founder of this institution once said: "We do not ask anybody to pay tithing, unless they are disposed to do so; but if you pretend to pay tithing, pay it like an honest man." (*Journal of Discourses*, Vol. VIII, p. 202). Fortunately, I am convinced there are very few members of this faculty who misrepresent what they pay. I hope hereafter there will be none. On the whole I feel confident the record of the faculty in the payment of tithing excels the good record of that of our student body, which it should. Indeed, it is from our faculty that our students get the motivation to pay tithing. So the record of our students is a tribute to the leadership and performance of our faculty.

If ever in my life I have had any doubt as to whether what I was paying was a full tithe—and this happened in days of adversity as well as prosperity—I always gave the Lord the benefit of doubt and paid the larger amount. I offer to you the same formula for putting your own business affairs in good order. When I am called upon this year to pass on proposed promotions in academic rank for members of the faculty, I hope I do not have to refuse any on the ground that the nominee does not adhere in practice to one of the qualifications approved by the faculty of this institution for advancement in academic rank, namely, "adherence to the principles and teachings of the Gospel as taught by The Church of Jesus Christ of Latter-day Saints," one of which is the payment of tithing. And I trust that such payment will be voluntary, for we do not want any person on this faculty to share his income with the Lord because of any coercion or compulsion.

Should there be any member of the faculty who does not voluntarily desire to pay his tithing the honorable and manly thing for that person to do is to resign his position. We shall be strong as individuals and collectively as a faculty only to the extent we exercise our free agency by freely choosing to obey the commandments and revelations of the Lord.

May we magnify our calling as teachers of the Lord Jesus Christ, I ask humbly in his name, Amen.

ADDENDUM BY THE AUTHOR

On reading the foregoing address, which I am informed has been distributed by the Public Relations Department of the University, I immediately noted one grave deficiency (undoubtedly there are many others). A number of the instances of the practice of tithing cited by me involved men who practiced this doctrine as a matter of personal conviction, even though the denominations of which they were members did not authoritatively preach that principle. Since they practiced this as a matter of personal conviction, apart from the doctrines of their particular church, they of course chose the particular charities which were the object of their bounty.

To those of us who belong to The Church of Jesus Christ of Latter-day Saints, the practice of tithing by revelation means that we pay the amount to our respective bishops, who in turn transmit it to the General Authorities of the Church for proper use by the Church. It is not for us as individuals to determine the particular purpose for which this tithing shall be spent.

ERNEST L. WILKINSON

"FAITH—THE MOTIVATION
OF ACTION"

(This address was given on the "Faith in Action" program of the NBC Radio Network on Sunday, March 18, 1956.)

This University, of which I have the honor to be president, is the product of faith of a great leader who generated faith in a great religious people.

One hundred nine years ago Brigham Young led the Mormon pioneers across the desolate plains to the barren Salt Lake Valley. As they passed near Fort Bridger, they met the colorful trapper and trader Jim Bridger. Bridger warned Brigham Young that starvation faced his people for the land was so dry and the growing season so short that edible crops would not mature. Tradition has it that he offered Brigham one thousand dollars for the first bushel of corn they grew in Salt Lake Valley. But this warning did not deter these pioneers, for they had faith in a divine promise that had been made to them that the desert would blossom as the rose and they would found a mighty commonwealth.

On arriving in the Salt Lake Valley these pioneers translated their faith into action—they damned up creeks, flooded the lands, and thus gave birth to modern irrigation. In due time the desert did blossom as the rose.

Under the leadership of this man of faith over one hundred thousand people crossed the plains; over three hundred towns and cities were colonized and a vigorous civilization was founded.

Brigham Young's great faith was inseparably connected with his deep belief in education and intelligence. Although he had had only eleven days of formal schooling in his life he believed that "the glory of God is intelligence"; that a man can be saved only as fast as he gains knowledge; and that the principle of knowledge is the principle of salvation.

With this educated faith he urged all his followers never to cease study or learning. Just two years before his death he founded this great University. His instructions to the faculty were that the school should be founded upon faith in the Lord Jesus Christ and that no teacher should teach even the multiplication tables or the alphabet without the inspiration of God. With that faith, without buildings or a budget, teachers began to teach without regular salaries, subsisting on vegetables or other farm produce which were accepted in lieu of regular tuition.

From that humble beginning of faith this University has now become the largest church-related University in the United States, with students from every state of the Union and from 31 foreign countries attending.

And, just as the Mormon pioneers were led to the Valley of the Great Salt Lake, and just as this school has grown, by faith and reliance upon our Lord Jesus Christ, so each individual, by recognizing he is accountable to his Creator for putting that same faith into action, may prosper in the fruition of his own talents.

In the early days of the University one boy who had little of this world's goods had such faith in his ability to succeed that he dug a cave in the foothills of the Rocky Mountains where he slept nights, spending each full day in the libary on the campus. He later became a prominent radio manufacturer.

Another boy had run out of funds to carry him through the spring term. Unable to obtain work, he walked every day to the post office hoping to receive a letter with expected funds from his father. One day, after several days

without food, he went to the post office fully intending
that unless he received an advance he would quit school.
The letter was there. The father explained the delay by
informing him that a large river had overflowed its banks
and had washed out the only bridge over which mail
could be transported. The father eventually had to swim
the swollen river with a gold coin tied to his neck. This
gold coin was enclosed in the letter. The faith of that
father was vindicated when his son later became superintendent of public instruction of his state.

These days of privation are not past. Just a year ago
we gave a scholarship consisting of full tuition and fees to
a little girl who had practically no means of continuing
her education. But with faith in her ability to achieve
she appeared for registration with her scholarship, a
grateful smile, and with the last five dollars her parents
had—this was to last her until she got a part-time job.
But she was grateful for the opportunity of providing for
herself. With faith in action she emerged at the end of
the year as one of the honor students of her class.

In the same way as faith in God and faith in oneself
bring personal success, so faith in God and the keeping of
his commandments, will bring forth great spiritual powers
and blessings. These spiritual powers such as manifested
by the Savior, when he healed the sick, caused the blind
to see, raised the dead, did not end with his death. They
are manifestations of the spirit of God—and can be enjoyed by his children today if they exercise the necessary faith and keep his commandments.

If you think that they have been taken from the earth,
listen to this dispatch of the United Press sent from
Honolulu on February 8, 1944:

> Some folks say that the day of miracles has passed. Yet here is
> a story of the battle of the Marshall Islands.
> The time was just before dawn when the great gray hulks,
> which were battleships, lay against the cool horizon of the blue
> Pacific. Aboard those ships the boys were anxiously awaiting the first
> signal which would announce the start of the drive to take one of the
> greatest of Japanese bases.

Being a war correspondent, my boat was going in behind the first line of men and we came upon two wounded marines in the water. One, from the stain of red around him, we could tell was wounded badly; the other, wounded too, was holding the other's head above water. We picked them up amidst a hail of shots from shore—then pulled back toward safer retreat to render first aid. The one seemed too far gone to need much help; the other refused aid until his wounded buddy was attended. But our help seemed insufficient, and we announced our decision through his comrade. Then it happened.

This young man, the better of the two, slowly got to his knees. His one arm was nearly gone but he placed the other on the head of his unconscious pal and uttered what to us seemed incredible words—words which to this moment are emblazoned in unforgettable letters across the doorway of my memory:

"In the name of Jesus Christ and by the virtue of the Holy Priesthood which I hold, I command you to remain alive until the necessary help can be obtained to secure the preservation of your life."

Today the three of us are here in Honolulu and he is still alive, in fact we walk down the beach together as we convalesce. He is the wonder of the medical unit, for—they say—he should be dead. Why he isn't, they don't know—but we do, for we were there, off the shores of Kwajelein.

Faith, in the case of these marines, had triumphed over death. The answer to all religious doubt is the answer given by Joaquin Miller in his "Christopher Columbus." When asked by his crew as to "What shall we do when hope is gone," Columbus answered, "like a leaping sword; Sail on! Sail on! Sail on and on!"

ADDRESSES
TO STUDENTS

Section 5

President Ernest L. Wilkinson of Brigham Young University with live cougar mascot "Sparrow."

Cosmo the Cougar, BYU mascot, counts as President Ernest L. Wilkinson does 44 pushups (at age 71) before a crowd during a basketball game February 13, 1971.

BE FRUITFUL AND MULTIPLY

(Taken from the Report and Address given at the 80th Commencement Exercises of Brigham Young University on June 3, 1955.)

Keeping the First Commandment

I am particularly pleased to report that past graduates of this University in their quest for material and professional success have not overlooked the more important matters of the spirit—in particular, that they have not forgotten the first commandment given to man, to "be fruitful" and "to multiply and replenish the earth and subdue it." (Genesis 1:28.) For a period of time the Population Reference Bureau, Inc., of Washington, D.C., which has on its Board of Trustees many of the best population experts in the United States, has been compiling a yearly record of the number of children born to both men and women graduates of the different universities and colleges of the country, who have been out of college for ten years and for 25 years, respectively. Through this study this Bureau now has a record, in which the BYU has participated, of the birthrate from each of the more than 100 participating universities, of six classes which have been out of college ten years, and six classes which have been out of college 25 years. The study of the birthrate for the first ten years out of college is a fair indication of whether the graduates have been postponing or curtailing the birth of children in their early married life. The study of the birthrate for the first 25 years out of college determines the complete size of the families (unless there is a second marriage) for presumably by that time the mothers are through their child-bearing age.

Out of six years in which the BYU participated in this national study, our men graduates who had been out of college 25 years ranked first four years and second two years; our men graduates who had been out of college for only ten years ranked first two years, second three years, and third one year. Our women graduates who had been out of college 25 years ranked first four years, fifth one year and sixth one year; our women graduates out of college for only ten years ranked first one year, second one year and third one year, but were not included in the first ten for the other three years. Presumably there were too many spinsters in three of the classes.

Grouping all four classifications together, however (men and women who had been out of college for 25 years and men and women who had been out of college for ten years), no other university or college matches the record of BYU. Furthermore, the number competing was so representative and the margin of difference so substantial that it can be said with confidence that, had all universities and colleges in the United States participated, the graduates of Brigham Young University would still be at the top of the list.

Because a different number of schools participated on different years and the published studies do not give the total number of children involved each year, it is impossible to give you an overall total as to the average number of children born to men and women graduates out of college for 25 years and 10 years, respectively. But the comparisons by years tell the story. Thus for the graduating classes of 1944, the last class so far canvassed, in which the graduates had been out of school 10 years, the BYU men had an average of 3.17 children per graduate as compared with 1.7 for the average male college graduate of 147 participating institutions. For the same year the

BYU women had an average of 2.08 children as compared with 1.39 for the average woman college graduate.

As respects the class of 1929, the last class canvassed in which the members had been out of college for 25 years, BYU women graduates had 3.78 children per graduate compared with an average of only 1.36 for the 121 participating colleges. The figure for BYU is almost three times as high as the average for the participating colleges. As to men of the same class, BYU men had 3.38 children per graduate as compared with an average of 1.95 for the participating colleges as a whole. Similar results are found for the 25-year graduates of the class of 1926. Brigham Young University had 2.62 children per graduate compared with 1.18, which is the average number of children per graduate for 121 colleges. BYU men had 3.88 children per graduate as compared with 1.84, the average for the graduates of 121 participating universities. In each of the latter cases the BYU figure is over twice as high as the average for all the participating colleges.

I am happy to state that the graduates of the Utah State Agricultural College and the University of Utah, universities in which the students are preponderantly Mormon, also, had a very high rating. The performance of the three Utah universities, in particular BYU, led Robert C. Cook, director of the Population Reference Bureau, to state in a letter written to me four days ago:

It is a remarkable record. When college graduates on the average are falling quite far short of replacing themselves, the graduates of these three Mormon universities have consistently shown a fertility well above replacement. Since in the kind of world we live, there is an even greater need for people with a high level of competence and ability, the importance of this can hardly be over-estimated. I sometimes tell my genetic classes at George Washington University that a college diploma comes high. Speaking statistically it amounts to almost semisterilization! That is not true in Utah. You should be very proud that this is so.

In an article in a bulletin published by the same Bureau Dr. Cook states:

This performance of the Mormon Colleges reflects . . . the high value which the Mormon religion places on children and large families.

As would be expected the same excellent performance is evident in the record of the BYU faculty. Dr. Bradford of our Sociology Department took a census this week of the children of faculty members and found that for faculty members whose wives are about 45 years of age (and therefore presumably beyond the child-bearing period) the average number of children per married faculty member was four. This is a much higher figure than the average for universities throughout the country. Indeed many faculties do not even perpetuate themselves.

For faculty members whose wives are under 45 years of age the average number of children per married member is well over three, even though many of them are newly married couples. The indications are that this latter group will substantially exceed the performance of the older faculty members. This increase among our younger faculty members demonstrates that our birth rate is not primarily due to the fact, as once theorized, that we are essentially a rural people, but is due basically to our religious beliefs and motivation.

I should add that I understand on June 6, 1955, the Population Reference Bureau will release to the press its study of the fertility of college classes for 1930, who have been out of college for 25 years, and for 1945, who have been out of college for 10 years. I have every confidence that, as in the past, taking men and women graduates together, BYU graduates will repeat their record of past performance. I hope you will be on the look-out for this expected news release.*

---

*The news release of June 6, 1955, more than vindicated the confidence of President Wilkinson. That release is as follows:

"Brigham Young University was announced as winner of the 'baby sweepstakes' competition among U.S. college graduates. BYU graduates captured first place in three out of four categories. The bureau studied 1945 and 1930 graduates of 178 colleges.

Leading the nation in number of children were BYU men of the class of 1930, with an average of 3.47; BYU men of the class of 1945 with 2.94, and BYU women of the class of 1930 with 2.75.

Women of the class of 1945 at Pacific University led the nation in their class, with an average of 2.40.

The bureau surveyed 29,494 graduates from the classes of 1945 and 1930.

This superior record of our graduates in being "fruitful" is a testimony to the integrity of this institution in teaching the commandments of the Lord, and to its graduates in observing those teachings—another evidence that it is the Lord's institution.

It springs, of course, from our revealed religious philosophy that marriage is ordained of God and is his sacred institution. In the words of President Joseph F. Smith, "While man was yet immortal, before sin had entered the world, our Heavenly Father himself performed the first marriage. He united our first parents in the bonds of holy matrimony and commanded them to be fruitful and to multiply and replenish the earth. This command has never been changed, abrogated or annulled; but it has continued in force throughout all the generations of mankind." (Jos. F. Smith, *Juvenile Instructor*, Vol. 37 [July 1, 1902], p. 400.) Accordingly, the faithful graduates of this institution are married in the temples of the Lord, not "until death do ye part," but "for time and all eternity."

In order that this class will not only follow but will surpass the unselfish record of prior graduating classes in this respect, I propose at this time, in lieu of a further traditional report, to do an unorthodox thing at a commencement exercise, and set forth what these teachings are. In doing so I propose to rely, not on my own interpretation, but largely on the wisdom and advice of the past and present prophets of this Church—the only Church named by the authority of and in the name of the Savior of the world. If I give too many quotations it shall be merely for the purpose of emphasis and to make use of what Dr.

It found that men of the class of 1945 have an average of 1.73 children, a 70% increase over the class of 1939 which averaged 1.02 children 10 years after graduation.

Women of the class of 1945 now have an average of 1.43 children, a 51% increase over the women of 1936.

Graduates of western colleges generally have more children than those in other sections of the country. But the report and figures for the West "are heavily weighted by large Mormon colleges in Utah."

University of Utah women graduates of the class of 1930 were second in the nation, with 2.44 children.

The bureau said the difference between the West and the other sections of the country "virtually disappears when the Mormon group is excluded from the regional totals." (United Press. Washington. Population Reference Bureau.)

Olds[1] and others will recognize as the doctrine of *stare decisis*. Even then I shall not read all the authorities in my written text but shall ask leave to revise and extend my remarks in the printed record.

Duty to Provide Tabernacles for Spirits of Men

Our belief in the eternity of the marriage covenant is a part of our belief that this life is only one of the steps in the plan of the eternal progression. Stated in the words of President Lorenzo Snow, "As man now is, God once was; and as God now is, man may become."

Speaking on this doctrine President J. Reuben Clark, Jr. has said: ". . . behind the great principle and commandment (to multiply and replenish the earth) lies the eternity of the marriage covenant, the creation of bodies to tabernacle spirits that Our Heavenly Father created and to bring them to this earth, so that they might have mortal bodies, live according to the commandments of God, that they might in their next estate begin and go on through all the eternities in eternal progression." (J. Reuben Clark, Jr., *121st Annual Conference of The Church of Jesus Christ of Latter-day Saints*, April 1951, p. 78 [hereafter referred to as *Conference Report*].)

Brigham Young, the founder of this institution, stated the same principle in the following language:

There are multitudes of pure and holy spirits waiting to take tabernacles, now what is our duty?—To prepare tabernacles for them: to take a course that will not tend to drive those spirits into the families of the wicked, where they will be trained in wickedness, debauchery, and every species of crime. It is the duty of every righteous man and woman to prepare tabernacles for all the spirits they can. (Brigham Young, *Journal of Discourses*, Vol. 4, p. 56.)

President Heber J. Grant carried forward the same doctrine when he said:

Providing opportunity for the spirit children of our Father in Heaven to come to earth and work out their own salvation is one of our sacred privileges and obligations. (Heber J. Grant, *Improvement Era*, Vol. 44, p. 329.)

[1]Dr. Irving S. Olds, retired chairman of the Board of Directors of United States Steel Corporation.

The late Melvin J. Ballard in a Mother's Day address delivered in the Salt Lake Tabernacle repeated the same divine truth:

There is a passage in our scriptures which the Latter-day Saints accept as divine: "This is the Glory of God—to bring to pass the immortality and eternal life of man." Likewise we could say that this is the glory of men and women—to bring to pass the mortality of sons and daughters of God, to give earth-life to the waiting children of our Father. . . The greatest mission of woman is to give life, earth-life, through honorable marriage, to the waiting spirits, our Father's spirit children who anxiously desire to come to dwell here in this mortal state. All the honor and glory that can come to men or women by the development of their talents, the homage and the praise they may receive from an applauding world, worshipping at their shrine of genius, is but a dim thing whose luster shall fade in comparison to the high honor, the eternal glory, the ever-enduring happiness that shall come to the woman who fulfills the first great duty and mission that devolves upon her to become the mother of the sons and daughters of God. (Melvin J. Ballard, "Mother's Day," *Sermons and Missionary Services*, pp. 203-4.)

Duty of Every Competent Person to Marry

Because of our duty to enable other spirits to enjoy a mortal existence, every competent man and every woman having the proper opportunity, has a divine obligation to marry.

President Joseph F. Smith has stated this duty in these words:

We believe that every man holding the Holy Priesthood should be married, with the very few exceptions of those who through infirmities of mind or body are not fit for marriage. Every man is a worse man in proportion as he is unfit for the married state . . . No man who is marriageable is fully living his religion who remains unmarried. He is doing a wrong to himself by retarding his progress, by narrowing his experiences, and to society by the undesirable example that he sets to others, as well as he, himself being a dangerous factor in the community. (Joseph F. Smith, *Juvenile Instructor*, Vol. 37 [July 1, 1902], p. 400.)

Duty to Marry Those of Like Spiritual Ideals and Attributes

The proper discharge of this marital responsibility imposes on you the responsibility to marry those of like spiritual ideals and attributes. All authorities on marriage —religious leaders, students of sociology, and others—agree that the prime requisite for success in marriage is that of a common religious culture and ideology. You should therefore make sure that you court those of like religious and spiritual beliefs. If that is done, you can then fall in love knowing that your marriage will glorify both yourself and your Heavenly Father. The unusual success of marriages resulting from romances on this campus arises from the fact that the participants enter into the holy and eternal bonds of matrimony imbued with the same divine mission, and with spiritual rather than materialistic motives dominant.

Mistake to Postpone Marriage Unduly

Your acceptance of the Mormon concept of marriage should discourage you from putting off marriage until the breadwinner has a competence. Any marriage for financial or social position is fraught with serious danger. On this point President Wilford Woodruff has spoken as follows:

. . . when the daughers of Zion are asked by the young men (of Zion) to join with them in marriage, instead of asking—"has this man a fine brick house, a span of fine horses and a fine carriage?" They should ask—"Is he a man of God? Has he the spirit of God with him? Has he got the spirit upon him to qualify him to build up the kingdom?" If he has that, never mind the carriage and brick house, take hold and unite yourself together according to the law of God. (Wilford Woodruff, *Journal of Discourses*, Vol. 18, pp. 129-130.)

Prophet Joseph F. Smith has given expression to the same thought:

I think that young men and young women, too, should be willing, even at this day, and in the present condition of things, to enter the sacred bonds of marriage together and fight their way together to success, meet their obstacles and their difficulties, and cleave together to success, and cooperate in their temporal affairs, so that they shall succeed. Then they will learn to love one another better, and will be more united throughout their lives, and the Lord will bless them more abundantly. (Joseph F. Smith, *Relief Society Magazine*, Vol. IV [June 1917], p. 314, et seq.)

Duty to Continue to Have Large Families

Once you have entered into the sacred bonds of matrimony you have a divine responsibility to follow the example of your forebearers in having large families rather than the example of most so-called educated men and women who very often do not reproduce themselves.

Our own living Prophet, President David O. McKay, states this duty in simple words:

The principal reason for marriage is to rear a family. Failure to do so is one of the conditions that causes love to wilt and eventually to die. (David O. McKay, *Improvement Era*, Vol. 46 [November, 1943], p. 657.)

Some young couples enter into marriage and procrastinate the bringing of children into their homes. They are running a great risk. Marriage is for the purpose of rearing a family, and youth is the time to do it. I admire these young mothers with four or five children around them now, still young, happy. (David O. McKay, *Church News* [weekly section of *Deseret News*], February 27, 1952, p. 3.)

His devoted and able counselor, President Stephen L Richards, in eloquent language warns us as follows:

To warn of great danger I must speak of it more specifically. I do so most reverently. If it shall please the Lord to send to your home a goodly number of children, I hope, I pray, you will not deny them entrance. If you should, it would cause you infinite sorrow and remorse.

One has said that he could wish his worst enemy no more hell than this, that in the life to come someone might approach him and say, "I might have come down into the land of America and done beyond computation, but if I came at all I had to come through your home and you were not man enough or woman enough to receive me. You broke down the frail footway on which I must cross and then you thought you had done a clever thing." (*112 Semi-Annual Conference of The Church of Jesus Christ of Latter-day Saints*, October, 1941, p. 108 [hereafter referred to as *Conference Report*].)

I have heard the late Melvin J. Ballard express his gratefulness to his parents because they did not stop with the fourteenth child; otherwise, he, the fifteenth, might never have been born.

Duty to Shun Birth Control

In the light of this advice you must never accept the principle or practice of birth control. On this point I call as my first witness the founder of this great institution. Nearly a hundred years ago, in language still applicable to the contemporary situation, Brigham Young stated:

To check the increase of our race has its advocates among the influential and powerful circles of society in our nation and in other nations. The same practice existed 45 years ago, and various devices were used by married persons to prevent the expenses and responsibilities of a family of children, which they must have incurred had they suffered nature's laws to rule preeminent. That which was practiced then in fear and against reproving conscience is now boldly trumpeted abroad as one of the best means of ameliorating the miseries and sorrows of humanity. The wife of the servant man is the mother of eight or ten healthy children, while the wife of his master is the mother of one or two poor, sickly children, devoid of vitality and constitution, and of daughters, unfit, in their turn, to be mothers, and the health and vitality which nature has denied them through the irregularities of their parents are not repaired in the least by their education. (Brigham Young, *Journal of Discourses* Vol 12, pp. 120-121.)

President David O. McKay has stated the view in these words:

Seeking the pleasures of conjugality without a willingness to assume the responsibilities of rearing a family is one of the onslaughts that now batter at the structure of the American home. Intelligence and mutual consideration should be ever-present factors in determining the coming of children to the household. When the husband and wife are healthy and free from inherited weaknesses and disease that might be transplanted with injury to their offspring, the use of contraceptives is to be condemned. (David O. McKay, *Improvement Era,* Vol. 51 [October, 1948], p. 618.)

I summon as my last witness on this point a dynamic moral as well as political leader of our country, one who returned to his Father before most of you students were born. After retiring from the Presidency of the United States, President Theodore Roosevelt led a national crusade against the demoralizing practice of birth control. In an article appearing in a national magazine in 1917 he summarized in constructive language the positive aspects inherent in quotations which I have already read, as follows:

What this nation vitally needs is not the negative preaching of birth control to a submerged tenth, and the tenth immediately adjoining, but the positive preaching of birth encouragement to the eight-tenths who make up the capable self-respecting American stock which we wish to see perpetuate itself. (Theodore Roosevelt, *Metropolitan*, October, 1917).

Inadvisability of Postponing Families

Now may I suggest to you that in these days of long preparation in which many of you will probably be required to spend at least two years in uniform in the service of your country, may be called upon for another two years of missionary service for the Church, and then spend from four to seven years in college, depending upon the degree and the extent of training your educational objective requires, it is more than ever a mistake for you either to postpone marriage or, after marriage, to postpone a family until you have acquired an education. I recognize that, according to the view of most educators in our country, this will be considered treason, for the prevailing view of the world is that you should acquire your professional training and be established in business before you should consider marriage. Under this view you would be from 26 to 30 years of age before entering into matrimony. Fortunately, it has not been the practice of members of prior graduating classes always to wait that long, and I am pleased to know that many of you have not postponed marriage until you have either acquired a competence or a college education.

I do not mean by this to give any countenance to child marriages or to give implied approval to children marrying while they are still in high school. Nor do I mean to say that the moment one enters college he or she is ready for marriage. There is a proper limit to the advice I am giving. Undoubtedly, there have been many students in this institution who, without having discharged either their military or their missionary duties, have married in their freshman or sophomore years but who would have been well advised to wait so that they could enter marriage with a little more maturity and judgment. No absolute rule as to age may be laid down. For ultimate wisdom on this question I again quote President McKay:

> How are we going to overcome some of the present-day difficulties (of young men and young women)? Postponement of marriage is not the answer. I know that there are many parents whose sons and daughters are struggling for an education who say it would be better if young couples postponed marriage until after they gained an education. I am not so sure about it. Each case must be considered on its own merits. The principal thing is to be sure the couple love each other. Marriage without love will bring misery. But if they are sure they are mated and have the same ideals, generally early marriages are best. (David O. McKay, *Improvement Era*, Vol. 51 [October, 1948] p. 618.)

The Fallacy that Young Couples Cannot Afford to Have a Family

I am, of course, aware of the objection often made by those who subordinate things of the spirit to the popular thinking of this world that young married couples are often in such economic circumstances that they cannot afford to have children. In the words of President David O. McKay:

> Hundreds are now saying, and hundreds more will say—"How can I marry and support a bride in a manner with which she has been accustomed? How can I get an education and support a family? I cannot even find a place in which to live?" (David O. McKay, *Improvement Era*, Vol. 51 [October, 1948], p. 618.)

The first answer to this question is that no young man of Mormon tradition and industry need resort to this specious excuse. Certainly members of this class cannot hide behind this selfish philosophy. According to figures compiled by the Bureau of the Census, elementary school graduates in this country may expect during their lifetime to earn a total of around $100,000; high school graduates on the average may expect to earn a total of around $200,000; college graduates on the average may expect to earn a total of around $263,000. In this situation certainly any college graduate should be ashamed to say that he cannot afford to have children, while at the same time those of inferior economic status are having large families.

The late Dr. John A. Widtsoe, the son of a widowed mother, who with his mother's help was one of the early leaders of our Church to acquire a coveted doctor's degree and who later was head of the Department of Agriculture at BYU and successively president of the Utah State Agricultural College and of the University of Utah, has made this sage observation:

> The future of the state and of the race depends upon the willingness of its citizens to beget and rear children without artificial interference. During the last centuries mankind has learned much. The comforts and blessings in every modest home surpass those of the emperors of old. Who shall inherit these gifts and the others in process of making?—Our children, of course, if we have any, and if they are numerous enough to claim consideration. It is a cruel fact, to which we must give heed, that those most highly prepared to enjoy and advance our civilization have a decreasing birthrate; while those of less training, or perhaps inferior gifts, continue fruitful. Many a college class of picked men and women half a century after graduation have fewer children than the original number of the class. It takes more than two children to keep the population from decreasing. The worldwide view is the same. The birth rate of the more advanced nations is failing rapidly; while that of the more backward peoples is large and increasing. (John A. Widtsoe, *Evidences & Reconciliations* [1943 edition], p. 250.)

When I read of prominent individuals advocating the limitation of families because of economic conditions I cannot help thinking of the faithful members of this faculty who on very modest compensation have become parents to as many as 10 to 12 children. I hope that, with the increased salaries that are being paid to present faculty members and which we hope will be even further increased, present members of the faculty will fulfill their spiritual obligations in the same manner as those patriarchs who through their loyalty have made this a great institution of spiritual and secular learning.

Quality vs. Quantity

I know also that the argument is sometimes made that it is better to have fewer children and give them a better education than to have more children who will have fewer opportunities. Stated another way, it is better to have

quality than quantity. But when I again observe that many
loyal members of our faculty have somehow managed to
give all of their children the opportunities of a college
education and to send them on two-year missions I realize
the superficiality of this argument. Small families just do
not connote higher quality. President Theodore Roosevelt
has stated the case when he said:

> To quiet their uneasy consciences, cheap and shallow men and
> women, when confronted with those facts, answered that "quality" is
> better than "quantity," and that decrease of numbers will mean
> increase in individual prosperity. It is false. When quantity falls off,
> thanks to willful sterility, the quality will go down too. (Theodore
> Roosevelt, *Outlook,* April 8, 1911, p. 765.)

Not Devitalizing to Mothers

Finally, the argument is made that it is too devitalizing for a mother to give birth to more than two or three
children. That, unfortunately, is the viewpoint of the elite
schools of the country whose graduates do not perpetuate
themselves. From conversations which I have had with
medical doctors and from having observed that most
women who make this argument seem to be in normal
health I suspect that this is more of an excuse than justification—you students have learned that one of the easiest
and most dangerous things you can do is to rationalize; I
am sure there is no scientific proof for such a thesis.

One year ago last week we named our 16 Heritage
Halls after 16 glorious pioneer women. They included
poetesses, legislators, artists, musicians, physicians, church
workers, and women in many other roles, but none regarded
any accomplishment higher than the calling of mother.
Although three were childless, they devoted their lives
to the service of children, and no appellation in their
honor was applied oftener or with deeper significance than
the word "mother." The thirteen remaining each gave birth
to an average of nine children, or 117 children in all.
That their unselfish obedience to the divine command to
"multiply and replenish the the earth" did not impair
their health nor shorten their lives is shown by the fact
that they lived all the way from 66 to 102 eventful years;

counting the present ages of three still living, these thirteen mothers as a group have already averaged a rich life span of over fourscore years. One of them, who gave birth to 12 children, is still living in her 102nd year. Rather than accept the philosophy that child-bearing is devitalizing, I suggest you young women study the lives and emulate the example of these great pioneer women.

Marriage is the Preserver of the Human Race

What I have said so far has been said from the standpoint of your individual welfare and happiness. It follows, as does the night the day, that individual obedience to the commandments of our Heavenly Father insures good homes. Good homes, in turn, guarantee a sound and righteous nation. In the words of President Joseph F. Smith:

Marriage is the preserver of the human race. Without it, the purposes of God would be frustrated; virtue would be destroyed to give place to vice and corruption, and the earth would be void and empty. (Joseph F. Smith, *Juvenile Instructor,* Vol. 37 [July 1, 1902], p. 400.)

This has been expressed by our baccalaureate speaker of last night, Elder Ezra Taft Benson, in the following words:

No nation can rise above its homes. The Church, the school, and even the nation stand helpless before a weakened and degraded home, in building character. The good home is the rock foundation— the cornerstone of civilization. If this, our nation, is to endure, the home must be safeguarded, strengthened, and restored to its rightful importance. [*Conference Report,* April, 1949], p. 196.)

President McKay has added his emphasis in the following language:

The home is the foundation of society. It is a sacred institution to members of the Church of Christ. We believe in the eternity of the marriage covenant, in harmony in the home. Indeed, our ideal is to have home just a little taste of heaven. Children constitute a very important part of the Latter-day Saint home. (*Conference Report,* April, 1954, p. 141.)

I recall that just after the turn of the last century President Theodore Roosevelt predicted that if France

still continued the practice of birth control, which was
then seizing the nation, it would not be long before that
country became a third-rate nation. That prophecy has now
been fulfilled. I again present the testimony of that great
American President:

> Voluntary sterility among married men and women of good
> life is, even more than military or physical cowardice in the ordin-
> ary man, the capital sin of civilization, whether in France or Scan-
> dinavia, New England or New Zealand. If the best classes do not
> reproduce themselves the nation of course will go down. (1916)
> (Theodore Roosevelt, Mem. Ed. IV 77; Nat. Ed. III, 249.)

> If the average woman does not marry and become the mother
> of enough children to permit the healthy increase of the race; and if
> the average man does not, above all other things, wish to marry in
> time of peace, and do his full duty in war if the need arises, then the
> race is decadent, and should be swept aside to make room for one
> that is better. Only that nation has a future whose sons and daughters
> recognize and obey the primary laws of their racial being. (1916) The-
> odore Roosevelt, Mem. Ed. IV 79; Nat. Ed. III, 251.)

I close with the words of our present Prophet, President McKay:

> Our most precious possessions are not our abundant harvest,
> nor our orchards yielding luscious fruit, nor our waterways, nor our
> million miles of paved highways, nor our oil wells, nor our rich mines
> of copper, silver, and gold, nor even our uranium—our most precious
> possessions, our treasures of eternity, are our children. These merit
> and should receive our greatest and our most constant care and
> guidance.
>
> Daniel Webster was right when he said:
>> "If we work upon marble, it will perish;
>> If we work upon brass, time will efface it;
>> If we rear temples, they will crumble into dust;
>> But if we work upon immortal souls,
>> If we imbue them with principles,
>> With the just fear of the Creator and love of fellow man,
>> We engrave on those tablets something which will brighten
>> eternity."
>
> The bringing of children into the world bears with it great
> responsibilities and opens to view the noblest purpose of life, namely,
> a co-partnership with deity "to bring to pass the immortality and
> eternal life of man." (Moses 1:39) (*Conference Report*, October, 1954,
> pp. 8-9.)

Personal Word of Appreciation

And now may I express my personal affection for each of you graduates. You and I both came to this institution four years ago. I preceded you only by a few months. You have accomplished your purposes and are now graduating. But the Board of Trustees apparently feels that I am not yet entitled to my graduation diploma. So while I am staying on, I shall always consider myself as one of your class—one who, however, never graduated within the allotted time. I think we have learned to love and respect each other. And when, ten years from now and, again, if God be willing, 25 years from now, I have the opportunity to review the annual report of the Population Reference Bureau, as to the record of our class in being fruitful, I trust that our record will not only be superior to that of any other graduating class in the United States, but that it will be so far superior that sincere and religious people will recognize that the spirit of the Lord animates and controls our lives.

God bless you and guide you and keep you, I ask in the name of his Son, Jesus Christ. Amen.

DREAM THE DREAMS
OF YOUTH

(*Charge to the graduates at Commencement Exercises in George Albert Smith Fieldhouse, June 6, 1958*)

I have only one charge for you tonight. I charge you to continue to dream the dreams of youth—dreams of what you may become, dreams of future achievement and accomplishment and lastly and always most important, dreams of service to your fellow men. This does not include dreaming to become an American millionaire—tempting as that may seem to you. If in the pursuit of service to your fellow men you happen to become a millionaire, so much the better. But I hope no one here will consider the acquisition of wealth, per se, to be a laudable ambition. So always continue to dream.

In these days of cheap jazz and non-inspiring television, I am afraid that you have little time for introspection —that there is a tendency for your minds to be occupied without ever being required to generate any thoughts of their own. You don't have the compulsive necessity which J. Willard Marriott and I had as boys of being compelled to dream in order to get something on our mind. I lived on the west side of Ogden across the tracks with all of the proper and improper connotations, but J. Willard lived across three additional railroad tracks. As he herded his father's sheep, and subsisted on strong mutton, he dreamed from day to day of the number of sheep he would some day own. I know he never dreamed that the time would come when in the course of one day (24 hours) he would actually serve that many sheep to his customers under the beguiling modern terminology of "choice tender lamb."

Whether that is true or not the arithmetic he learned in dreaming about and counting his sheep now stands him in good stead in counting the tens of thousands of meals served to satisfied customers in his restaurants every year, and the millions which go through his dependable cash registers.

So never forget to dream and to execute those dreams —not by the guillotine but by going on and giving them creative existence. James Hanaker once wrote: "All men of action are dreamers," and Adelaide Ann Proctor concluded, "Dreams grow holy put in action."

I owe my entire education to the educational dreams and standards of three great men: to Brigham Young, who founded this great institution—to him and his educational ideals I owe the guiding philosophy of my life; to George Washington, the Father of Our Country, in whose honor George Washington University was founded and which under the imaginative and dynamic leadership of Dr. Marvin has become a great institution of learning—to that institution I owe my basic training in the field of law (a field hallowed by our first President) as a result of which I in turn have been able, I hope, to make a small contribution to society; to John Harvard, who bequeathed his fortune to found Harvard College—to that institution and therefore to John Harvard I owe a debt of gratitude for raising my scholastic objectives and helping me to evaluate matters objectively.

This institution, I am sure, still proves true to the dreams which led Brigham Young to found it. I am sure the Father of Our Country is proud of the training given by the school consistent with his dreams and founded in his honor. While Harvard College has in many respects

98 EARNESTLY YOURS

departed the dreams of its founder—a school for the education of the ministry, "for the education of others who might better serve their God"—yet it is nevertheless a beacon light of secular learning in this country. God bless these three dreamers for what they gave to me and are still giving to thousands of others.

And just as dreams are a part of youth, may I suggest that you never become other than youthful. There are some members of our faculty today who, though forty years older in physical age, are still younger in spirit than some of you. I know of no persons who so personify in my mind the spirit of youth—of quest of knowledge, of zest for life, of a desire to serve—as President Clark and President Marvin. I can suggest nothing more helpful than that you emulate them, in which event you will be happy all the days of your life. There is no need to labor the point. I need merely quote the Credo of General Douglas MacArthur, hero of both World Wars I and II, now nearing eighty years of age and chairman of the Board of Remington Rand, Inc. In the enthusiasms of his present youth he recently wrote:

Youth is not entirely a time of life—it is a state of mind. It is not wholly a matter of ripe cheeks, red lips or supple knees. It is a temper of the will, a quality of the imagination, a vigor of the emotions, a freshness of the deep springs of life. It means a temperamental predominance of courage over timidity, of an appetite for adventure over love of ease.

Nobody grows old by merely living a number of years. People grow old only by deserting their ideals. Years may wrinkle the skin, but to give up interest wrinkles the soul. Worry, self-distrust, fear and despair—these are the long, long years that bow the head and turn the growing spirit back to dust.

Whatever your years, there is in every being's heart the love of wonder, the undaunted challenge of events, the unfailing childlike appetite for what's next, and the joy and the game of life.

You are as young as your faith, as old as your doubt; as young as your self-confidence, as old as your fear; as young as your hope, as old as your despair.

In the central place of every heart there is a recording chamber; so long as it receives messages of beauty, hope, cheer and courage, so long as are you young.

When the wires are all down and your heart is covered with

the snows of pessimism and the ice of cynicism, then, and then only
are you grown old.

By that standard may you never grow old! May life
be to you just one "commencement" after another! May
you always be imaginative, have a "vigor of emotions,"
always have an "undaunted challenge of events," have a
zest to solve all problems as they present themselves—yes,
even the problems which we shall meet in the hereafter.

Woodrow Wilson once said there were three kinds of
people who came to Washington—those who shrivel and
pass on unnoticed and who have no influence on the
course of events in their times; those who swell and expire
by their own limitation; finally, those who grow and solve
the problems of the day. Please dream and grow and
transform your dreams into living realities. By doing that
you may somehow become as God now is. Amen.

THE PRICE OF SUCCESS

(This address at Commencement Exercises of the LDS Institute of Religion at Cedar City was given May 27, 1955, when Dr. Wilkinson was chancellor of the Unified Church School System, and simultaneously president of Brigham Young University)

I congratulate members of the graduating class tonight on your graduation from this Institute of Religion because, in your quest for truth at the College of Southern Utah, you have not neglected the quest that comes from the study of our revealed gospel and from your willingness to live in accordance with its commandments. Your graduation represents another step forward in your own lives, and we are all governed by the law of eternal progression. There is no such thing in this life as standing still. We either move forward or we slip backward. And I am very happy to be able to congratulate all of you because, so far at least, you are moving forward.

In these days of formal education, first in high school and also in college, formal education is a great aid in the educational process. In fact, college education is something that is becoming almost indispensable. The true purpose of education, says one author, is to cherish and unfold the seed of immortality already sown within us, to develop to the fullest extent the capacities of every kind with which the God who made us has endowed us. You remember the definition of President Brigham Young, a definition which was sent to the World's Fair in San Francisco near the turn of the century, and which received the plaudits of educators all over the country. While Brigham Young did not have the benefits of the formal education which you students have received at this time, he knew probably as much as any other man the ingredients necessary to a well-rounded education. He defined education as "the power to think clearly, the power to act well in the world's work, and the power to appreciate life." The Prophet Joseph Smith, in one of those great declarations for which he was noted, said that "man was created to dress the earth, to cultivate his mind, and to glorify God." In these days of formal education, let me give you a few facts to show that it is almost indispensable for our individual progress that to-day we have not only a high school education but also a college education.

In 1900—and that was just two years after the College of Southern Utah was founded—only two out of every ten children of high-school age in the United States were in high school. Today, throughout the country, eight out of every ten are in high school. The figures have just been reversed. In 1900, only two out of every hundred college-age youth were in college. Today the ratio is twenty out of every one hundred. Just ten times as many students are going to college today as there were in 1900, based on population; and it is estimated that by 1970, another fifteen years, there will be two times as many of our students going to college as there are in 1955. In other words, by 1970 there will be twenty students going to college compared to every one who went to college in 1900.

You will be interested in knowing, also, that the income of these students is almost directly related to the amount of education which they obtain. The United States Chamber of Commerce recently published some very interesting statistics revealing that eighty-two per cent of all the people in the United States who have an income of $10,000 or more have a college or at least a high school education; that those with an eighth grade education or less constituted seventy-seven per cent of the people in the country who had incomes of $5,000 or less. The United States Bureau of the Census—and this will be interesting to the students who are graduating—recently reported that the average lifetime income expectancy of a young man starting out today is in excess of $150,000. That's an average for everyone. If you have no high school education all you may expect to make, on the average, is a total of $100,000. A high school diploma raises the expectancy to $200,000—just twice the amount of one without a high-school education. The college graduate will generally earn a lifetime average of around $268,000.

Have You Developed Love for Knowledge?

In giving these figures, let it be understood that in my philosophy the measurement of an education in dollars and cents is the least important result of a broad spiritual and secular education. I should just like to ask this graduating class at this time, each one of you, how much do you think you are educated? What attributes of an educated man or an educated woman do you have? For the test I should like to suggest is not whether you have gone through two years of college, but whether two years of college have gone through you—and whether or not you have retained the rudiments of that penetration. *Have you developed in the first place a curiosity for knowledge, an urge to know more? Would you like to know more about something than anyone else in the world so that you could be called the top expert in that particular field?* And are you willing to pay the price of learning more?

Let me tell you one story, a story of ambitious youth. It's a story of the early part of this century. An alert young scientist went west with his bride to teach in a small church-related college—not one of our church, but a Protestant college. He wanted a modern research laboratory. A bishop of that church on a tour of inspection visited the college and questioned this young scientist. The bishop was not impressed by the arguments for a laboratory. He asked what good it would do.

"We might discover something new," the young scientist replied, "perhaps even some great invention."

"Nonsense," said the bishop, "preposterous. What things yet remain to be invented? Can you name one?"

And timidly this young scientist replied, "I think that man may sometime learn to fly, to fly faster even than the birds."

"And for that," thundered this bishop, "you will fry in hell. Flying, young man, is reserved for the angels."

That bishop was the father of Wilbur and Orville Wright, the inventors of modern aviation.

And so I say to you graduates that if you have acquired that mental curiosity, without which you cannot be an educated man or an educated woman, you will not stop now with your education. We had the privilege at Brigham Young University just this last week of having the New York Philharmonic Orchestra. The maestro of that orchestra spoke to our student body. He told the typical success story—now the leader of the greatest orchestra in the world. But he said the secret of his success was that when he was offered the position, he was ready for it. By his training over the years, although he had never expected an offer of that kind, he was prepared when the time came.

To those of you who seek opportunities in other professions, there will often be the temptation to take a job before you are ready for it, or to take a job that pays handsomely in the beginning even though there may be little opportunity for future advancement, and I should like to suggest that you not surrender to that temptation. Dr. Karl G. Maeser, the founder of Brigham Young University, tells of his father who trained to be an artist. In his youth he wanted to paint masterpieces, and he was so gifted and promising that at an early age he was persuaded to give up his great ambition of painting masterpieces and accept a position and a good salary as a painter of china. Later on in his life he told his son, Karl, "Except for the premature glint of gold, I might have been one of the great painters of Europe. The masterpieces that adorn the art galleries of Europe might have been mine." Little wonder, therefore, that his son, Karl, later told his own students at Brigham Young University: "Eagerness to earn bread and butter has overshadowed many a golden opportunity."

Have You Learned to Think?

May I ask you graduates, in the second place, *whether you have really learned to think, or do you get some other student to do your thinking, or go to the teacher and have him do it for you?* Henry Ford once made the statement that the hardest thing there is to do in life is to think, which is the reason so few people do so little of it. Thomas Edison once made the statement that most people will go to no limit of work to avoid doing a little thinking. I walked through a room the other day at Brigham Young University with one of our great scientist teachers, Dr. Harvey Fletcher, and as we walked along over some carpets he purposely dragged his foot for a moment. We could almost see the electricity, and he made the comment to me, "I don't know why it took the world so long to find out about electricity. It seems to me that anyone ought to have been curious enough to find out from walking over a carpet what electricity was." Benjamin Franklin, one of those who helped discover electricity, left us with this great statement: "If a man empties his purse into his head, no one can take it away from him. An investment in knowledge is always the best insurance and pays the highest rate of interest."

And so I should like to suggest again to you graduates that the true end of education is to discipline rather than to furnish your mind with facts, for if you once learn or acquire the ability to think under any circumstances, you then will be able to ascertain the facts for any problem you face. Arnold Bennett once said, "I think it's rather fine, the necessity for thinking, the necessity for the tense bracing of the will before anything worthwhile is done. I rather like it myself. I feel it to be the chief thing that differentiates me from the cat by the fire."

Have You Learned to Work?

May I ask you graduates, in the third place, *whether you have so learned to work that you can get as much enjoyment out of work as you do out of pleasure?* If you do not get just as much fun out of the work you are doing, then I should like to suggest to you that you have missed one of the fine attributes of education. Some of you in this class have already achieved more than others, but whether you will achieve more will depend upon your own determination and upon your own perseverance and upon your willingness to learn even more. In the race ahead, some of you who are now out in front will tire and drop by the roadside; others will emerge as the real leaders, for the race, according to the Apostle Paul, is not to the swift and the strong, but to him who endureth to the end. In a letter to a major in the army, President Lincoln once wrote:

> The lady bearer of this letter says she has two sons who want to work. Set them at it as fast as you can! Wanting to work is so rare a merit that it should be encouraged.

I had always thought that in the days of Lincoln, people wanted to work more than we do in these thirty-five and forty hour weeks, but apparently many were lazy then also.

One of the great orators in the history of this country was Joseph Choate. Someone at one time asked him for his formula for success, and he replied that there were three ingredients. The first was work, the second was more work, and the third was still more work. One time when he was on a vacation to Switzerland, he was so popular that the American tourists got together and invited him to address them at the end of the following week. After his address, many of the tourists gathered around and complimented him on his marvelous ability to give a speech of that kind without any preparation. Indignant, his daughter who stood at his side exclaimed, "Yes, he has ruined my entire vacation by spending all week preparing this talk for you." Charles Kingley in his famous Town and Country Sermon

states the case for work as follows, and I hope you graduates
will remember this. He says:

Thank God every morning when you get up that you have
something to do that day which must be done whether you like it or
not. Being forced to work and forced to do your best will breed in
you temperance and self-control, diligence and strength of will,
cheerfulness and content, and a hundred virtues the idle will never
know.

You have heard the story of Abraham Lincoln as
written by an anonymous author:

When Abraham Lincoln was a young man, he ran for the
legislature and was badly defeated.

Next he entered business, failed and spent seventeen years of
his life paying the debts of a worthless partner.

He was in love with a beautiful young lady to whom he was
engaged, and she died.

Entering politics again, he ran for Congress and was badly
defeated.

He then tried to get an appointment to the General Land
Office of the United States and failed.

He became a candidate for the vice-presidency in 1856 and was
defeated. He was again defeated by Douglas in 1858.

One failure after another, bad failures and great set-backs. But
in the face of it all he finally became one of the country's great men.

May I just, in all earnestness, say to you graduates
that if twenty, thirty, or forty years from now you want to
be one of the leaders of your generation, I can tell you how.
You need to follow only one fundamental rule of success.
Curiously, there is no secret to it, yet many college graduates
and most people think it is shrouded in mystery. They fail
to realize that such a rule has been public property ever
since the beginning of the world and is not the subject
of any patent or copyright. Assuming a fair degree of intelligence, normal health, and a willingness to live a righteous
life so that you may receive the blessings of your Heavenly
Father, the only remaining ingredient for success is constant, day in and day out, hard work. And on this let me
quote one of the most significant statements that I read as
a student some thirty years ago and which I never forgot.
It is taken from the *Principles of Psychology* by William
James:

Nothing we ever do is, in strict literalness, wiped out. Of course, this has its good side as well as its bad one. As we become permanent drunkards by so many separate drinks, so we become saints in the moral, and authorities and experts in the practical and scientific spheres by so many separate acts and hours of work.

Let no youth have any anxiety about the upshot of his education, whatever the line of it may be; if he keeps faithfully busy every hour of the working day, he may safely leave the final result to itself. He can, with perfect certainty, count on waking up some fine morning to find himself one of the competent ones of his generation in whatever pursuit he may have singled out. Silently, between all of the details of his business, the power of judging in all that class of matter will have built itself up within him as a possession that will never pass away. Young people should know this truth in advance. The ignorance of it has probably engendered more discouragement and more faint-heartedness in youth embarking on arduous careers than all other causes put together.

I recall as a boy that one of the leaders of this great state of ours used to give his two rules of success; first, that he was always eager every morning to get to work before anyone else in his office; second, that he stayed at work long after all others in the office had left. Elbert Hubbard puts it in this quaint language: "Parties who want milk should not seat themselves on a stool in the middle of a field in the hope that a cow will back up to them."

Have You Learned to Uphold Standards?

And now may I, in the *fourth place, ask you whether your education has taught you that it never pays to depart from your own standards?* Let me give you just two illustrations. In 1938 when I was in Washington, D.C., a young man of my own age came to Washington. He had been a state agricultural agent in the State of Idaho. He was called there by the Board of Directors consisting of about thirty members of the National Council of Farmer Cooperatives. They were looking for an executive secretary, the chief administrative officer for that organization. And there sat these thirty men, and they called this young man before them.

After he had been interrogated at length, the chairman of the board said to him, "Mr. Benson, we should like to offer you now the highest administrative post of this organization. Will you take it?"

And young Ezra Taft Benson—he was then still in his thirties—turned to them and said, "Gentlemen, I've been in Washington a few days. I know that this job involves representing you before the committees of Congress. I am led to believe that a great deal of this lobbying and other work in Congress consists of meeting people around the cocktail tables and doing other things which I cannot do. I am sorry but I will have to decline your offer."

Then Judge Miller, the chairman, a distinguished judge from the State of Pennsylvania with white hair, arose and said, "Mr. Benson, we know you are a member of the Mormon Church. We know what your standards are. We know that if you come back here you will not be engaging in any cocktail parties, and it's for that reason, among others, that we have decided to offer this position to you. You can have it on your own terms. But if you take it, we also will be disappointed if you prove false to the standards of your religion."

On those terms, Ezra Benson accepted the position, later became a member of the Quorum of Twelve Apostles and is now the Secretary of Agriculture, the first man in our Church to be a member of the President's Cabinet.

Let me give you another example of the reverse. Once in a great while at Brigham Young University we have some student who proves false to his trust. It is not often. When I was a young practicing lawyer in New York City in the office of the Honorable Charles Evans Hughes, later Chief Justice of the United States Supreme Court, I was assigned one day to investigate an application that had come to one of their clients from a young man who represented himself as just being out of Yale University and who wanted a very prominent job in that organization. He had been in the city of New York for only a few weeks. He had immediately joined some of the social clubs. He was displaying prominently a block "Y" on the theory that he was from Yale. Something came up to cause the employer to be just a little suspicious, and the Hughes firm was asked to investigate. I, a young Mormon attorney in that firm, was to do the investigating. And I found this boy was a graduate of Brigham Young University. He never got the job.

After thirty years in New York City, that boy has practically no better job today than he had when he went there. But coming with him at the same time was a young man from BYU who was willing to pay the price of advancement by hard work. The one boy who represented himself as being from Yale wanted to start out at the top at a high salary. The other boy was willing to take a very humble salary if he could get the kind of a job that would train him to be one of the best security analysts in America; and for a few years he almost starved. He took a job that hardly paid him enough to live. Some of his friends thought that he would never make the grade. In order to cut down on expenses, his family lived throughout the winter in a summer cabin near the ocean. But in the course of about fifteen years, after he had received the training that he was willing to pay the price to receive, he began to forge ahead. And one of my first jobs at Brigham Young University was to ask William F. Edwards, our dean of commerce and now vice-president, to give up a job which at that time paid him $40,000 per year, and by now would have paid him $100,000 per year, to come back to Brigham Young University as dean of our College of Commerce.

Have You Learned Service?

May I say, in the fifth place, has *your education taught you that the truly educated man never measures his service in terms of dollars, but rather in terms of service?* I have already indicated that it was my good fortune to begin the practice of law with the Honorable Charles Evans Hughes, who later became Chief Justice of the United States. You may be interested in knowing that Judge Hughes seldom set a fee for himself, at least in his latter years of practice. He would always let the client set the fee, but because of the excellence of his service, because his clients knew that they always got everything there was in it to be obtained, he

always, I am sure, received more in that way than if he
had set his own fee. Elbert Hubbard states the same rule
in this language: *"He who never does any more than he gets
paid for never gets paid for any more than he does."* And should
there be any in this graduating class who eventually intend
to be teachers, let me just read this from the famous
Rousseau:

> The calling of a teacher should not be taken up for reward.
> There are callings so great that they cannot be undertaken for
> money without showing our unfitness for them; such callings are
> those of the soldier and the teacher.

In these days of crass materialism, too many of us set
a price on our services instead of letting others set the
price for us.

Do You Appreciate Your Opportunities?

And finally may I ask you, *has your education taught
you that the greatest blessing in life consists in appreciating your
opportunities and in learning to glorify your Heavenly Father?* On
one occasion Aristotle was asked how much an educated
man was superior to an uneducated man. He replied, "As
much as the living are to the dead." That is what he
thought of a well-rounded, true education. Another author
says:

> Education is a companion which no misfortune can depress—
> no crime destroy, no enemy alienate—no despotism enslave. At home,
> a friend; abroad, an introduction; in solitude, a solace; and in
> society, an ornament. Without it, what is man? A splendid slave, a
> reasoning savage.

Dr. George H. Brimhall wrote a parable with which
I should like to close. According to this parable—

> The camel merchants of Arabia, in order to determine the
> value of a camel, examine him as he would a horse, but that is only
> a preliminary examination. The final examination, upon which is
> based the value of the dromedary, is that of leading him to the
> watering trough. There he is saddled. The trough is filled with
> bright, sparkling water. And he is led up to it. If he rubs his nose
> in the water, splashes around a little and then turns and looks this
> way and that way and sniffs the air, he is turned down as a fourth-
> rate camel. If he drinks a little, he is a third-rate camel. If he drinks

moderately, he is branded as a second-rate camel and his value is proportional. But if he drinks copiously, drains the trough, he is the highest priced camel—and why? Because the sniffler that simply splashes the water with his nose, the gazer from side to side, the looker into the distance as though he could travel the whole desert when he is loaded and started would perish on the desert.

It is only the camel that drinks profoundly that can get across the desert. And so may I say to you graduates, drink deeply of every educational and spiritual opportunity which you have; and if you drink deeply, are willing to work, have a curiosity for knowledge and are willing to pay the price for success, you may rest assured that in your day you will be one of the competent ones of your generation.

May the Lord bless you that you may drink deeply, that you may prove true to your faith, that you may be of service to mankind, I humbly ask in the name of the Lord, Jesus Christ. Amen.

WHAT IS RELEVANT?

(*Excerpt from message at Commencement Exercises of Brigham Young University, May 29, 1969*)

And now having told you something about your own class at Brigham Young University, may I express the deep gratitude of the Board of Trustees, the administration and the faculty for your exemplary conduct in a year in which student disturbances and rioting have convulsed the nation.

We congratulate you for having come to learn and not to riot. I have letters from all over the country congratulating you and your fellow students on the example you have set for higher education in America. We hope that by our conduct in future years we can prove worthy of the trust that dedicated Americans and people of good will everywhere are placing in us.

The student disturbances have plagued, as you know, not only public institutions, but private institutions as well. Indeed some of the most serious disturbances and riots have been in such prestigious institutions as Columbia, Harvard, Dartmouth, Princeton, Cornell, Colgate, Brandeis, Chicago, Northwestern, Claremont, Stanford, and even among some of the private women's institutions such as Radcliffe. These disturbances have not only been an avenue for vigorous dissent but they have consisted of unlawful activities such as criminal trespassing, serious breaches of the peace, the breaking in and destruction of private property, the looting of files of the presidents, the destruction of research projects which cannot be replaced, and even the burning of buildings.

In most cases these criminal activities have been carried on in *alleged support of more relevant education*. So that you may see what these student rioters classify as relevant, let me outline to you some of the demands that have been made on the various universities.

Relevance or Regression?

Many of them, falsely asserted under the concept of freedom of speech, relate to a relaxation of moral standards on university campuses, that there be open visitation privileges in the rooms of the opposite sex at all hours of the day and night, that women students "be permitted to drink and stay out all night," that students be permitted to distribute any kind of literature and openly to exhibit obscene literature, and that students have the freedom to create their own standards of morality, and impose them on the university.

Other demands also urged under the banner of relevance relate directly to the academic life and courses of the university. They demand the admission of minority groups regardless of their academic qualifications; joint student and faculty control of course requirements, of grades, and of the dismissal and promotion of the faculty. Time and again revolutionary and dissident students have tried by intimidation and force to prevent war-related industries such as Dow Chemical from recruiting on university campuses and have disrupted and even burned the facilities of ROTC units where loyal American students are preparing for the defense of our country. On this campus we welcome Dow Chemical and we are increasing and enlarging our ROTC units.

The most serious of the announced purposes of some of these militant students is that of defiant "opposition to the middle class" and openly proclaimed "destruction of our existing social order." Indeed the hard-core militants on some campuses openly admit that they are communists and that they are engaged in revolution. The organization called "Students for a Democratic Society" is the top leader of the hard-core revolutionists on our campuses. During the riots at Columbia, members wrote on college buildings, "Lenin won, Castro won, and we will win too." In some of their rioting they have carried the red flag of the Communist Revolution and the black flag of anarchy.

Michael Klonsky, national secretary of SDS, has written, "The National Liberation Front in Vietnam and the oppressed peoples in the U. S. are fighting the same enemy, American Imperialism . . . . Remember Ho, Mao, Fidel, etc." In an address which he gave to the national convention of the SDS at the University of Texas, Klonsky said, "Our primary task it to 'build a Marxist Leninist revolutionary movement.'"

Now it may be true there are some who mistakenly see communism as the root of all evils in our country, but I submit that no one who has kept abreast of what is going on and who reads the literature of our day can deny that some avowed communists and their associates have played a large part in the disorder, revolution and anarchy on our campuses beginning with the original two student leaders at Berkeley, Mario Savio and Bettina Aptheker, who first denied and then admitted they were communists.

Unworthy of Their Country

In my judgment students who would destroy either the government which gives them more opportunities than any other nation in the world for both their material and spiritual advancement, or who would destroy the educational institutions created by our government or made possible by our system of free enterprise, should have their dreams fulfilled by having their citizenship revoked and, like Philip Nolan, be made men without a country. And I think it is time that trustees of universities take stern action with administrators who coddle these revolutionists, who provide sanctuaries for them on their campuses by failing in their first duty as citizens to report any and all violations of law to the police and to assist the police not only in making arrests but in prosecuting the criminals. Theodore Roosevelt once said that no person is above or below the law. Why, therefore, should students be protected from criminal punishment by presidents of universities refusing to call the police and to enforce the law? I submit that university students should be the first to obey the law, and the most relevant of all teachings in our present school disorders should be that there will be vigorous enforcement of the law against student and non-student alike.

In order to gain immunity for the unlawful acts which they have already committed and still threaten to commit, many of the rioters such as those at Columbia are demanding amnesty for all of their violations of law; others, such as students at the University of Colorado, would remove from college administrators all rights to discipline any student and would have the discipline in each case administered by the courts; and to cap it all, students at the State University of New York at Onconta are now demanding that agitating students be given a weekly allowance of twenty-five dollars for spending money so they can continue their agitation.

One of the practices advocated by some of the extremists is that of free love. In some cases, as I have suggested, it masquerades under the demand for free access to women's dormitories at any time; in other cases it openly advocates premarital sex. I ask you again what is relevant about this to the building of a more decent and greater society—to public morality?

One student revolutionist recently described the burning of buildings as "relevant and meaningful arson." What is there relevant about the destruction of educational buildings built through the generosity of the philanthropists or extracted from the pockets of the taxpayers for the very education of those who burn them?

Many of these acts are of course violations of criminal law; they constitute violent anarchy which no government can tolerate or endure. I merely ask you again since these practices are pursued by those clamoring for *relevancy in education*, what relevance they have in improving our educational system or in making the world a better place in which to live? In fact they would destroy our educational systems and cause civilization to revert to the Dark Ages.

Military a Basic Issue

Probably the current issues which the rioters press most vigorously for inclusion in our curricula are the related issues of our military draft and Vietnam. They of course do not want objective courses covering these questions—they want emotional courses condemning both the draft and our involvement in Vietnam. Time does not permit me to discuss the question of whether we were justified in the first place in going into Vietnam, although on the basis of sacred covenants, national honor and our commitment to freedom for all people, I can justify it. But whether right or wrong, we are there for a noble purpose—that of assuring freedom to the people of Vietnam, and every loyal American should give his full support to that cause.

Nevertheless, we have an amazing number of demagogues who are inflaming the populace by unpatriotic, immoral and seditious utterances on both of these issues. One of these is George Wald of Harvard, a Nobel Prize winner in medicine, but who shows abysmal ignorance of American ideals, national honor and world leadership.

In the name of relevancy he goes around the country urging unilateral withdrawal from Vietnam and often concludes his comments by the unthinking childish quip, "How do we get out of Vietnam—why by ships."

I will answer the unpatriotic Wald in the words of Kenneth Crawford:

> Withdrawal from Vietnam in ships, no questions asked, would leave South Vietnam at the mercy of the same Ho Chi Minh who executed some 50,000 of his fellow countrymen and sent another 100,000 into forced labor because he considered them politically unreliable when he took control of North Vietnam. Not to have committed the crime of war a quarter century ago would have left Europe

at the mercy of Hitler. To forswear nuclear weapons now would be to open the world to Soviet leaders who seem to be reverting to Stalinism.

I may add that not to have committed the crime of the Revolutionary War would mean that we would still be subjects of Great Britain; not to have committed the crime of the Civil War would have perpetuated slavery in this country, and not to have committed the crime of World War I would probably have resulted in the destruction of Europe.

To my mind all these wars in the interest of freedom have been highly relevant, the underlying purposes of which are amply supported by Holy Writ.

Education Is Relevant

Most of the complaints of the dissident students are against what they call "the establishment," which has been responsible for the greatest educational system in the history of the world. Many of them would substitute revolutionary ideas lacking in moral integrity for the curriculum which has been developed.

What could be more relevant than English and mathematics to those whose lack of skill in these basic areas has condemned them to inferior jobs and exploitation by those who prey on the ignorant? A limited vocabulary is often a more serious handicap than a squalid environment. Until comprehension improves, it is difficult to release anyone from the prison of his own inexperience. Those who must compete in a dominant culture must master that culture.

What could be more relevant for a historian than a study of history?

What could be more relevant for a nurse than to study the facts of physiology and health which are necessary for her work?

What could be more relevant, for those who would truly understand the world, than skill in a language other than one's own? BYU has been a national leader in developing an oral-aural approach to language teaching that turns what is often mere passive accomplishment into a living instrument. Our very successful semesters abroad in Austria, France, Spain, and Jerusalem, and the numerous tours sponsored by the University truly make the world our campus.

What is more relevant for a physical scientist than to study physics, chemistry and geology?

What could be more relevant for engineers, teachers, lawyers, doctors, dentists and others aspiring to be professional men and women than to study the knowledge of centuries pertaining to their respective professions?

In the crescendo of condemnation which is rising on many campuses, only a few voices are heard asking such fundamental questions as, Are the colleges to supplant welfare agencies? Are faculty associations to usurp the functions of city councils and state legislatures? These questions are not answered by citing what some think is legislative apathy or heartrending urgency. The function of a university is still that of education, not that of political or social reform, much of which today is socialistic and at variance with our form of government. Universities which attempt to be all things to all men succeed only in diffusing and weakening their impact or confusing the publics they serve.

Finally, while I cannot speak for higher education in general, I can say that BYU is trying to chart a course which we believe both relevant and responsible. We recognize that symptoms cannot be ignored in searching for causes, and we have a successful—and expensive—program designed to help those succeed in college who come to us from disadvantaged backgrounds. We have tried to avoid token solutions and romantic gestures. We are short on slogans but long on patience. Education is relevant to the degree that it enables a student to gain an educational understanding concerning his relationship to God, to himself, to his fellowmen and to the extent that it equips him with tools to serve.

A Special Relevance at BYU

There is a special relevance in the curriculum of BYU
—a curriculum which, in addition to the subjects taught
in secular institutions, teaches us that:

1. God is real; he presides over a universe of order.
What is more relevant than to search out the real purpose
of life and existence?

2. God is a God of law and order, and also a God of
justice and mercy. What could be more relevant in our
world of chaos and anarchy than the understanding that
God upholds law and order and justice? And what could be
more relevant in our world of sin and sorrow than an understanding of the law of mercy, namely—the application
of the law of repentance and the atonement of the Savior
for our sins.

3. The teachings of the Lord (including the Ten Commandments and the Sermon on the Mount) still represent
the moral code for a Christian and orderly society. What
could be more relevant today than the words of the Lord
to Moses on Mt. Sinai, "Thou shalt not kill . . . Thou
shalt not commit adultery . . . Thou shalt not steal . . .
Thou shalt not bear false witness." (Deuteronomy 5:17-20)
And what could be more relevant today than the teachings
of the Savior, "Thou shalt love thy neighbor as thyself
. . . pray for your enemies . . . do good to those who would
despitefully use you or persecute you."

4. The gift of free agency which postulates that we
are responsible for our own welfare politically, economically
and spiritually is still our guiding compass both in this
life and the life to come. What could be more relevant
than the belief that the world does not owe us a living,
or a college education, but that we must acquire such
through our own efforts?

5. What could be more relevant than the belief that
our Constitution is what Gladstone said it was, "the greatest document ever struck off at a given time by the brain
and purpose of man!" We teach that it is a document
which, according to divine revelation, the Lord himself

"suffered to be established, and should be maintained for the rights and protection of all flesh, according to just and holy principles," that it was established "by the hands of wise men whom the Lord raised up for that purpose," and as the Lord said, this land was redeemed by the shedding of blood. Is anything more relevant than the preservation of our government even at the expense of the shedding of blood, for it was intended as a model for the righteous people of all nations, and as the late President J. Reuben Clark, Jr. said, "If our liberties are lost we shall never regain them except at the price of blood." God grant that the virtue and sovereignty of our republic shall never be surrendered or impaired by any organization or in any other way.

6. Most relevant of all is the training that virtually every student receives in the ten stakes and ninety wards on this campus. For it should always be remembered that "relevant" originally ment "uplifting." We haven't neglected that meaning at BYU. Eternal principles are always relevant and they provide a temporal triangulation that is sober comfort in a relative and shifting world. For there are certain principles which were, are, and will forever be relevant. They are the revealed words of God, from the prophets of the Old Testament down to the present, and we stand on that rock in undismayed confidence. In the words of the Apostle Paul, we may be "troubled on every side, but we are not distressed; we are perplexed, but not in despair." We pledge our continuing commitment at BYU to help all who come to us. We are determined that no one who asks for bread at this Institution shall receive a stone.

BYU is vigorously in the world, but we do not overestimate our ability to shape that world directly. We concede to no institution, however, our ability to train those whose skill and moral and spiritual integrity may have world-wide impact.

An ancient writer has told us that unless our knowledge is in order the more knowledge we have the more will be our confusion. In my judgment it is the absence of these orderly teachings, hallowed at Mt. Sinai and validated by centuries of history in other institutions of learning, which is the main cause of the chaos and revolution abroad today. Because man-made secular learning has been substituted for the teachings of the prophets and the Master, some of our university students have pyramided confusion upon confusion, and would today destroy their own birthright.

My fervent prayer is that as representatives of Brigham Young University you will ever abide by these concepts, and if you do you will maintain a relevancy in life and never join in the irrelevant and irreverent revolution which is today threatening our country.

I congratulate you this day for your achievement, and pray for the blessings of our Eternal Father on all of you in the name of his Son, Jesus Christ. Amen.

MAKE HONOR THE
STANDARD WITH ALL MEN

(Excerpts from an address on honesty to the students of Brigham Young University in Devotional Assembly, October 15, 1957.)

The distinguished German educator, Karl G. Maeser, came to Provo and held his first class at the Brigham Young Academy on April 24, 1876. The minutes of the meeting record that there were present the principal, Karl G. Maeser, twenty-nine students, and some members of the Board of Trustees. A hymn was sung, with Brother Maeser both leading and playing the organ. Prayer was offered, and then Brother Maeser made his first official address to the students. He said, "I trust you all. I give you my confidence. I hope you will do nothing to weaken that confidence. I put you all on your word of honor."

This short, meaningful address of Brother Maeser, given at the first assembly at the BYU, I adopt as my text today.

Later on, in another address, Brother Maeser gave further definition of what he meant by honor. "My young friends," he said, "I have been asked what I mean by 'word of honor.' I will tell you. Place me behind prison walls—walls of stone ever so high, ever so thick, reaching ever so far into the ground—there is a possibility that in some way or another I may be able to escape; but stand me on the floor and draw a chalk line around me and have me give my word of honor never to cross it. Can I get out of that circle? No, never! I'd die first."

These statements of Karl G. Maeser have been basic to the philosophy of this institution from the beginning. We trust all of you from the time you enter this institution and hope that you will never do anything to be found unworthy of that trust.

Consistent with this philosophy, the Blue Key National Honorary Fraternity, with the intention of developing integrity and honor in every student, about 1948 began a movement to encourage the students to adopt their own honor code. This culminated on May 12, 1949, in the studentbody adopting an honor system as a part of the Constitution of the Associated Students of the Brigham Young University. The honor system is therefore the creature of the student body itself, designed to give vitality, by the students themselves, to the charge that Brother Maeser gave to the student body in 1876.

(Editor's note: In 1968 the Honor Code was replaced by the Code of Conduct, which is administered by the Dean of Students, although many of the same principles apply.)

The Honor Code itself of the Brigham Young University reads as follows:

We, the students of Brigham Young University, in order to secure a more general adherence to our ideals and standards of personal integrity and social responsibility, do establish the following Honor Code:

We take for granted that enrollment in this University assumes acceptance by the individual of the moral ideals and standards of The Church of Jesus Christ of Latter-day Saints.

We feel it an obligation to respect the personal rights of others in our use of University facilities, in our participation in school activities, and in all our personal relationships with one another.

We believe that the *property* rights of others are sacred and should not be violated. Since we all share in the use of University grounds and facilities, we feel that it is our responsibility to respect and preserve them.

We believe a high sense of personal honor and integrity is imperative; that honesty must prevail in all *academic work;* that our lives can be enriched only to the extent that our academic achievement is the result of our own effort.

We believe that adherence to these ideals and standards by all students can be more effectively brought about through the establishment of an Honor Council selected from the studentbody. It is our aim through the Honor System to improve the quality of our university life.

This Honor Code is the student body's reaffirmation of the standards of conduct for BYU students stated in the catalog of this institution, which require of every student the maintenance of standards of honor and integrity, of graciousness in personal behavior, of Christian ideals in every day living, of a single standard of morality and of an abstinence from the use of alcohol and tobacco. The student body realized, in the words of former President Elliott of Harvard University, that "there are some things that the honorable man never does—he never wrongs or degrades a woman, he never oppresses or cheats a person weaker or poorer than himself, he never betrays a trust, he is honest, sincere, candid and generous." Applied to our scholastic work, he never obtains any academic grade under false pretenses; he never accepts a degree knowing that it is a product of deception to which he is not entitled.

The written Honor Code procedure defines *academic* misconduct as that "of giving or receiving aid in examinations, or in the preparation of individual work done in or out of the classroom unless the instructor has specified that giving or receiving aid in such work is permissible." Examples of this misconduct are those of copying from some author without giving that author proper credit; of preparing a theme for someone else, or handing in as a theme someone else's product; or of plain cheating during examination. Summarily stated, academic misconduct means receiving academic credit under false pretenses, which in ordinary business life would be the occasion for criminal prosecution.

Your Student Code defines *non-academic misconduct* as consisting of "any violation of Christian standards of proper conduct, including without limitation, any infractions of personal honor, integrity, or morality, and any other conduct not in keeping with the ideals and standards of The Church of Jesus Christ of Latter-day Saints, whether committed on or off the campus." Examples of this misconduct are acts of stealing, which make you a thief; bearing false witness against another student, which in ordinary business practice may be of such a nature as to subject you to criminal prosecution; dishonesty in business dealings, which in ordinary commercial life is the cause of many people being in the penitentiary; or failure to observe the single standard of morality which, under the Latter-day Saint code, is one of the greatest of moral sins. Instances of dishonesty on a campus may take many forms, such as trying to get two meals on one cafeteria ticket; trying to beat a traffic ticket by claiming another was driving; signing a contract with a landlord for a room, giving a check in payment therefor, and then cancelling payment on the check; the stealing of property of another such as books or money. In this institution, also, in accordance with a revelation of the Lord to the Prophet Joseph Smith, the use of tobacco and alcohol are moral offenses because they are injurious to our "tabernacle of flesh" which we call our body.

There are other offenses which are equally serious for one who claims to be a faithful member of the Church which supports this institution. I am sure it is just as offensive to our Heavenly Father for us selfishly to refuse to pay a full tithing as it is for us to use alcohol; but because tithing records are confidential between the tithe payer and his bishop, this is one phase of conduct which the Honor Council will be unable to investigate.

With respect to faculty responsibility, the Code of Honor procedure for the University says: "It is recognized that without full cooperation of the faculty, the honor system will not succeed. Faculty members shall therefore acquaint themselves with and support the Honor Code and its procedure and shall cooperate with respect to its philosophy and enforcement. Members of the faculty shall report any violations of the Honor System either to the President of the University or to the Honor Council."

In accordance with this provision in the Honor Code

adopted by the students themselves, the faculty member will generally leave the room during an examination, unless the examination be of such a nature that questions may arise and it would be helpful to the students for the teacher to be on hand to answer such questions, or there be some other reason for his being present. The examination may also be of such a type that the teacher may want to know how long it takes for students to answer the questions, and may therefore stay around to see when most students finish. Generally, however, the teacher will leave the room. When the teacher does leave the room, you will be entirely on your own; whether you are a person of character and integrity will then reveal itself. For the test of any person's character is that which he does when he is alone, accountable only to himself.

This means that in examinations you are on your honor, that your classmate is on his honor, that in the interest of the integrity of this institution, you are all honor bound to maintain the honor of the institution. This means not only that you shall demean yourself in a manner worthy of your better self, but also that in the interest of fairness to yourself, you report those who are honoring neither themselves nor their school. It means that no one is to tolerate cheating. For the very integrity of our marking system is at stake if cheating is condoned by any of us.

The tradition that has grown up on the campus is that if anyone sees anyone else cheating, he raps his pencil on his desk. If the person cheating does not desist from his wrong practice at that time, the other student should arise and state that someone in the room is cheating. If that is done, I am sure the cheating will not continue.

I know there is a natural instinct for students not to report on someone else, but I would like to suggest to you that good citizenship requires that you make such a report. If you see someone committing a robbery, do you think you are a good citizen if you do not report that person to the police? If you should see someone stealing an automobile, would you be a good citizen if you sat by and made no report of it? If you were competing for an engineering job and you saw that your competitor cheated in examination by going to some book and copying from it, would it be fair for you to sit by and not report the wrongdoing of the other person? It is equally wrong for you to sit by in a class and permit someone else to cheat, when your comparative grades are going to be based on your relative performance in that examination.

If, in private and public life, we did not report the wrongdoings of others, there would be a complete breakdown in law enforcement. May I suggest, therefore, that you have the same student responsibility at the University as you do civic responsibility at home—even more so; and that for you to fail to report wrongdoing does not represent manliness on your part, but a lack of courage and a lack of respect for the standards of this institution. You will yourselves never grow to the stature of men and women if you fail to do your own duty.

Lesson in History

The Honor Code on this campus, set up by the students, is a guide for your future conduct in life. Whether you will succeed or not will depend more upon your reputation for honesty than upon your reputation for brilliance or for getting by. We all very soon in life learn to trust a man who is honest, even though he may not be brilliant. We never trust a dishonest man, even though he be brilliant. His brilliance makes him all the more dangerous and dishonorable. I am satisfied that one of the basic reasons why Abraham Lincoln became President of the United States was because of his reputation of honesty. His opponent, Stephen A. Douglas, had a greater reputation for brilliance, but he was lacking in the fundamental prerequisite of honesty. Judge Douglas had been a great friend of the Prophet Joseph Smith, and on many occasions bore testimony to the integrity and ideals of the Prophet. When however, the Saints in Illinois became unpopular and it was politically popular for Douglas to denounce the Saints, he chose to do so.

William Clayton, one of the Saints who kept a faithful daily journal of events, recorded in his diary of May 18,
1843, that he had had dinner with Judge Douglas and
the Prophet Joseph, and that at the end of this dinner
the Prophet Joseph arose and said, "Judge, you will aspire
to the Presidency of the United States; and if you ever
turn your hand against me or the Latter-day Saints, you
will feel the weight of the hand of the Almighty upon you;
and you will live to see and know that I have testified the
truth to you; for the conversation of this day will stay
with you for life." This prophecy was made some seventeen years before Douglas ran for the Presidency in 1860,
and was published in the *Deseret News* in Utah on September 24, 1856, some four years before that election.

In 1860 the Democratic Convention nominated
Douglas as its candidate for the Presidency. When he was
nominated, no man in the history of American politics
had more reason to hope for success. The political party
of which he was the leader had, in the preceding election,
polled 60% of both the electoral and popular votes. That
is an unusually high vote in this country. Three years
prior to this nomination, however, and fourteen years
after the interview with the Prophet, Judge Douglas gave
a speech at Springfield against the Mormons, in which he
suggested that the Congress "repeal the organic law of
the Territory of Utah on the ground that the Mormons
are alien enemies and outlaws, unfit citizens of one of the
free and independent states of this Confederacy." After
this speech, the Deseret News, in its issue of September 2,
1857, had the following to say.

In your last paragraph (of the Springfield speech) you say: "I
have thus presented to you plainly and fairly my views of the Utah
question." With at least equal plainness and with far more fairness
have your views now been commented upon. And inasmuch as you
were well acquainted with Joseph Smith, and his people, also with
the character of our maligners, and did know their allegations were
false, but must bark with the dogs who were snapping at our heels, to
let them know that you were a dog with them; and also that you may
have a testimony of the truth of the assertion that you did know
Joseph Smith and his people and the character of their enemies (and

neither class have changed, only as the saints have grown better and their enemies worse:) and also that you may thoroughly understand that you have voluntarily, knowingly, and of choice sealed your damnation, and by your own chosen course have closed your chance for the presidential chair, through disobeying the counsel of Joseph which you formerly sought and prospered by following, and that you in common with us, may testify to all the world that Joseph was a true prophet, the following extract from the history of Joseph Smith is again printed for your benefit, and is kindly recommended to your careful perusal and most candid consideration.

The *Deseret News* then printed the advice and warning which the Prophet Joseph had given to him as early as 1843.

When the electoral votes for President were counted in the 1860 election, Douglas had the fewest votes of the four candidates who ran.

In contrast to the dishonesty of Douglas, let me give you another incident. It was my privilege as a young lawyer to become employed in the law office of the Honorable Charles Evans Hughes, who later became chief justice of the U.S. and was recognized among lawyers as the greatest chief justice since the days of John Marshall. Judge Hughes had already been governor of New York State, was later associate justice of the United States Supreme Court, and had run for the Presidency of the United States against Woodrow Wilson. He later was secretary of state for the United States and he then returned to private practice, when it was my rare privilege to become employed in his office.

Integrity of a Great Man

A jury in New Jersey had awarded some $6 million against the Aluminum Company of America, on the theory that the Aluminum Company had conspired with Duke, the tobacco magnate, to violate the anti-trust laws. It was at this point in the case that Mr. Hughes was engaged to appeal the case, and I was one of his assistants in preparing the appeal. I well remember going with him to Philadelphia, where he argued the case before the Circuit Court of Appeals. As he came to the core of his argument, he informed the court that in his judgment there was only one small bit of evidence in the entire record of thousands of pages to justify any inference that there had been a conspiracy, and that that one bit of evidence did not justify the decision of the jury. I remember the chief justice of the Circuit Court of Appeals stopping Mr. Hughes and saying, "Mr. Hughes, we as a court are willing to rely entirely on your statement. If you will give us the page on which that evidence is recorded, we will examine it carefully." All of the five judges thereupon made a note of the evidence which Mr. Hughes said was the only relevant evidence in the record to prove a conspiracy. A month later the justices handed down an opinion in which they relied completely on the statement of Mr. Hughes as an attorney in the case, stating that there was only one bit of evidence to support the charge of a conspiracy, and that this was insufficient to support the jury verdict. They thereupon reversed the decision of the lower court.

I had another experience with this same man. Through hard work, strength of character and sound judgment, Judge Hughes had risen to the top of the legal profession. Now there is probably no greater variation in income in any profession than that of the law. A very large number of lawyers starve and have to change professions; some make large fortunes. Judge Hughes was of such eminence that he had ceased to set a price for his services. He also allowed his clients to determine what his fees should be; and incidentally, in that way he got more money than if he had set the price himself.

He had been engaged by one of the large oil companies in the country to determine whether a certain business transaction which they proposed to enter into violated the anti-trust act. He, with two or three of us as assistants, had worked months in preparing the opinion. It was a case for which, because of his pre-eminence, he could easily have charged a fee of $100,000. He was to deliver the opinion in person one afternoon to the board of trustees of the oil company. That morning before the meeting of the board of trustees, he sat in his office with the opinion be-

fore him, all ready to sign. Before he did so, however, he
reviewed the opinion again and again. As a young lawyer,
I was sitting across his desk, and he would occasionally
ask me whether I had checked this or that aspect of the
matter.

When he was just ready to sign the document, the
telephone rang. I could tell from the expression on his face
that it was a confidential call and that he wanted me to
leave the room, which I did. I walked up and down the
hall outside his room, waiting to be called back in. When
he did call me, he looked at me and said, "Mr. Wilkinson,
better leave me alone for a few moments. I don't think
this opinion will ever be given." Mystified as to this turn
in events, I was called back in half an hour and was informed that the person on the other end of the line had
been President Hoover of the United States, who had
asked Hughes to become the chief justice of the United
States Supreme Court. Mr. Hughes said to me, "Now we
have prepared this opinion. We have not been influenced
in any way. The work is all done. I have not yet been
sworn in as chief justice, but nevertheless, I have told
President Hoover I would accept, and having told him
I would accept the position of chief justice of the Supreme
Court, I cannot, in fairness to my profession, give this
opinion. I may have to pass on this particular case when
I become chief justice." The opinion was never given,
and the $100,000 fee never collected.

In San Francisco there is a very prominent publishing
company by the name of Whitney-Bancroft, which pub-
lishes a great many periodicals for the legal profession.
Shortly after the turn of the century, the office of this
company, with all of its accounts receivable, was burned.
The company therefore, had no record of the amount
owed to it by thousands of lawyers throughout the United
States. Faced with this situation, the officers of the company wrote a letter to each of the lawyers with whom
they had done business, stating frankly that the records
of accounts receivable had been destroyed and that they
therefore did not know whether the lawyer to whom the

letter was addressed owed them or not, but if he did, they would be grateful if he would inform them as to the amount he owed, and would be even more grateful to receive payment. In due time, this company collected 102% of all of the accounts outstanding at the time of the fire. With this income they constructed a new building, and on the front of the building are carved the words, "We serve an honorable profession."

Scrupulous In Details

One of the boasts of this institution is that we aim to produce men of honesty and integrity. It was my privilege as a youngster in Washington, D. C., to know a former governor of this state, William Spry, who had subsequently been appointed United States land commissioner. His life, he told me, had been greatly influenced by Karl G. Maeser. When he became commissioner of the General Land Office in Washington, D. C., fountain pens were just coming on the market. Not many people had them. The government supplied him with a fountain pen for his work at his desk, which pen he carried in his pocket during his work. But every night when he left the office, he took that pen out of his pocket and left it on his desk, for he told his office force that that was property of the government, and he had no right to use it for private purposes.

In those days he and his secretaries had an old manual press for getting out carbon copies of letters, and by the time Governor Spry got through his work each day, he often would have a purple ink on his hands. The government had a special kind of soap which could be used for taking this ink off his hands. One of his secretaries one day put a couple bars of the government soap in Governor Spry's pocket so that when he went home that night he would have this soap to erase the ink from his hands. The Governor did not notice the bars of soap in his pocket until after he left the building, but when he discovered they were there, he brought them back to the office before he went home and informed his secretary that that was government property and that he had no right to use it except for the purposes intended in the office.

I remember at one time, as a youngster, hearing old Brother Morton of the Deseret Sunday School Union, who was an Irish convert to the Church, tell the story of a prominent man in this state riding on a streetcar, the fare for which was a nickel for all over six years of age. This man would take along his seven-year-old son, and every time the conductor came to collect fares the father would push the son down in the seat so that he could pass as a five-year-old. This son, when he grew up, became a shyster in his profession and finally had to pay for his misdeeds by serving time in the penitentiary. Brother Morton used to always conclude his story by saying that the father was the one who should have served the time; that the child was so stunted in character by being made to appear less than six years of age, that he never measured up to his age or his inner capacity.

Many of you may have seen placards on the class-rooms of this University containing a quotation from Joseph Smith which reads, "Make honor the standard of all men." Many of you may not know that statement comes from the political platform on which Joseph Smith aspired to be President of the United States. In that platform, some sixteen years before the outbreak of the Civil War, he urged:

Petition . . . your legislators to abolish slavery by the year 1850 . . . Pray Congress to pay every man a reasonable price for his slaves out of the surplus revenue arising from the sale of public lands, and from the deduction of pay from the members of Congress. Break off the shackles from the poor black man, and hire them to labor like other human beings; for "an hour of virtuous liberty on earth is worth a whole eternity of bondage!" Abolish the practice in the army and navy of trying men by court martial for desertion; if a soldier or marine runs away, send him his wages, with this instruction that his country will never trust him again, he has forfeited his honor. Make HONOR the standard with all men.

We congratulate you as a student body on making honor the standard for all students. It follows in this school that if a student violates his word or breaches the Honor Code in any way, you will have to say to him, "You have not been honorable with yourself, and in the interest of the honor of this institution, I will have to maintain my own honor and see that your dishonorable conduct is made known." And in some flagrant cases the administration may have to say, as the Prophet Joseph said, "This school will never again trust you; you have forfeited your honor. You shall no longer pollute the halls of this sanctuary."

We know that there will be some violations. If there were not—if we were all perfect—we would be lifted up to heaven like the Children of Enoch.

In a student body of 9,000 there are certain to be some who cannot measure up to our standards. The obligation for the rest of us is that we not tolerate such conduct, for it is unbecoming a student of this institution. For we know that adherence to standards of integrity and honesty for this studentbody is very high. As one example, I am happy to report to you that during the school year of 1956-7 the students of this University found and turned into the Lost and Found Department some 8,665 articles having an estimated value of $65,759.27.

A School of Honor

One of my predecessors, President George H. Brimhall, in an address given to an earlier student body, told of one of the greatest schools ever to be taught by mortal man. It was not a very large school; there were but thirteen students, and it was held on an island. The school building was a barn, and the laboratory was the rocks, the waves, the sands, and the washings of the sea. The great teacher was Agassiz, in whose honor academic societies have been organized all over the world. When he went to this island he took eleven males, nine of whom were gentlemen. Two ladies were also enrolled in this school. There was some objection to the ladies' going, but the great teacher believed in co-education. The barn was partitioned off, one end for the ladies, the other for the men, and between was the dining room and the experiment hall.

It happened one evening that two of the male members of the school—in a half-playful way, as they tried to make the professor believe—indulged in some indelicacy of subject or conduct. The next morning the great teacher was grieved and grave. At the breakfast table he took a note that he had written and read it. The contents of the note were this: "At 9 o'clock this morning a boat will touch at this land. Mr. so-and-so and Mr. so-and-so will embark. They will not return." Of course it was like a thunderbolt to those two persons. They pleaded to be reinstated, but the teacher was firm and in his greatness said, "We want men, we want men; we thought we had men." They never returned. Of the eleven, the two ladies and the nine men who remained, each one has become famous. That is why it is called the greatest school in the world, because it turned out a greater percent of its students as successful graduates.

The two who were expelled from the island spent most of their time in endeavoring to belittle this great teacher and lessen the influence of his school. But the nine men and the two women who remained carried his name high on the ladder of fame and in so doing made their names great.

The Agassiz school required that the moral standard and the intellectual standard be parallel. We have the same requirement here.

The Honor Council is to be commended for its desire to have the *Honor Code* executed in an honorable way by honorable students. We give it our complete support. May you, through prayer, self-restraint, and will power, make it the best administered honor code of any university.

If you are tempted to cheat, remember the charge of Karl G. Maeser "My young friends," he said. "I have been asked what I mean by word of honor. I will tell you. Place me behind prison walls—walls of stone ever so high, ever so thick, reaching ever so far into the ground—there is a possibility that in some way or another I may be able to escape; but stand me on the floor and draw a chalk line around men and have me give my word of honor never to cross it. Can I get out of that circle? No, never! I'd die first!"

In that way you will maintain the maxim of George

Washington, who wrote, "I hope I shall possess firmness and virtue enough to maintain what I consider the most enviable of all titles, the character of an 'Honest Man.'"

PEACE WILL COME ONLY THROUGH RIGHTEOUSNESS

(Conclusion from Dr. Ernest L. Wilkinson's acceptance address at his inauguration as president of Brigham Young University, October 8, 1951)

We want our students, especially those entering their country's service as members of the ROTC, to know that our approval of their becoming a part of our armed services is a reluctant one. We give it only because our so-called civilization so far has failed to follow the teachings of the Master, which would make war with all of its human slaughter and carnage unnecessary.

Because man has not permitted love for fellow men or the golden rule to be determinative of his conduct, wars have cursed the world since the dawn of history. In our own time, Mussolini is authority for the statement that the normal course of events in Europe is to have a war every twenty-five years. Until World War I we thought we were comparatively safe from the recurring ravages of these wars.

In the spring of 1914, Dr. David Starr Jordan, president of Leland Stanford University, made a nationwide tour of our country, in which he espoused the thesis that we had at last arrived at that state of our civilization when nations, like individuals, would conciliate or adjudicate their differences, and that there would be war no more. His last address of the series was given in the Salt Lake Tabernacle. After the conclusion of his address, Dr. James E.

Talmage, a member of the Quorum of the Twelve and a
friend of Dr. Jordan, approached him and said in substance, "Dr. Jordan, because you have failed to take into
account the prophecies contained in Holy Writ you have
arrived at the wrong answer. There will continue to be
wars until the advent of the millennium."

That was the spring of 1914. August of the same year
saw the outbreak of World War I.

Now I do not want you to conclude from this that
wars are necessary—that wars are foreordained as a part
of the plan governing the universe. All we can safely derive from that prophecy of Elder Talmage is that the
Prophets of the Lord are sometimes able to foresee the consequences of man's failure to follow the teachings of the
Master.

When and if our young men are actually called into
service in the uniform of their country we hope they will
go as ambassadors of peace toward all men of good will—
that they will ever pray for divine guidance—that they
will keep hate out of their hearts—that they will place
their ultimate reliance upon the Lord and not upon arma-
ments (not even the atomic bomb) for in the long run, victory and finally peace will come to that nation which
serves the Lord. We hope they will keep in mind the historical narrative of Gideon and the Midianites as portrayed in the Old Testament (Judges, Chapters 6-8).

Because the Children of Israel became wicked they
were delivered into the hands of the Midianites. When they
repented, the Lord through their prophet-leader Gideon
planned for their deliverance. For that purpose Gideon
assembled an army of 32,000 which in itself was exceed-
ingly small as compared with the army of the Midianites.
The Lord, nevertheless, told him this army of 32,000 was
too large, because if they won, they would themselves
claim credit for the victory. He instructed Gideon to let
all those who were "fearful and afraid" depart. Of the
32,000 some 22,000 departed, leaving only 10,000. Of these
ten thousand the Lord chose only three hundred who were
righteous and faithful, and excused the others. With this

tiny army of three hundred and the help of the Lord, Gideon overcame the Midianites who were so numerous they "lay along the valley like grasshoppers for multitude."

This nation will be well-advised if it relies more upon spiritual obedience to the commandments of the Lord than upon the atomic bomb.

Security

As a necessary corollary of this truism, individual and group security will come to us through individual righteousness and faith in the Lord, rather than through arming to the hilt.

In some societies, the individual who goes unarmed is regarded as a fool. Tell a Bedouin that among us no one ever carries arms and he will protest with amazement: "But how do you ever survive?" The answer is that we are really much safer than if we carried arms, and that such a peculiar and paradoxical solution to the problem of security is known as civilization. We would be completely safe if we were sufficiently righteous to rely on the promised protection of our Lord.

No figure of antiquity had more stories told about him than Dionysius of Syracuse, a man who, through his own wits and daring, had attained the position of top man in the whole world of his time. From then on he became obsessed with a desire for security, and that made him the most miserable man on earth. Every measure that he took to insure his safety only limited his own freedom of action and made him feel more insecure, until finally he died, hidden away in a prison of his own making, where no enemy could get at him.

The only real security lies in the intellectual development of individuals so that they can think effectively, and more important, in their spiritual development so that they can voice, and have the courage to carry out their convictions. In that way they will avoid falling victims to error. We can never be saved from the vicissitudes and heartaches and labor of life. When we attempt to do so and surround ourselves with walls of security—when we turn our

attention from a positive desire for further endeavor and
follow a negative search for static security—all progress
has ceased. It shall be the objective of this University to
teach its students that security will come by losing themselves in the service of mankind—rather than by trying to
obtain some selfish security for themselves.

This was the message of Christ at a time when the
world was also an armed camp. When he came to make
it possible for mankind to be redeemed, the Hebrews
were in bondage to the Romans. In the great Greek city of
Athens, three-fifths of its population were slaves, and a
similar condition existed over the Mediterranean world.
Individuals convicted of crime were executed in the most
brutal fashion, often being hanged on crosses along public
roads and in the market places as examples to others. Fear
was the chief restraining influence upon men. In parts of
the Roman Empire the sick and aged were left upon
mountainsides to perish. Starvation of the poor was commonplace. The natural affections for blood kin seemed woe-
fully lacking. Brothers murdered brothers for gain; wives
poisoned their husbands, and husbands destroyed their
wives. Even the great Constantine murdered his wife and
one of his sons without arousing much comment among a
people depraved by sin.

The Jewish historian, Josephus, says of the Jews who
lived in Jerusalem shortly after the death of Jesus "that
a more wicked generation of men had not been upon the
earth since the days of Noah."

Yet the Saviour's plan for saving that sick world was
not a political one—nowhere did the Saviour urge collective or state-imposed security. His entire emphasis was
on personal integrity, personal initiative, and personal
goodness. "He who saves his life will lose it; he who gives
his life, for my sake, will save it."* The same emphasis is
contained in the revelations to the Prophet Joseph Smith.

Ultimate Mission

The ultimate mission of this school is, therefore, to
teach the Gospel of Jesus Christ in its fullness. If you think

---

*See Matt. 10:39, Luke 17:33, John 12:25.

that is not realistic, let me summon as my witnesses three great generals. I start with Napoleon Bonaparte, who said: "Alexander, Caesar, Charlemagne and I myself have founded empires; but upon what do these creations of our genius depend? Upon force! Jesus alone founded his empire upon love; and to this day millions would die for him."

I come next to General MacArthur. In a recent address in which he attempted to analyze the ills of the world, he stated: "The problem basically is theological and involves a spiritual recrudescense and improvement of human character that will synchronize with our almost matchless advance in science and art, literature and all natural and cultural developments of the past two thousand years. It must be of the spirit if we are to save the flesh."

I come finally to General Omar Bradley, our chief of staff. In an Armistice speech of two years ago, he said: "With the monstrous weapons man already has, humanity is in danger of being trapped in this world by its moral adolescence. Our knowledge of science has clearly outstripped our capacity to control it. We have too many men of science; too few men of God. We have grasped the mystery of the atom and rejected the Sermon on the Mount. Man is stumbling blindly through a spiritual darkness while toying with the precarious secrets of life and death. The world has achieved brilliance without wisdom, power without conscience. Ours is a world of nuclear giants and ethical infants. We know more about war than we know about peace, more about killing than we know about living. This is our twentieth century's claim to distinction and to progress."

While we do not agree that there are too many men of science (in fact, we intend to train more) we intend to train those scientists so that they also will be men of God. As desired by President Brigham Young we intend here that science and religion will implement and strengthen each other.

As long ago as 1909 the prime minister of Great Britain made a speech before a large audience at the University of Edinburgh. The title of his speech was "The Moral Values Which Unite the Nations." He discussed in a very able manner: (1) common knowledge among nations, (2) common commercial interests, (3) the intercourse of diplomatic relationships, and (4) the bond of human friendship.

The audience greeted the masterful discourse with a great outburst of applause. The presiding officer arose to express the appreciation of himself and the audience, and as he did so, a Japanese student doing graduate work at the University stood up and leaning over the balcony said, "But, Mr. Balfour, what about Jesus Christ?"

Mr. Robert Spear, who reported the incident, wrote: "One could have heard a pin drop in the hall. Everyone felt at once the justice of the rebuke. The leading statesman of what was then considered the greatest Christian empire in the world had been dealing with the different ties that are to unite mankind, and had omitted the one fundamental and essential bond. And the reminder of his forgetfulness had come from a Japanese student from a far-away non-Christian land."

The tragic epilogue to that story is that Christ and his plan in its fullness have continued to be forgotten by our so-called Christian civilization. I conceive it to be the mission of this school to understand and remember his mission, and to prepare the world for the advent of the millennium, when Christ will reign personally upon the earth, and there will be war no more. In the meantime we can all participate in the blessings of the Master when he said, "Peace I leave with you, my peace I give unto you' not as the world giveth, give I unto you. Let not your heart be troubled, neither let it be afraid." (John 14:27) And again:

"Come unto me, all ye that labour and are heavy laden, and I will give you rest." (Matt. 11:28)

To that end I dedicate the services of the faculty and myself, in the name of the Master. Amen.

THE HELPING HAND

(Excerpts from commencement message at Brigham Young University, August 21, 1969)

Now may I tell you of some of the things we are doing on our campus to maintain our reputation of being a friendly institution. In the light of the educational scene over the last few years throughout our country, it is occurring to more and more people that the truly helping hand is the open hand—not the aggressive, closed fist. In no area of our national experience is this becoming more evident than in higher education. The fragile rationality upon which all education is based has been no match for mindless muscle when the shouting and the shoving have started. Nor has dramatizing the problems generated easy solutions. Indeed in a disheartening number of cases, conciliation has been almost precluded by confrontation.

If the essential ineffectiveness of physical coercion is being recognized more generally, a far more subtle temptation still claims a host of students and faculty who are determined to reform higher education in America. These would agree that the open hand and not the clenched fist is the appropriate symbol, but the open hand to them suggests lavish governmental support. The so-called "disadvantaged" become, in effect, wards of Washington.

While the consequences have been less dubious here

than in efforts resorting to force, few who have been deeply involved in massive government financing of higher education feel easy about past experience or future prospects. Inequities abound, questionable programs remain unevaluated, and sources of funding rather than interest or capability coerce research efforts.

When everything that money can do is done for you, the tendency to remain a totally passive recipient is overwhelming.

At BYU the open hand is not a symbol of largess but of invitation. If you are not able to reach out and grasp the helping hand offered to you, we cannot do it for you. Help for students at this University is not a matter of careless dispensing and thoughtless receiving. We care too much about you to be party to such a demoralizing situation. Yet, since the times have a tendency to keep us from recognizing help that is simply available rather than lavished upon us, I want to rehearse today some of the ways in which the BYU community stands ready to help.

Admissions Advising—We have appointed and trained admissions advisers for most stakes in the Church. Our Admissions Office not only keeps them supplied with the latest information concerning BYU, but they are brought together from time to time and instructed concerning standards and policies which prospective students—and families of prospective students—need to be aware of if they hope to attend this University. We believe that education is a family affair, and we encourage our admissions advisers to discuss possible enrollment at BYU in a family setting.

Guidance Center—Although academic requirements at BYU are now so demanding that not all those who apply can be accepted, we are as concerned for those we deny or defer as those we enroll. In cooperation with the Seminaries and Institutes of the Church, we have set up on campus an Educational Information and Guidance Center. Here trained and sympathetic counselors help young members of the Church explore various educational alternatives. Those whose current preparation appears deficient for matriculation at BYU are given explicit direction for remedying these deficiencies or advice as to other institutions where they may obtain an education fitted to their needs. Occasionally a disturbed parent demands that we give his child "the right to fail." In his disappointment such a parent does not foresee what a traumatic experience failure can be for an impressionable 18-year-old. Out of much experience and deep concern we are committed to an admissions and counseling policy which emphasizes the probability of success instead of the right to fail.

Orientation—When students arrive on campus, they are assigned to a so-called "Y group" which takes them through a process of orientation to the entire school. Such groups are small and informal. Under the leadership of upperclassmen, these units provide an opportunity for questions, candid discussion of problems, and an immediate identity with approximately a dozen and a half young people who are about equally apprehensive concerning their new life at college. While many universities have elaborate orientation programs, the "Y groups" concept is uniquely a product of BYU. The many schools which are now trying to emulate it testify to its worth.

Counseling—While the size and complexity of our institution make registration for classes a bit overwhelming to the entering student, we make up for that by conceding to no school the hours spent in individual counseling by faculty and administration during this period. Deans, department chairmen, teaching faculty, and the dedicated staff who do the actual processing *all care* and try to translate that concern into programs which put the welfare of the student first.

Job Placement—For those who must work part time to remain in school (and during a four-year course this usually involves 75 percent of our students), an especially efficient Placement Center is available, rated by recruiters who recruit at 81 western universities as the number one university recruiting center. This year over 13,700 students registered with the center seeking employment. This employment center participated in filling 13,400 positions of which 11,200 were on campus and 2,200 off campus. On an average day about 8,200 of our students are employed. No other major university approaches the percentage of its students which BYU hires from its own funds. This has been made possible by our policy of hiring as few as possible full-time employees for the physical operation of the University, in order that the manifold operations, such as housing, feeding, farming, and building maintenance may be done by our students.

What is not generally known is the unusual effort made by the center to help students with special placement problems. For instance, information was gathered for a student with visual impairment which made it possible for him to make contact with over fifty possible employers. Through the help of one of them, he is now in a graduate program which promises to utilize his abilities totally. Another physical education major lost the use of her legs and was confined to a wheelchair. She gives much of the credit for her successful employment as a physical education director with a major school district in the state to the efforts of BYU's Placement Center. The large number of foreign students on this campus pose an unusual placement problem also. Since many of these need extensive individual help in preparing letters and resumes, the center has allocated special help to aid them.

Study Help—Individual colleges have all been developing ways in which they could participate more meaningfully in each student's achievement. In the College of Religious Instruction, for instance, we will try this fall to keep introductory courses at a size which will make it possible for instructors to give individual help. We are also arranging for study-discussion groups which will meet several times each week for those who wish to attend. In addition a large amount of supplementary material for the beginning Book of Mormon course has been videotaped and will be shown at nine different times each week so students can fit this viewing into their own schedules.

In nursing each student enrolled in a nursing sequence is given National League of Nursing Achievement Examinations at the close of each semester. Those who have scored below a certain percentile are invited to attend a special help session with instructors from the college whose background make it possible to give specialized instruction in that particular subject. As a result of this concerted and individual help, out of a total of 471 graduates from our nursing program, 471 or 100 percent have been able to pass the licensing examination and become registered nurses!

Indian Program—BYU has also received national attention for its program with American Indian students. The success of this program, however, is less dependent upon innovative techniques than it is upon convincing students for whom college is a severe cultural shock that someone does understand these problems, that he is willing to spend time helping, and that he truly thinks of himself as the Indian's brother. Perhaps the most exciting result of this mutual respect and affection is the sense of personal responsibility it is engendering in individual students.

Decision Making—The General College tries to help the 1,800 students who come to BYU without deciding on a major. In our present program we offer an eight-week block course which not only acquaints students with possible majors, but supplements this with extensive testing and counseling. The result is that over 60 percent of those that take this course decide on a major their first year. Only 20 percent of those who do not avail themselves of this help are able to choose a major during a comparable time.

While I could cite instances from all colleges, let me round out this discussion of academic help by mentioning some specific instances in which colleges or academic units cooperate with student groups effectively.

Tutoring—Students from the Honors Program have supplemented the tutoring available on a fee basis by volunteering to tutor beginning students in chemistry, English, history, psychology, mathematics, and languages without charge. In the College of Education there are three student groups which attempt to introduce prospective teachers to their chosen profession.

Rehabilitation—Possibly the best known of the on-campus agencies which are organized to aid students come under the direction of the Dean of Students. If the disciplinary functions which the University Standards Office must perform are a traditional target for campus criticism and humor, it should be remembered that the primary function of this office is to counsel and rehabilitate. Even in cases in which penalties must be imposed, great care is exercised to see that those who might speak in behalf of an erring student—people such as his bishop —are available.

Personal Planning—The Counseling Center provides direct, individual service to students who need assistance in formulating educational and vocational plans. It also serves to identify and treat those with interpersonal problems.

The Academic Standards Office not only keeps students apprised of their academic standing when deficiencies occur, but it also makes available specific materials on effective study, and, in cooperation with college advisers, suggests steps which might be taken to continue normal progress toward a degree.

Church Activity—The final area in which significant help is available to all BYU students is through their ward and stake organizations. Pioneered at BYU, the campus ward is now a vital part of many campuses on which there are a number of LDS students. This next year we will have 10 stakes and 92 wards on campus. Not only does membership in a campus ward provide opportunity for spiritual growth and a developing awareness of Church procedure, it also provides a relatively small group with which a student may feel strong social identification. Additionally, in most cases, campus bishops are also associated with the University and can supplement the academic and personal counseling generally available.

Summarily stated, BYU, as the University founded by the "only true and living Church," is dedicated to the Christian ideal that it is our duty to be concerned about the whole life of every student—his social, religious, and moral life as well as his intellectual development. In this way we differ from many institutions of higher learning who have abandoned the concept that institutions are *in loco parentis* or foster parents.

Thus at a recent meeting of members of boards of trustees representing most of the educational institutions of the country, held at the University of Missouri, one of the leading educators in America from one of the most reputable institutions judged by secular learning spent his keynote address to demolish the idea that a university had any responsibility to its students other than educating their minds. All other academic speakers like sheep followed his lead; no one of them gave him any argument. Then a student who was president of the student body of the University of Missouri was called upon to speak. Referring to the speaker who had first advanced the idea, he said in effect, "Of course you realize, Doctor, that this leaves a whole lot of us with no parents at all; your philosophy is the philosophy that is destroying our educational institutions."

In this sharp reprimand to leading educators this student recognized that in our day many students come from homes where they had no spiritual or other stabilizing influences and desperately need the university to set up spiritual and social standards, and that all students from wherever they come need the constant guiding hand of criteria which has been tested through the centuries and which are enunciated in the Ten Commandments and the Sermon on the Mount.

Since BYU unreservedly accepts its role of foster parents to those who matriculate here, we are trying to be sensitive to student need without prolonging or indulging youthful dependence. Ours is the open hand of invitation to shared responsibility in the finest education available to the "youth of a noble birthright."

In the name of Jesus Christ. Amen.

ADDRESSES TO THE
FACULTY

Section 6

Dr. and Mrs. Wilkinson on the day he was inaugurated president of Brigham Young University, Oct. 8, 1951

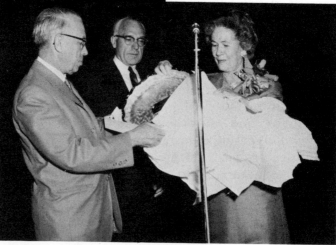

Representing the BYU faculty, Dr. Stewart Grow presents a silver tray to Dr. and Mrs. Wilkinson at a banquet in 1964.

THE CALLING OF BYU

(*Address given to the faculty of the Brigham Young University on September 18, 1962 in the Annual Preschool Faculty Workshop.*)

As school begins this year we see signs on every hand that we are living in a *universe,* not just a world, of change and ferment. Our modern vocabulary is filled with terms unknown a few years ago, but now on the lips of every literate person, such as astronaut, cosmonaut, countdown, Telstar, anti-missile missile, etc. This is truly a scientific and complex environment—one fraught with great potentials for good but beset with grave dangers as well.

Man has left evidence of his existence in the implements he used, the cities he built, his burial places, memorials, public structures, roads, and irrigation canals; yes in the civilizations he built—some of which he destroyed from without, and others of which disintegrated from within. His mode of travel and transport has been extended from foot to flight, and from musclebound back to mighty and versatile machine. The fantastic means of communication today are miraculous compared with the primitive grimace, gesture, and grunt.

The material and physical state of man has been advanced from an animal existence to the luxury of thermostatically-controlled, air-conditioned, soap-scented, fluorescent-lighted, push-button comfort. He is clothed in

synthetic fabrics of rainbow hues, amply nourished, replete
with vitamins; irradiated, inoculated, and chlorinated.

Today's concerns, in America at least, are more apt
to be those of obesity and geriatrics than starvation and
pediatrics. In short, to "live like a king" has lost its appeal.
Regal luxury has become commonplace—and free from a
king's responsibility!

The prophetic novels of Jules Verne, or Edward Bel-
lamy, seemed fantastic to their early readers. Today so
many scientific marvels have become reality that the speed
of sound is a unit of aircraft velocity, and the speed of
light a term in the equation of space travel. The electron
and the atom are hard at work in man's service and the
fourth dimension is no longer a science fiction nightmare.

The sky is no longer the limit. The real limit, today,
is only the boundary of man's vision and ability, and both
are a measure of his training for the future. It was recently observed that of all the scientists who have ever
walked the earth, 90% of them are living today! Furthermore, it is estimated that during the past decade more
learned data has been accumulated than during all the
preceding period of recorded history! Undoubtedly, we
are living in a stunning era of accelerated knowledge. In
reality, we are in danger of being "submerged" by data—
of all kinds, in all fields of leadership.

But, this staggering challenge instead of discouraging
our pursuit of knowledge, must inspire us on to greater
intellectual mastery. Despite the overdone hysteria of the
recent "Sputnik" achievement, we still must recognize
that we of the free Western world are locked in mortal
combat with the enslaved East presently under the domination of the Union of Soviet Socialist Republics. No amount
of propaganda can disguise this basic issue.

In this fearful struggle, the quality of education and
our willingness to abide by it become supremely important. This means our willingness to pursue the truth, and
our willingness to live in accordance with the truth. These
qualitative factors alone may determine our survival or
destruction. It would be absurdly ostrich-like to rationalize

away the solid achievements of Soviet science; rather they should be the cause of sober reflection on our part. But, on the other hand, it would be equally absurd to surrender to panic and downgrade everything in American education. However, we should be honest enough to recognize our serious shortcomings and resolute enough to correct errors.

The pathetic aspect of Soviet education is that the effective and powerful marshalling of zeal and talent should be used for such evil ends. Though we maintain our ends are infinitely more to man's benefit, we could well emulate Soviet dedication to the tasks at hand, rather than trying, as some modernists do, to debunk our accomplishments and de-glamorize our progress as free men.

Actually, American education is but a *mirror* for our culture. We cannot expect our educational system to be pluperfect when we ourselves tolerate a growing contempt for work, barbarous music and art, a sensual and sensational press, tawdry drama, and corrupted media of communication. We might fight constantly against the rising obscenity and growing vulgarity of our society. BYU should be in the vanguard of those who would fight for the highest standards in life—including those of the intellectual order. What, then, can be done at this institution?

I would submit that we should *persistently struggle for greater academic attainment.* We need a toughened attitude *toward our curriculum,* on the part of both teachers and students. Some research psychologists estimate that, at best, men use only 10% of their potential thinking capacity. What a challenge for intellectual progress! We also know that greater application of reasoning power is obtained where the challenge is most severe and exciting. There is no doubt in my mind that we should do everything possible on this campus to stimulate the latent intellectual talent of our students.

Furthermore, we should also *recognize the danger,* on the part of each member of our campus community, to *use the unreliable gauge* of sheer and mere social activity to judge student performances, rather than insisting upon the highest standards of academic scholarship. As a friendly outgoing people, Mormons may be prone to place greater stress on active social adjustment than upon intellectual discipline. At this point, it might be well to bear in mind the famous statement of John W. Gardner:

> We must learn to honor excellence, even to demand it, in every socially accepted human activity, and to scorn shoddiness, however exalted the activity . . . The society that scorns excellence in plumbing because plumbing is a humble activity and tolerates shoddiness in philosophy because philosophy is an exalted activity, will have neither good plumbing nor good philosophy. Neither its pipes nor its theories will hold water.

We should sponsor an enthusiastic revival of stern and conscientious study habits. The definition of Brigham Young which adorns one of the walls of the Smoot Administration Building that "Education is the power to think clearly, to act well in the world's work, and the power to appreciate life" must never be forgotten at this institution. Students should be taught how to think, encouraged to actually *do* some thinking, and inspired to take action on the *results* of their thinking, and then taught a reverence for and appreciation of life in all its component parts. Above all, we must remember that *quality,* not quantity is the true yardstick of education. It is far better to have one outstanding scientist, for example, than ten mediocre ones. Also, we should frankly recognize that we cannot possibly compete with the Soviet world on a *quantitative* level—we are "out-gunned" at the very start by their bigger population base.

There is a sore need for more emphasis on *solid core subjects* of learning, and a de-emphasis on the "softer" fringe courses dealing with problems of life adjustment and behavior patterns. However, this is not a case for swinging the pendulum of education to another extreme point. American schools, on all levels, must continue to stress training for *citizenship and character* because these are the qualities essential to freedom.

But a delicate balance is required. We minimize the stern and exacting disciplines at our own peril in an age fraught with unimaginable danger. However, if in the process of emphasizing these disciplines we lose sight of the more subtle qualities absolutely necessary to human freedom we may reap the bitter harvest of trading *shadow for substance.* Our citizenship and character training can never become so nebulous as to lose significant meaning, nor can it be discarded as a mere "frill." We need *both* specialized and generalized outlooks on life and its challenges. We should not be forced to choose between, but should strive for quality in both approaches to education.

At BYU, I submit that the faculty should definitely demand more of our students. I do not mean to suggest that increased demands have not already been made. On the contrary, I think our academic environment has improved greatly in recent years. But I do feel that the circumstances of our time in history justify demands of sterner stuff.

On the other hand, these demands by the faculty should be just, and of basic value. The young Ph.D. should not try to wrap in one course all that he learned in his conquest of that "union" trademark. On the other hand, no teacher should ever give "make-work" projects which have little real purpose except to consume both time and energy. We can no longer afford such academic waste. Most students of any reasonable intellectual quality will be excited by the challenge of a good teacher who has an exciting standard and up-to-date information which he maintains honestly in his own work. No student will thrive on lectures upholstered when the professor himself graduated from college which have never been thereafter refurbished. A teacher once complained to a university president over his lack of progress. He said he had had 15 years of experience at the university. The president replied that he was sorry, but he had had the same experience 15 times.

But above all else, we must remember that the youths we teach here will be the future leaders of the Church, the nation, and the world. We must not fail them! Let us provide them with the intellectual tools they will need to meet the test of their times.

This age-old dilemma of knowledge which can elevate and at the same time submerge us confronts us on many fronts. Uppermost, of course, in our minds, is the urgent crisis of civilization itself that is inherent in the existence of nuclear research. But if the others are less serious, they are by no means simple. As medicine and nutritional science progress, the general population and proportion of older people rise. Shifts to new automated technology bring temporary unemployment and make certain skills obsolete. Increasing leisure, accompanied by lack of inspiration for its intelligent use, nourishes frustration and dilutes spiritual values. The horrible prospect of a future society resembling George Orwell's "1984" cannot be ignored, or taken lightly.

So far, our generation has not always been wise in its adaptation to the advances of our society. While we have increased the span of life, we attempt to decrease the span of working years. And while some argue for the reduction of the working week, they also insist on overtime so that their compensation may be increased. This does not make very much sense!

But growth of knowledge no matter how rapid and how spectacular, even though sometimes misapplied, can never become a threat to true education if accompanied by constant critical vigilance and by a never-ending process of sifting which will separate the universal principle from the practical application, and the firm truth from the wild guess. However, this sober task is becoming increasingly difficult. Society demands vast numbers of people trained in a vast variety of skills. In response to this sharp demand, universities tend to multiply their course offerings, to sponsor specialized projects, and are inexorably forced to *train* rather than *educate* the students.

We are tempted to tell our students that the field they want to study has grown so enormously and has become so complex and so intricate that they must specialize as soon as possible. Further, that once embarked upon the process of specialization, they'll have little or no time for anything else, and it will take all their time to keep up with the developments in their own specialty. After some years of this brain-washing process, decorated perhaps with the "Order of the Ph.D.", the young scholar will go out to attempt himself to contribute to the growth of knowledge in his specialty, while at the same time forgetting the other values of life. I submit that this type of counsel should never be given on this campus! As I see it, the true purpose of education in the Latter-day Saint environment is not to awe or frighten with vastness and complexity but rather to impress with the simplicity that comes from real insight—not to depress and discourage students by the bewildering array of data, but to bring order out of the chaos of information and inspire them with the great spiritual principles which bring harmony, order, joy, and happiness in human life.

We must therefore teach our students about the divine nature of man. Each human being has a tremendous potential for good or evil. But we should recognize that evil does not automatically disappear because we have higher standards of living or better housing or that it will disappear with socialized medicine. On the contrary, the evil in the world could very well increase! All around us, in today's public drama, we see vigorous activity apparently geared to the premise (which I consider false) that the best policy for man is that which is directed solely toward the pursuit of a higher standard of living. Is this the way life should be? I think not!

> For what is a man profited, if he shall gain the whole world, and lose his own soul? Or what shall a man give in exchange for his soul? (Matthew 16:26.)

In considering the awesome importance of the BYU teacher in this learning process affecting our students, I sincerely believe that these scriptures are also very relevant here:

> And they shall also teach their children to pray, and to walk uprightly before the Lord. (D&C 68:28.)
>
> Let him that is ignorant learn wisdom by humbling himself and calling upon the Lord his God, that his eyes may be opened that he may see, and his ears opened that he may hear. (D&C 136:32.)

O that cunning plan of the evil one! O the vainness, and the frailties, and the foolishness of men! When they are learned they think they are wise, and they hearken not unto the counsel of God, for they set it aside, supposing they know of themselves, wherefore their wisdom is foolishness and it profiteth them not. And they shall perish. But to be learned is good if they hearken unto the counsels of God. (2 Nephi 9:28-29.)

At BYU, we have a two-fold responsibility—a grave responsibility which demands a great deal of our faculty and staff:

1. *Proper academic development*—to meet the tests and challenges of the world.
2. *Proper spiritual development*—to meet the basic inner needs of the student, and help him understand his relationship to his fellow man and to God, the Heavenly Father.

It is especially important that faculty and staff remember this responsibility always. Each classroom, each office, and each workshop should be affected strongly, in its own way, by the gospel of Jesus Christ. This attitude of basic reverence for eternal principles should be the hallmark of BYU.

Basically, our University, in attempting to teach students that man, as a son of God, is a free agent with unlimited possibilities for eternal development, and in constantly emphasizing a never-ending search for truth and a proper understanding of that truth, should be keenly interested in supporting certain steps, taken to insure the most optimum environment.

1. The first step is that of strong encouragement for the proper development of a deep-seated interest in LDS spiritual values. Superficiality should not be tolerated. Thorough understanding of one's religious perspective is essential.

On this subject I get from time to time reports that a student's testimony has been impaired or actually destroyed by some thoughtless or irreverent teacher. On investigation I occasionally find the accusation to be true. In those rare and unusual cases where I have found such a deed to have been done purposely and premeditated by the teacher we have had to terminate his services. Obviously he had no testimony of the divinity of our restored gospel himself and therefore either came to our faculty under false pretenses or apostatized after he arrived. Sometimes, however, a teacher will carelessly affect the life of a young student by destroying the bridge which supports his testimony without at the same time providing a stronger and more enduring bridge in its place. Admitting that the testimonies of some students are immature and indeed sometimes not solidly based, we must never be guilty of impairing their faith in an all-wise creator and in the divinity of the restored gospel. It is our duty to improve and enlarge, not impair or crush the testimonies of our students. I urge all of you to give serious consideration to this duty that none of us by flippant comment, sarcastic innuendo, or irreverent attitude or otherwise, be guilty of depriving a student of the motivating spiritual power which his parents probably sent him here to obtain and retain. Such irresponsible conduct in this institution is tantamount to blasphemy.

In the meetings of the Board of Trustees President McKay has often suggested that the greatest opportunity for a teacher at this institution is to teach some principle of the gospel in a class in chemistry or geology or sociology. In that respect we have more freedom of speech in this University than we would have in a public institution, for there we would be forbidden to teach Mormon doctrines.

2. The second step is that of a constant emphasis upon the basic religious nature of *all* knowledge. To accept the common authorship of God for all spheres of learning is the cornerstone of LDS education.

The acceptance of this truism comes to us direct from the Doctrine & Covenants.

And I give unto you a commandment that you shall teach one another the doctrine of the kingdom. Teach ye diligently and my grace shall attend you, that you may be instructed more perfectly in theory, in principle, in doctrine, in the law of the Gospel, in all things that pertain unto the kingdom of God, that are expedient for you to understand;

Of things both in heaven and in the earth, and under the earth; Things which have been, things which are, things which must shortly come to pass; things which are at home, things which are abroad; the wars and the perplexities of the nations, and the judgments which are on the land; and a knowledge also of countries and of kingdoms. (D&C 88:77-79.)

The founder of this institution preached the same doctrine:

Every accomplishment, every polished grace, every useful attainment in mathematics, music, and in all science and art belong to the Saints, and they should avail themselves as expeditiously as possible of the wealth of knowledge the sciences offer to every diligent and persevering scholar. (*Journal of Discourses,* IX, 370.)

again:

There is nothing I would like better than to learn chemistry, botany, geology, and mineralogy, so that I could tell what I walk on, the properties of the air I breathe, and what I drink. (*Journal of Discourses,* IX, 3.)

again:

Let them also learn all the truth pertaining to the arts and sciences and how to apply the same to their temporal wants. Let them study things that are upon the earth and that are in the heavens. (*Journal of Discourses,* VIII, 39-40.)

and finally:

We should be a people of profound learning pertaining to the things of the world. We should be familiar with the various languages, for we wish to send men to the different nations and to the isles of the sea. We wish missionaries who may go to France to be able to speak the French language fluently, and those who may go to Germany, Italy, Spain, and so on to all nations, to be familiar with the languages of those nations.

We also wish them to understand the geography, habits, customs and laws of nations and kingdoms whether they be barbarous or civilized. (*Journal of Discourses,* VIII, 9.)

3. The third step is a determination to place LDS religious values in all of the activities of the institution— not merely in the academic field, but also in the non- academic areas. Are we truly living up to the gospel of Jesus Christ in all of our various facets of university life? It is essential that all of us, faculty and staff, recognize this responsibility.

4. The fourth step is a definite program to combat effectively those aspects of university life on all levels which tend to create a secular environment. No LDS institution can possibly give aid and comfort to those persons or forces which are obviously inimical to the highest ideals of the Church.

5. The fifth step is a recognition that the University has an obligation to produce a student who is fully appreciative of the principles of the Latter-day Saint faith, and of his role in the universe as a sacred and independent individual. Brother Maeser gave utterance to this thought when he said, "There is a Mt. Sinai for every child if only he can be inspired to climb it." Every student should therefore be encouraged to recognize the great inherent power which he possesses as a human being and as a son of God. But this is not the only result. The individual who goes forward from BYU should also realize that his individual strength is not to be used for himself alone. Through the spiritual influence of the campus community, he should have acquired the vision and the inspiration to be concerned about his fellowmen, to be truly interested in rendering service wherever it is needed.

In practical effect, this means that each of us at BYU should be living and walking examples of the gospel of Jesus Christ. We should strive as mightily as we can to live up to the principles of the Church every day of the week, and not just on the Sabbath. For good or for ill, we stand as examples before our students. Any member of the faculty or staff who may scoff at and deride spiritual values is impairing his usefulness at this University. Though he clothes his skepticism in brilliant and fascinating verbiage, he will ultimately be an unhappy person on this particular campus community. Further, what can a student's evaluation be when he observes that some of us pay only nominal attention to the spiritual principles that the institution publicly espouses? I strongly declare that once we become associated with this institution we also carry upon our shoulders the responsibility of exemplary living. This may not be easy, but it is certainly a realistic factor in our lives. If we treat this obligation lightly we could unwittingly, as well as deliberately, offend or disillusion a student to the point that he finds it very difficult to gain or retain a testimony of the faith.

I confess to you as I prepared this address and wrote these words that I was almost afraid to utter them for I know that I do not fully measure up to this test. But I hereby pledge myself to make a more strenuous effort to approach the proper standard and I hope that others of you will do so also. Although I have now been here for nearly 12 years never have I felt so keenly the responsibilities of my office and the need for spiritual guidance. I therefore pray humbly for that strength and for your spiritual support.

No student can truly succeed in this modern world— by the gauge of the *whole* man—without the firm support of religious devotion. His physical achievements of the future, no matter how impressive from the secular viewpoint, are but a mockery if he fails to recognize his deep obligation to God the Father. If the student does not become deeply aware of his great personal need for spiritual motivation, and does not work actively to obtain it, then our world is truly lost! Thus, the obligation upon us, who deal so intimately with the youth of today, is indeed sacred and of pre-eminent importance.

We should give loving attention to each student in our charge. I implore all of you as you are engaged in counselling students to take this responsibility to heart. These young men and women need guidance and counsel every step of the way. I'm not advocating pampering, but I feel that we should do everything in our power to avoid the pitiless and coldly impersonal attitude so prevalent on the campuses of many large universities. Each student is not only significant as a human being, but particularly as a brother or sister, and child of God. With our spiritual background, we should not only be concerned about the students assigned to us, but feel a personal responsibility for the success or failure of each student so assigned. And this concern must be expressed in kindness and understanding. The late John C. Swenson often told of his becoming so discouraged as a young student that he decided to return home. On his way to the railway station he met Karl G. Maeser. Sensing the worried expression on the boy's face, Brother Maeser put his arm around him, spoke a word of encouragement and John C. turned around and came back to the campus. In his lifetime Brother Swenson in turn gave encouragement to hundreds of his students. I hope you will do likewise.

May I urge all of you to have regular and thorough physical examinations. If you have not recently had one, I urgently suggest that you take this common sense step for your own personal welfare.

Furthermore, watch your diet carefully. Ask your doctor, or our College of Family Living, for counsel on the proper foods you should consume, and try to avoid obesity in every way you can.

Never neglect regular proper physical exercise; it will improve both your muscular tone and your emotional outlook. However, avoid excessive exercise which might produce a heavy strain upon your strength and physical resources.

Finally, a word of cautious counsel to those who are 50 years "young" and over. Don't forget to take proper rest at regular intervals. I suggest a brief noon-day nap. It will give the necessary vigor and vitality to finish out the day without expending any diminution of your strength and will add years to your life. I knew of a celebrated surgeon in the East who began taking a noon-day nap at the age of 30. He was a high-strung individual who consumed a lot of energy, but through a good nap he exhibited no fatigue. If you will pardon a personal example, may I comment that if I follow the advice of my doctors, given after my heart episode and take a short nap at noon, I can leave the office at 7:00 at night feeling almost as fresh as when I reported to the office at 8:00 in the morning. I hope you will acquire this habit. For years, before my heart attack I resisted taking a "nap" thinking that such a break in the day's work was only for a "sissy." Now I recognize that it is nature's way of permitting one to continue to function as a mature man.

Lastly, develop a wholesome attitude toward your work and toward your associates, and avoid worrying about your problems, which we all have. Your mental attitude is as important to your health as anything else.

You have often heard someone say of a friend who passed on that he "worked too hard." Rarely does anyone work too hard if he takes proper care of his health. I remember working late one Saturday night in the office of the late Chief Justice Charles E. Hughes with whom I began the practice of the law. Near midnight Judge Hughes came to the office himself to pick up a book that he wanted to study over the weekend. Noting that I was there, he came to my office and commended me for being at the office that time of night. I remember him looking straight at me and saying, "Mr. Wilkinson, don't let anyone ever tell you that hard work will ruin your health. I have heard that said of many of my legal associates over the years, but when I have investigated each instance I have generally found that it was not hard work but bad habits or family tensions or mental attitudes that was the cause of their demise." With that philosophy it is not surprising that Chief Justice Hughes continued to be chief justice of the United States until after 80 years of age.

I offer you this counsel only in the interest of your own personal health. Each of you should try to do everything possible to *maximize* rather than *minimize* his reservoir of health.

In conclusion, permit me to express my personal affection and gratitude to each and every one of you. Brigham Young University is certainly a large university with an attractive campus and modern buildings. But all these advantages, while extremely significant, means virtually nothing unless they are bolstered by the devoted and dedicated efforts of our faculty and staff. I know you have given freely of your devotion and dedication—often at considerable personal sacrifice—to the "Y". What progress we

have achieved here is due largely to the outstanding contributions you have made—individually and as a group—
to the improvement of our academic standards, and the
personal interest you have shown in guiding our students
into proper and wholesome channels. If you have not already read the little booklet we published last year on "A
Unique Faculty" I urge you to do so.

I heartily urge you to continue the fine record which
you have already made. We need your help to fulfill
the great and stimulating destiny of BYU. I humbly pray
that the Lord will bless all our righteous endeavors in
this direction.

THE RETURN OF FULL VALUE

(Address given to the faculty of the Brigham Young University on September 21, 1959, in the Annual Preschool Faculty Workshop.)

The General Authorities apparently believe that from the standpoint of the future destiny of the Church both the Institutes of Religion and the BYU are good investments. Having expressed this confidence in us, the question becomes that of what we can do as teachers and members of the BYU staff to vindicate the judgment of the Authorities and to make sure that the faithful tithe payers of the Church obtain the greatest possible return on their investment at the BYU.

I propose today to suggest certain ways in which we may do this—how we as teachers and employees may further the sacred mission of the Church in carrying the gospel to every nation, kindred, tongue and people and in establishing world peace through individual righteousness. I submit there are three broad areas in which each of us may make our contribution to that sacred mission and that unless we do so, we are failing in our duties. These areas are:

1. Developing our individual testimonies of the gospel of Jesus Christ and sharing them with our students.

2. Infusing the gospel into the entire educational program of the University.

3. Creating in our students the profound belief and conviction that accepting the gospel of Jesus Christ implies practicing it—that they will be failures unless they dedicate their lives to the service of their fellow men.

Developing and Sharing Testimonies

In view of the mission of our Church, and of BYU, I submit that it is implicit that every member of the Church on the staff of this University should be a member in good standing—and not only that, but that he should be active and faithful and a leader in helping the Church to fulfill the full measure of its sacred mission.

Good membership implies the possession of a firm testimony that God truly lives, that Jesus is the Christ, that Joseph Smith was indeed a modern-day prophet of the restored gospel, and that the present constituted General Authorities of the Church from President David O. McKay on down are the present authoritative promulgators of the gospel of Jesus Christ.

Of course, men arrive at their personal testimonies via different paths.

To some it is given by the Holy Ghost to know that Jesus Christ is the Son of God and that he was crucified for the sins of the world.

To others it is given to believe on their words that they also might have eternal life if they continue faithful. (D&C 46:12-13.)

To some a testimony of the gospel comes from study and knowledge, coupled with a devout desire to know the truth. This is the manner in which most of us on this faculty obtained our testimonies.

Others obtain their testimonies by having faith to be healed; others by having faith to heal; others by the working of miracles; others by gift of prophecy; others by the discerning of spirits; others by the gift of tongues; others by the interpretation of tongues; but unto all of us who are humble and keep the commandments and share our talents and substance with others it is given in some way or another that we may of a verity know that this gospel is true. (D&C 46:17-25.)

But unless a member of the Church on the faculty or staff of this University has that testimony, and is willing to stand up and be so counted, he has no place at this University! In so stating, I am not suggesting an inquisition, or a massive investigation into the fealty of all of us at the Y, for I am confident that the overwhelming sentiment of our administration and faculty is one of deep loyalty to the principles and to the leadership of our inspired Church.

But if there be some among you who may be sorely troubled on this vital matter, may I suggest that you earnestly seek counsel and guidance from God, and from our General Authorities. If this path does not bring forth the desired peace of mind and soul, then the only reasonable alternative is for you to find a niche elsewhere. While I would regret such an alternative, it is the only decent and honorable decision for a doubting Thomas. The law of free agency gives everyone the right to accept or reject the gospel as he sees fit. But if a skeptic were to remain in the BYU environment, with its emphasis on the spiritual rather than upon secularism, he would become increasingly embittered and unhappy. Such a frame of reference, for any unbeliever, would be entirely frustrating to him. Furthermore, he would, by his very presence and example, tend to undermine much of the strength and integrity now extant at our University. I do not wish to over-dramatize the problem, nor appear brutal in my evaluation, but in our situation, the words from the Book of Mormon are completely applicable and entirely pertinent:

. . . It is better that one man should perish than that a nation should dwindle and perish in unbelief. (1 Nephi 4:13)

That is why this faculty a few years ago approved of certain requirements for appointment on this faculty. The first of these requirements, applicable to all except those not of our faith who have honored us with membership on our faculty or staff, reads:

Belief in and adherence to the principles and teachings of the gospel, taught by The Church of Jesus Christ of Latter-day Saints.

For a number of years I accepted this requirement as a restatement of the traditional policy of BYU and as a guide for administrative action with respect to hiring and promoting members on this faculty. This year it was, together with the other criteria adopted by the faculty, officially adopted by the Board of Trustees.

Inasmuch as there would be no purpose for the continued existence of Brigham Young University except to make better Latter-day Saints of the thousands of sons and daughters entrusted to us by faithful parents of the Church, I was requested by the Board to make sure that each faculty member has a strong testimony of the divinity of the Savior, belief in the divine mission of the Prophet Joseph Smith, and his successors, and that he or she adheres to the principles and standards of the Church, including the payment of tithing. To this end and in order that there will be no misunderstanding as to performance, each member of the faculty is urged to attend tithing settlement, and to accurately inform the bishop whether the amount paid is a tithe (representing a full 10% of one's income) or merely a contribution toward tithing, commonly but erroneously known as part tithing.

In response to that request I have charged the deans with the initial responsibility of encouraging adherence to the views of the Board. I want to make it plain, however, that since one of the fundamental principles of the gospel is the doctrine of free agency, no member of the faculty should adhere to any of the principles, including the payment of tithing, just to retain his position on the faculty or obtain a promotion. I do not want to coerce any member of the faculty to follow any standard of conduct which he does not voluntarily favor. If, therefore, any member of the faculty does not believe in and adhere to the standards of the Church, I would appreciate his being honest and forthright about the matter. He should inform me that he does not want his contract renewed for the school year 1960-61. This will save embarrassment to all persons concerned. Should any faculty member have any question about the interpretation or application of this policy in his particular case, I shall be available to discuss the matter fully with him.

I am aware that there may be some who say that there cannot help but be coercion if adherence to the standards of the Church including the payment of tithing are requisites for continued employment on the BYU faculty. My answer is that unless you believe in and practice these principles you yourself have exercised your own free agency by choosing not to be on the faculty of the BYU, for you do not come within the qualifications laid down by the faculty or Board of Trustees for membership on this faculty. You have yourself made the decision.

In making this statement I express my deep appreciation to the overwhelming membership of our faculty and staff who recognize their obligation to serve as worthy examples for all who come within their sphere of influence. I believe that only by the proper living of its faculty and staff will this University receive the blessings to which it is entitled.

Destruction of Faith

There is nothing more tragic in the life of any young man or young woman than to have his or her faith destroyed by a teacher. Brother Maeser used to say that he would sooner have his child tossed into a den of serpents than to have that same child taught by a teacher who had no faith in God.

I should like to modernize that utterance by stating that it is just as disloyal to this institution to destroy the faith of a child, as it is disloyal to our country to divulge any secret of national security. And that constitutes treason! I believe it is just as self-condemnatory for any individual to accept the tithing of this Church for the purpose of teaching doctrines which destroy faith in this Church as it was for Judas to accept 30 pieces of silver to betray the Master.

We are not here to teach whatever heretic doctrine we may be susceptible to ourselves. We are here as the servants of not only the leaders but also the humble members of this Church—widows who send their children here to be inspired and to receive the inspiration which they have missed because of being fatherless—and God shall hold us responsible if we abuse that trust.

It follows that under no circumstances can we permit teachers to remain on our faculty who destroy in our students the very faith which this institution was founded to inculcate. Neither may we condone the hiring of an agnostic or an unbeliever, for any faculty member of that kind would, pro tanto, defeat and destroy the purpose of the BYU and make it an unprofitable institution to those whose tithing is used to support it.

Lest it be charged that this is a deprivation of free speech, may I answer that no loyal member will want to exercise his right of free speech to teach doctrines destructive of our faith. May I further state that for those who desire to teach the divinity of Christ we have more freedom of speech on our campus than we would have in a state institution where teachers are forbidden to teach the Gospel in its fullness. There we would be paid from taxes to teach only secular subjects. We are here paid from the tithing of the Church to teach the revealed word of God. Whether therefore we consider that we are deprived of our right of free speech depends on what we desire to teach. If the freedom of speech we want is that of ridiculing the Gospel of the Lord Jesus Christ, we should go elsewhere where we may have that freedom. If the freedom of speech we want is that of expounding the word of the Lord in its fullness, this campus is the place where we may enjoy that freedom of speech.

The view has sometimes been expressed that BYU can never be a great university because we cannot have freedom of expression in postulating religious truths. Those who hold to that view, by their very statement, admit either that they do not accept in entirety the restored gospel as interpreted by its leaders, or that they think man may improve upon it.

Those who hold to that view arrogantly assume that man is more capable of formulating religious truth than the

Creator of man. The answer is that the entire period of
recorded history belies this viewpoint. The recurring
periods of apostacy in Old Testament and Book of Mormon
history, the Dark Ages, and the great apostacy, recurring
periods of pagan worship, the failure of churches throughout the world today to inspire people to live in righteousness and peace, all attest to the failure of man-made
religions and religious truth. Revealed religious truth
throughout the ages has been the only safe guide and
anchor for the orderly progress of civilization. Whenever
humanity has departed from this revealed truth retrogres-
sion has set in. I submit, therefore, that this University will
become the University of Destiny, not by following religious
patterns which from time immemorial have failed, but by
clinging to the word of God as revealed to his prophets,
both ancient and modern. By pursuing that course we
will build a faculty, which, while it may not be the most
scholarly in secular learning, will nevertheless because of
its reliance on both secular and revealed knowledge, be
better able than any other faculty in the world to pre-
scribe for the ills of the world and the brotherhood of
man. This combination of Christian goodness and reverent
scholarship will make it the greatest university in the
world.

Over a century ago, President Timothy Dwight of
Yale University was planning to organize a new Chemistry
Department. He needed a chairman in whom he had confidence. After considerable thought, he selected a promising
graduate student and offered the new post to him. Silliman, the student, had absolutely no knowledge of chemistry
and was amazed at Dwight's offer. But the president
simply indicated that the young man could obtain leave
to study his subject matter in Europe and then return to
Yale. When Silliman asked why he had been chosen for
the great honor, Dwight replied: "Because it is far more
difficult to find a *good man* than it is to find a good chemistry professor!" Silliman studied abroad and came back
to spend many brilliant years at Yale, blazing an outstanding trail in American chemistry. Dwight's confidence

was amply justified. Obviously, the man is far more important than the subject matter! This truth holds valid for today, especially for the BYU faculty.

The young men and women who enter our halls are searching for something meaningful in their lives. They have a right to find the answers here. They deserve the inspiration and uplifting influence of our testimonies. They will admire and respect a university leader who stands committed and dedicated to a spiritual cause.

Once in a while one of our number becomes imbued with that element of modern secularism which insists upon "objectivity" in all areas of learning and experience. He lacks the faith necessary to believe in the pre-existence, the resurrection and hereafter, or the divinely inspired plan of eternal progress. He does not believe in anything which he cannot demonstrate. I submit that this attitude, especially at Brigham Young University, is fundamentally unsound. And I am convinced that no student will have respect for a teacher or an administrator who vainly seeks refuge in a watered-down objectivity.

BYU, of course, cleaves to the highest standards of truth. Our academic frame of reference must always be a ceaseless, diligent, and brilliant search for validity everywhere. We cannot live by any other code. This reference, however, does not mean that we are to be deprived of conviction, or to the promptings of the still small voice. A man has a responsibility to his Father in Heaven, and to himself, to search for truth and then to declare that truth to all who will hear it.

I realize that there is a great temptation today among many church-related institutions to obtain the services of charming and scholarly skeptics. The temptation is made more alluring by the so-called "sophisticated intellectualist" trend which aims at secularizing all education, even in the Christian colleges. Unfortunately, this fear of being ridiculed for preaching what is termed "sectarian bias and indoctrination" has stilled the voices of many fine men. It is this fear which has caused educators in Utah, living under the shadow of the temple, timidly to shy away from any religious subjects in the Utah Conference on Higher Education. This spiritual paralysis has actually promoted religious indifference, and left the academic battleground in the harsh custody of militant secularists. Ironically, the pipe dream of "objectivity" becomes the tool of secularism in its onslaught against Christian values. I am convinced that under the influence of our General Authorities such a plight will never befall this institution.

Infusing the Gospel

In addition to the actual commitment of faith, both by precept and example, we as university leaders have a responsibility to instill the noble light of the gospel of Jesus Christ into our work, in all areas and on all levels.

A teacher is obligated to bring his spiritual insight to bear upon the subject matter of every course he teaches.

I realize that some may declare such an approach appropriate to only certain subjects and not to all. I strongly disagree with this evaluation. If the teacher has a firm grasp of the fundamentals of his subject and also is blessed with a strong testimony of the gospel, he cannot fail to see the golden bridge which links the two categories. And he will sense a spirit of noble purpose as he brings his reconciliation and vision to the minds and hearts of his students. No teacher could ever receive greater satisfaction than this!

And no student could ever be inspired more than this, as has often been brought to my attention by students who have transferred to this institution from secular institutions of higher learning. I remember one young man bursting into my office without even knocking at the door. He was still under the spell of a very rich and rewarding spiritual and intellectual experience. Without waiting for any introduction, he exclaimed, "This is the greatest university in the world. I just came from a class in chemistry where the teacher took time out to explain a principle of the gospel. I have never heard anything like that before in any other university." I hope that young man's ecstasy will be the experience of thousands of students on this campus. I need not point out to you that a principle of theology is often accepted with better grace when it is taught in mathematics or chemistry than when it is taught in a course in religion.

I know from many comments he has made in meetings of the Board of Trustees that President McKay feels that this opportunity and practice, namely, to teach the Gospel in any class in the curriculum, is one of the most important reasons, if not the most important, for the continued existence of this University.

The contrary practice existent in most universities, that of separating the religious from the intellectual, has brought the following condemnation from Dr. M. E. Sadler, President of Texas Christian University:

> Certainly an educational institution cannot make itself meaningfully Christian by encouraging the establishment of any number of religious side shows around about its program. As a matter of fact, many thoughtful educational leaders wonder if the establishment of these peripheral religious projects have not dulled the conscience of some institutions and kept them from developing more fundamental programs.
>
> The program cannot be solved merely by adding a course here, or a department there, nor by having any number of prescribed chapel or so-called religious services.

"The full solution of this problem," according to Dr. Sadler, "involves a complete conversion, a new direction, a return to vital religion as the focal center of *all* sound education." "It will not suffice," says he, "to have religion merely as one stone in the total educational building. It must be the overreaching beam, the focalizing center, the permeating spirit, the uniting force which gives meaning and significance to *all* subjects and *all* courses. If God is the ultimate and controlling reality of life, learning is obviously inadequate unless it does confess Him as its Foundation. John Henry Newman, in his "On the Scope and Nature of University Education," is speaking with deep insight when he says, "Religious truth is not only a portion, but a condition of general knowledge."

This recognition of religion as the focal center of all educational direction is basic in our educational program at this school. It means that we shall not only preserve and uphold the traditions of Brother Maeser, but that we shall enlarge upon them. There is no reason why, with our advanced training and added facilities, we should not do a better job, not only in secular education, but also in character building. Indeed, the dichotomy between sacred and secular knowledge, now extant in the world, is a false and deceptive notion. True, such separatism serves the purpose of convenience, but it has also led men—some of great promise—into paths of confusion. The division of God's truth into sacred and secular channels is purely arbitrary and artificial. Our society has been cursed by this tragic dualism. We have been tempted to reject the basic truth of the divine root of all knowledge by grasping at the straw of mere convenience. We have become too wedded to certain scientific advances that we have forgotten the Sermon on the Mount. Men struggle against the reality of God's existence by insisting upon secular, or non-spiritual, standards for the measures of all things.

Of the two great enemies which our Christian world now faces—communism and secularism—I sincerely believe that the latter is the most dangerous to us. We are forewarned about communism. But secularism creeps upon many of us unarmed and unrecognized. Through its insidious appeal of naturalism, which now permeates our academic communities, we are led to an outrageous denial of objective standards for morality and Christianity—as cherished and embraced at this institution. Man has been tempted to take God's place. And, inevitably, he does not destroy God in so trying, but really destroys only himself. Furthermore, I submit that communism could never be successful in the world unless its way had been well paved by the minions of secularism.

But extremes and false dichotomies should be avoided at all times. There may be some of us, perhaps in indignant reaction against secularists, who unwisely become virulently "anti-reason" in sentiment. However, it is obvious folly to condemn the legitimate and well-founded discoveries of so-called secular learning. There is no place at the "Y" for a grand inquisition against honest intellectualism. Our search for truth must proceed unhampered or else we have poor excuse for this University. In insisting upon the verities of the restored gospel, we must never close our minds to new truths.

On the other hand, we must always vigorously oppose the extremists who arrogantly reject the basic theme of a gospel-centered education. These misguided zealots unfortunately cannot discern the absurdity of using man—and man alone—as the measure of truth in our universe. Members of this extremist group can have no real home at the BYU. Their corrosive intellectual enticements will injure rather than enrich the lives of our students.

The gospel of Jesus Christ is the precious cement that binds us all as individuals, and also unites our various academic disciplines. Without the gospel as a unifying force, our lives are aimless and our knowledge disjointed and fragmentary. Faith and reason must be fused together into a glorious, enlightened whole. Reason without faith is harsh, distorted and fantastic, Faith without reason is nebulous, intangible and sometimes mystical.

A true Latter-day Saint environment must continue to flourish and prosper at our institution. Every teacher permeates his class, inevitably, with his testimony, or creates a vacuum by his lack of testimony. But no vacuum can be tolerated at BYU. Nor can it be disguised or hidden by hypocrisy or faint-hearted allegiance to the gospel; nor is it proper for a teacher at this institution to give his secular *opinions* the force of *fact;* and thus mislead the immature and inexperienced student. Always he must have in mind the impression that is being registered in the soul of the student.

Creating in our Students a Desire to Dedicate Their Lives to the Service of Their Fellowmen

If we continually develop and share our testimonies with our students and infuse the principles of the gospel into all of our classes, we will have gone a long way in creating in our students the profound belief and conviction that a proper dedication to the gospel of Jesus Christ requires that they dedicate their lives to the service of their fellowman. Altogether too few of our students are doing this. In an age which is regnant with materialism, I have noted that many of our students, in seeking employment after they leave here, are concerned primarily, and in some cases almost exclusively, with the monetary compensation which they are to receive. That is basically wrong and a reflection upon our tutelage of them.

We should teach our students to enter into occupations where they can render a real service to their fellowmen, regardless of the compensation involved. I take particular pride each year in our nursing graduates who sometimes obtain not much more than half of what other graduates, even in the field of teaching, receive. I am sure that a kind and responsive Heavenly Father will bless them for what they have done.

A few years ago Brother Stewart Grow sent me a quotation that he proposed be placed on the entrance to Brigham Young University which reads:

"Enter to Learn, Go Forth to Serve." Unless we can get a better slogan than that, it will be emblazoned on the permanent entrance to this University.

On a visit to New York some time ago, one of the main officers of the Ford Foundation told me that the week previous the minister of education of Indonesia had been to see him with respect to the future plan of education for that country. To assist this minister he took him to call on the president of Yale University. The president spent the entire conversation talking about the intellectual standards of that institution and their plans to further elevate those standards. The Ford Foundation representative then took this minister to the president of Temple University where the president talked only of the service that students of Temple University were rendering. As the director of the Ford Foundation was about to leave the Indonesian minister, the latter commented, "I have thought a lot about the conversations I have had with the presidents of Yale and Temple. I think we are going to need in Indonesia a few Yales where intellectual standards can be set, but we're going to need scores of Temples for service." That same spirit of service must ever be one of the guiding standards for this University.

Conclusion

In summary may I state that I do not believe that any faculty member or administrative officer of BYU will measure up to his responsibilities as a teacher at this institution unless:

1. He constantly reaffirms his fundamental testimony in all of his classes and pledges himself to act dynamically in full support of it.

2. He constantly emphasizes the exalted level of revealed truth.

3. He constantly recognizes that human reason must be limited to legitimate criticism, evaluation and reflection, and that human reason can never become the prime basis for the Kingdom of God.

4. He cultivates a genuine dedication and humility for scholarly learning and research, but one that is clearly aware of the finite limitations of man.

5. He constantly instills in his students the dedicated desire, regardless of the monetary consideration involved, to serve his fellowmen.

I suggest that each of us as we try to evaluate whether in a given quarter we have been successful as members of the BYU staff constantly ask ourselves:

1. Has my testimony of the restored gospel been strengthened this quarter?

2. Have I shared my testimony with others? Have I strengthened the testimony of others? How many? Are there any students who are remaining in school who would not have remained except for my encouragement?

3. Have I lived a better Christian life this quarter? Has my performance more nearly accorded to the standards of my Church? Have I put into my work more than I got out of it? Or have I gotten by with as little as I could and devoted most of my time to activities other than my primary job of teaching?

4. Have I succeeded in inspiring students to higher endeavor? To lives of greater service? Which ones? What greater lives of service are they performing?

Unless you can abundantly answer these questions in the affirmative you are not growing and perhaps should consider a change, either of institutions or professions. There is no place for either a "jack" or a "coat-tail" Mormon on the faculty of this institution.

Our University, because of the blessings of the Lord, the fine support of the General Authorities, and your own diligent efforts, has made remarkable progress. But we face stimulating challenges in the future. There are many more things to be done than have been done. How will BYU acquit itself in the unknown conflicts ahead? I have no doubt as to the favorable outcome if we remain true to the faith.

But if Brigham Young University should ever lose the gospel of Jesus Christ as its primary motivation, it would have no excuse for a continued existence. It would justly deserve being discarded by our General Authorities, and scornfully rejected by the members of the Church. A university that has departed from God is like a ship without anchorage. It will drift aimlessly, buffeted by the fickle and fleeting passions or whims of the moment. Attempts to root a university in a naturalistic environment are like the feeble efforts of grappling for firm anchorage on a sandy ocean floor.

Let us then stand united this day, as administration and faculty, in the common goal of strengthening the anchorage of Brigham Young University. Let us return full value to our Church for the valuable and beneficial investment currently being made in education. Let us prayerfully examine our personal testimonies, and determine ways in which we can bring our light to those young people in our charge. And, finally, let us constantly remember that the gospel is the sacred binding power that can bring great purpose to our lives, and give true life, color and depth to the work of this great University. To the end that we shall be successful in this cherished venture, I humbly pray in the name of Jesus Christ. Amen.

BEYOND THE CALL OF DUTY

(Part of an address to the Brigham Young University faculty at a Preschool Conference September 11, 1961)

I think it is obvious to any objective observer that academic excellence must be the heart of any great university. Only the highest standards of scholarship are acceptable at an institution aspiring to be a center of learning. This is true at BYU as elsewhere. But this scholarship and learning at BYU means not only the expanding of man's horizons of knowledge in terms of acquiring secular facts and data, but also in the sense of obtaining the inspiration and ennobling influence of the gospel of Jesus Christ. To me, as I have said many times before, this combination of the secular and spiritual comprises the only valid path for man to traverse on his journey to true wisdom and salvation, and is the only reason for the perpetuation and enlargement of this institution.

The success of any institution of higher learning and the value of its contribution to society as a whole rests primarily upon its faculty. At Brigham Young University, faculty members are chosen, as in other great universities, for academic scholarship and competence; degrees and distinctions; for achievement and competence in research and creative endeavors; but primarily for worth as outstanding teachers; and also, *our emblem of special significance,* for a spirit of service, loyalty, and adherence to the principles of The Church of Jesus Christ of Latter-day Saints.

The faculty of Brigham Young University is primarily a teaching faculty. As we all know, our school has always emphasized as a major obligation the skillful dissemination of existing knowledge rather than the acquisition of new knowledge. On this point, suffice it to say that whenever a future history of BYU is written, I venture the prediction that its main claim to fame will be the combination of its lofty ideals and its superior teaching.

We take great pride at this institution, or at least I do, in recounting the dynamic teaching ability of Karl G. Maeser, and yet I think that we often fail to realize that each of us on the present faculty has greater opportunities in inspiring and serving the lives of students than did Brother Maeser. When he came to this institution in 1876 the entire studentbody consisted of only 29 students. Each of you have an opportunity to influence the lives of more students than that. With all the humility of my soul, I urge you to consider that it is your privilege and opportunity and duty to motivate your students even more so than Karl G. Maeser. I hope that some of you with the added opportunities you have had for training (opportunities which Karl G. Maeser never had) will be able to coin even better phrases than those coined by Karl G. Maeser which electrified his students. Let me read you some of them and I do this in particular for those of you who are new on our faculty:

Infidelity is consumption of the soul.

Eagerness to earn bread and butter has overshadowed many a golden opportunity.

Everyone of you, sooner or later, must stand at the forks of the road, and choose between personal interests and some principle of right.

You can pray best when you feel most like praying, but you should pray most when you feel least like it.

There is a Mount Sinai for every child of God, if he only knows how to climb it.

Our patriarchal blessings are paragraphs from the book of our possibilities.

Boys, when you are tempted to go into a saloon, think of me, your teacher.

I would rather trust my child to a serpent than to a teacher who does not believe in God.

I challenge each of you to give the same kind of spiritual and intellectual leadership at this University as was given by Karl G. Maeser. If you do that, Brother Maeser's statement that the influence of Brigham Young University would extend to every hearthstone of the Church will become a present-day reality.

In order to give each of you more time for creative thinking so as to better inspire your students (which after all is the dominant purpose of your position), the teaching load of our faculty has been reduced to about one-half of what some teachers formerly carried (some instructors during President Brimhall's administration on campus taught as much as 28 hours per week). With this lighter teaching load, I certainly hope that you will have the desire and find the time to do research, writing, or other creative work—all of which contribute to the richness of academic background and enhance the teaching skills. But with all this additional creative work we, as teachers, must never lose sight of the fact that our students will love us because of our teaching ability and because we take a personal interest in their spiritual as well as in their intellectual growth.

Students at this institution will revere and bless you for the inspiration and attention you give them. And I do not mean by this that you are to be friendly but soft in your teaching. It doesn't take a college student long to size up a teacher who doesn't prepare or who has little to offer. As soon as he can he will want to change teachers or sup at some other trough.

Last year we had the senior students tell us their best teachers. As is always true in this situation, those who received the highest rating were those who demanded the most from their students—and they generally got it.

At the present time, (1961) we have enrolled at the University a total of 530 full-time faculty members, 66 per cent of whom have received at least one of their degrees from BYU. We have sometimes deliberated over whether this meant too much inbreeding of our faculty, but we concluded that it did not because with a small number of exceptions all of them have received their terminal degrees at 96 other colleges and universities located in 41 states and 5 foreign countries. I shall not take time to read the list of 96 institutions from which our faculty have graduated. Suffice it to say that they represent all of the great institutions of learning in this country and some institutions abroad such as Oxford, University of Bordeau, Munster University and West Phalian Wilhelms University. It may be of interest to you to know that 39 of our faculty have degrees from the University of California, 30 from Stanford, 28 from Columbia and 21 from Harvard.

It will further interest you to know that apart from 350 degrees having been conferred on this faculty by BYU, other private institutions of higher learning have conferred 204 degrees and public institutions of learning have conferred 487 degrees. This makes a total of 1,041 degrees held by our faculty members, 554 being from private and 487 from public institutions of higher learning.

I take great pride in the fact that our faculty members are devoted, active members of the Church, serving in a variety of positions on all levels. According to a special survey taken recently, faculty members currently hold the following Church callings: general board members, 33; stake presidencies, 14; stake patriarchs, 2; stake high councilmen, 51; stake clerks, 6; members of stake boards, 68; ward bishoprics, 44; ward clerks, 14; ward auxiliary heads, 29. In addition, 5 former mission presidents are members of our faculty, and slightly over 40 per cent of our teachers have served a full-time mission for the Church. Over 48 per cent of our male faculty members are high priests.

On the personal side, almost 90% of our faculty members are married and are blessed with a total of over 1600 children. It is especially praiseworthy that, even though many are newly married and have only begun their families, 3 of the faculty have over 8 children apiece, and almost 25 per cent of our faculty children are three years of age and younger, with many more yet to be born. The German Department, a unit of our Department of Modern Languages, apparently leads the big family parade. The five teachers in this unit have a total of 34 children—for an average of almost 7 children per teacher! Our Art Department, selected completely at random in the survey, now consists of 13 teachers. Over half of these have 5 or more children.

A great many of our faculty members are active in service units and political organizations. Several are leaders and officers in the various public service clubs of our neighboring communities. Among them are also found the former chairman of the Utah County Republican organization, and a vice president of the Young Democrats of Utah.

On this campus we encourage, rather than discourage participation in civic and political responsibilities. All who participate in those activities, however, (and I am one of them) should remember that in doing so we should stand for principles rather than party expediency or the parties to which our parents and grandparents belonged, for no political party can be accused of consistency in the principles it espouses. We should also be careful to have proper respect and tolerance for the viewpoint of others. And even though we do this as individuals and not as members of the BYU faculty, we should always remember that our audiences often cannot distinguish between the two. We should, therefore, always speak and act with proper restraint, for what we do and say we always do at our own peril. I, for one, am willing to take the risk of that peril to actively practice my rights of citizenship, but I must always realize that I should so demean myself that my usefulness to the University is not impaired.

In a variety of ways BYU faculty members have demonstrated unusual courage, and devotion to this institution and to their quest for added learning. Some have carried on with great distinction despite ill health and physical affliction.

Another kind of courage and devotion is demonstrated in those who are working on advanced degrees. One faculty member had 12 children while seeking his degree. Another embarked on a doctoral program, even though he had a wife and six children to support. One mother (a BYU faculty member) used every summer and vacation period for ten years in order to obtain her Ph.D. Such sacrifice and determination is typical of scores of faculty members employed at Brigham Young University.

Less colorful and less often recognized are examples of our faculty members who devote much of their life (beyond class instruction time and class preparation time) to helping students, bettering themselves as teachers, and bettering their departments or colleges. Not unusual is one older faculty member, long past retirement age, who after having served for several decades as teacher and chairman (William H. Snell) still can be seen coming to school early in the morning, staying late at night, and frequently returning on Saturdays.

We are happy that many teachers contribute regularly to scholarly journals; produce mongraphs and other scholarly letters; compose music and direct numerous groups, as well as exhibit a variety of musical skills; direct and produce plays; write poetry, prose fiction of various types, and non-fiction; and do research in all fields. I am proud and happy to state that much of this scholarship has been reflected primarily in top-quality teaching.

Lest some of you may feel that I am pressing this point of teaching responsibility in undue fashion, let me refer to an address of five years ago by Professor Dexter Perkins, one of America's most eminent historians. On the occasion of his inauguration as the new president of the American Historical Association, he gave an address entitled "We Shall Gladly Teach." Strangely enough, this was the first time in the more than 70 years of history of the association that any president had mentioned the subject of teaching.

Professor Perkins has constantly reminded his fellow historians that they have tended to exalt the written over the spoken word in the academic profession. Although he himself is the author of a dozen books on American history, he would prefer to be remembered as a *teacher* of history, rather than as a *writer* of history.

Dr. Perkins has been practicing what he preaches for more than 40 years. He taught at the University of Rochester for over 36 years and then for another period at Cornell. He holds the unusual distinction of being professor emeritus at both institutions. Early in his career, Professor Perkins acknowledged that he was content to go along giving part of his time to teaching and part to writing—trying mentally to keep each function in a separate compartment. He soon became convinced that the separation was a false one. He also became convinced that the arena in which historians can play their most importantant role is the classroom. In his own words: "Here is our greatest chance of usefulness, our largest hope. The young men and women who participate in our instruction are eager and anxious to learn from us; they are capable of benefiting by our multiplied historical experience; they may be warmed by our personalities and find yet a generous view of life and a wider view of knowledge."

It is in this spirit of intellectual fellowship so admirably stated by Dr. Perkins that I earnestly solicit your support for this most precious jewel of our overall academic environment. We must press forward constantly to stress the quality of our teaching endeavor. Of course, we must also recognize our obligation to explore new areas and frontiers of knowledge through research. But under no condition, in the tradition of life at Brigham Young University, should we ever permit the proverbial tail to wag the dog! One truth in our society today is almost evident: deadening and destructive mediocrity is creeping into key places. It is therefore extremely vital that we provide a cultural climate in which the intellect is stimulated by superb teaching, and the moral and spiritual principles of individual dignity and responsibility are propagated.

Perhaps a small number of dedicated souls cannot ameliorate or mitigate the mass degeneration that seems to threaten us. Perhaps as a people we have been anesthetized by our leisure and wealth. It could well be that our vitality has been mortally sapped and we no longer have the vigor to voluntarily blaze new frontiers, both intellectual and physical. It may be that that is why both political parties, instead of appealing to our patriotism as free men to rise to higher endeavors, resort to regimentation by force of law.

But I am not pessimistic enough to accept this thoroughly gloomy outlook on life. I am firmly convinced that we at Brigham Young University have the wonderful prospect of becoming the veritable leaven in the lump. Also, I am confident that we can inspire, if we but exert the effort, our whole world to rise to the challenge and destroy the blight of mediocrity and lock-step conformity which seems to overshadow us in our culture today.

Important as our building program has been and will continue to be, I shall be very sad if those who succeed us at this institution shall record that our chief contribution during this period of growth consisted in the construction of great buildings. It was the boast of Augustus Caesar that he found Rome of brick and left it of marble. But he also found Romans free; and he left them slaves. He found Romans hard-working, self-reliant, and self-supporting; he left them indolent, dependent on the state for their sustenance and other subsidies. I hope that in the history of this institution our progress over the last several years will not be measured in terms of our material progesss, but rather that the buildings which have been constructed will be recognized merely as tabernacles of learning and of spiritual growth for the choice children of God's covenant people.

May our Father in Heaven give all of us the strong testimony and dedication we need to achieve the glorious goal of inspiring and uplifting our students, I humbly pray in the name of Jesus Christ. Amen.

RESPONSIVE AND
RESPONSIBLE TEACHERS

(This excerpt concluded Dr. Wilkinson's address to the Brigham Young University faculty at the opening faculty orientation meeting September 15, 1969)

This great assembly represents the response of the leadership and loyalty of the members of our Church to the instructions given by Brigham Young to Karl G. Maeser when some 93 years ago he called him into his office and gave him the simple instructions, "You are to teach not even the multiplication tables or the alphabet without the aid and inspiration of the Spirit of God. That is all— God bless you."

A little over 12 years after these instructions were given by Brigham Young the *Utah Enquirer* in one of its issues published on January 3, 1888, recorded as follows:

President Brigham Young organized by a deed of trust, October 16, 1875, the educational institution bearing his name. The aim was to build an institution surpassed by none. During the first year of its existence, President Brigham Young died, thus leaving the responsibility of carrying out his plans upon others. Thus thrown, as it were, upon its own resources, the B.Y. Academy had to look for its support to the interest taken by its students, the faithfulness and efficiency of its Board of Trustees, and above all, the blessings of Almighty God.

May I add to that that the Brigham Young Academy and University has had to look for its support to its faithful faculty throughout the years, for without their dedication we would not be gathering here today. We are the inheritors of the legacies they left us just as I hope those who come after us will be the beneficiaries of our efforts.

Although Brigham Young died within a year after he had executed the deed of trust founding the Brigham Young Academy, he had in the meantime given the responsibility to Abraham O. Smoot, president of the Utah Stake of Zion and president of the Board of Trustees, to finance this institution, and Brother Smoot carried this responsibility with very little help from Salt Lake City up until the time of his death in 1895. When he died he was personally indebted to the banks of Provo for $30,000 which he had borrowed to finance the Academy. I have been told by some bankers that this would probably be the equivalent of one-half million dollars today. His entire estate had to be sold to satisfy the indebtedness, including the homes of his three wives. Fortunately Uncle Jesse Knight stepped forward and purchased the three homes and gave them back to the wives. It was not until 1897 that the First Presidency assumed full financial responsibility for financing Brigham Young Academy.

This response of Abraham O. Smoot was equalled by the response of the faculty, who on various occasions accepted vegetables and agricultural produce in lieu of any cash salary—produce which had been tendered to the institution by the students in payment of their tuition.

On one occasion Brother Maeser became so discouraged that he decided he would have to forsake the assignment given him by Brigham Young—that he would accept a position at the University of Deseret in Salt Lake City where he would get regular compensation on which his family could live. He went so far in making this decision that he told his wife and daughter that they should pack their trunks preparatory to moving to Salt Lake City. After packing and sitting on these trunks for several days, his daughter finally summoned enough courage to ask her father as to the time of departure. Brother Maeser replied that he had changed his mind—that he had had a dream in which he had seen Temple Hill (which is the hill on which we are located) dotted with beautiful buildings comprising a temple of learning and that he wanted to respond to that dream by devoting his life to its fulfill-ment. I hope he is able to look down on this campus and this audience at this time and that he will also be able to witness the ground-breaking ceremonies of a real temple this afternoon.

Even after the Church assumed the burden of financ-ing this institution, great responses and sacrifices have been made by succeeding faculties. When I was a student here some faculty members were receiving as little as $2,000 per year. When I was honored by being appointed president I found that Thomas L. Martin, who was dean of the College of Applied Sciences, and who probably made as great a contribution to this school as any teacher outside of Karl G. Maeser, was receiving a salary of only about $4,700. When we raised his salary to over $5,000 he responded by coming to my office and doing a "jig."

With this background, what has been the response of the Church and its membership to the sacrifices of those who dedicated their lives to this institution? Probably the most notable response lies in the fact that beginning with a membership of only 29 students in 1876, this year we will have 24,000 students, coming from all 50 states of the Union and about 70 foreign countries, making us the largest private university in the United States. I do not believe that Brother Maeser ever dreamed of a student body of that size.

The second most notable response is the fact that this year we will have a distinguished faculty of 1,001 full-time and 166 part-time members. The faculty alone is nearly three times the size of both the high school and college student body when some of us attended school here as students.

The third most notable evidence of response is the beautiful campus located under the shadow of the majes-tic Wasatch Mountains, which many of our friends tell us is the most beautiful campus in the country and one in which the Church has now invested scores of millions of dollars.

A fourth notable response is the fact that the graduates of this University are now recognized throughout the country as men and women of character, competence and compassion.

I am happy to report to you that of the two Life Science Buildings one, which will be named after Thomas L. Martin, is now ready for occupancy and was used for Church services yesterday. It is a very serviceable building which will accommodate 2,308 students at one time. Stated differently, this building can alone accommodate more students than we expect the increase will be in our fall registration. Included in this edifice are classrooms large enough to accommodate eight wards of the Church.

Dr. Martin first came to BYU as a boy of 15 from the coal mines of Wales, and later joined our faculty as a Ph.D. graduate of Cornell in agronomy. Because of his diminutive height of only 5 feet he was affectionately referred to by the students as "Tommy." His short stature was the result of malnutrition in his youth, some of his brothers having actually died of starvation. Shortly before his death he was honored by the Soil Science Society of America for having inspired more students to become soil scientists than any other teacher in the nation.

Because of his enthusiasm, which bubbled incessantly, seventy-five of his students in agronomy acquired Ph.D. degrees in that subject in eastern institutions. Although "Tommy" was refused appointment to the faculty of Cornell because he was a member of the Mormon Church, one of his BYU students later became chairman of the Department of Agronomy of that institution—in fact dean of the school that included agronomy. One of my objections to some of our teachers of today is that they so worship the cult of objectivity and neutrality that they never acquire the conviction and enthusiasm of "Tommy" Martin. I hope you all appreciate that each of you has a greater opportunity to mold the minds and develop the character of students than even Karl G. Maeser, for each of you will be involved in the lives of far more students than did the first president of this institution.

The other of the two Life Science Buildings will be devoted exclusively to laboratories and offices and will be ready for occupancy a year from now. It will constitute one of the largest academic buildings on our campus. This will be named after Dr. John A. Widtsoe, an immigrant from Norway, a member of the faculty at Brigham Young University, from which he was appointed successively president of Utah State University and the University of Utah. In giving his name to this new building we recognize the contribution which he made to all three of these universities, and to education in general in the State, as well as his contribution to our Church.

I repeat what I have asserted before. While we do not proclaim Mormon chemistry, some of our disciplines are charged throughout with our theological beliefs. And even the most objective experiment and the most carefully documented fact take on an added dimension when they are presented by a man or woman who is a worthy recipient of divine inspiration. Such teaching is not the mere dissemination of knowledge or the refining of skills. Teaching and directing research at BYU makes possible an educational impact that should be without peer in the world. Our concern for the whole student—his spiritual as well as his academic development and the way he lives as much as what he studies—is not unique in American higher education, but it is rare for a major university. We are neither dismayed by our lack of company nor made disdainful of others who choose a different course. We must continue on our own course.

And I should like to emphasize that this approach is not the result of an overwrought concern for our "image." We find comfort in the fact that many visitors—particularly nonmembers of the Church—find our campus and our concerns to be refreshingly distinctive, but we are embarrassed by accounts—some widely published—which praise us for what we are not and describe us in terms which suit their special interests.

Only to the extent that our image reflects principles which we hold sacred are we concerned with appearance.

I'll confess that it is thrilling to me to walk through our buildings and find them in beautiful condition—the walls not defaced and the furniture unscarred. A recent visitor to our campus from a distinguished liberal arts college found many things which interested him, but he marvelled openly that we could display fine paintings in our student center without having them slashed, marked up or stolen. In reflecting on this, I marvelled at how much we can take for granted in our students and faculty. While there is no question but that the young people who are attracted to BYU are as much above average in character as they are in academic potential, I recognize that the example set for them by their teachers is a critical factor in their developing maturity. One of the most disappointing aspects of current unrest on university and college campuses is the extent to which students are inflamed by dissident faculty. The crude use of force, which has often had open or tacit approval of large numbers of faculty at some of our most distinguished institutions, is an embarrassing rejection of the rationality upon which all education is founded.

Richard Bushman, who is currently on leave from our history department to work at the Charles Warren Center in Boston, reported recently that many faculty at Harvard were having painful second thoughts about their failures to help influence students during last year's uprisings. One reported to him, rather gloomily, that the threat upon the personal safety of faculty was now so real that the legitimacy of student complaint was becoming incidental and that any university which could guarantee the physical security of its teachers would soon be able to attract the best men in the country.

While there may be a few scholars from the Ivy League whom we would like to recruit, for we are a bit short of Nobel laureates at the moment, I honestly believe we now have the *best* faculty in the country. For you expect more of yourselves than scholarship and teaching skill. Your example is convincing evidence that profound learning and a devout testimony of the gospel are compatible.

We need you to help young members of the Church develop personal standards which are in harmony with Church teachings. No effort—or combination of efforts—will be so effective in stressing standards of modesty and personal grooming as a teacher's comments. If upholding BYU standards of dress and conduct is turned over to the Dean of Students' Office exclusively, we retreat to a program which is inevitably coercive. If teachers will help by speaking their support of standards which have been approved by the Board of Trustees and carefully sent to every potential student at BYU this fall, our efforts can remain persuasive. A flippant or sardonic comment by a teacher, however, may delude a student into believing that he has your support in flouting University standards. At that point you are a significant part of whatever problem he may be nursing. We do not want faculty members to be policemen. A simple statement in your class that you support the dress and grooming regulations and expect your students to do the same will take care of all but the deliberately rebellious. We really expect very few of these, but we will try to involve campus bishops as well as the Dean of Students' Office in helping them.

Quite simply, we are asking that you be *responsive* and *responsible* in this area of student behavior as well as in the conventional areas which might be expected of you elsewhere. Your attitude sets the tone of the campus. We recognize how dependent we are upon you and earnestly solicit your support. The Board of Trustees is equally aware that the role of teacher at BYU is an unusually demanding one. They deeply appreciate your commitment to an ideal of higher education which is infused with gospel standards and given impetus by spiritual as well as secular goals. Their confidence in you is manifest in their willingness to approve the number of new programs which I have reported to you. The Brethren trust that, whatever the discipline, our impact upon the lives of those who come to prepare themselves here will be total—and totally positive.

It is obvious that BYU may become an increasingly

inviting target for disruptive forces. While some of these
may be allied to the revolutionary groups which have
beachheads on other campuses, I suspect that we will feel
our greatest pressures from those who try to strike at the
Church through us. If these pressures build up—as I pray
they won't—we must face them calmly but firmly. We do
not intend to engage in shrill interchanges with anyone or
any group. To avoid situations which may be exploited, or
which may lead to fruitless discussion, we urge all faculty
members to be alert to the use that a careless statement or
light-hearted jibe on our part may be put. You may identify your comments as personal speculation, but no dis-
claimer on your part will erase from every mind in your
classes the semi-official aura which your words carry. May I
suggest, in this regard, that many of you grossly overestimate the capacity of your students to appreciate academic irony. Hardly a week goes by without my office
receiving indignant letters from parents who quote soberly
what a teacher has obviously meant humorously. While we
can handle them—and we try to do it tactfully without
even letting you know about them—they do point up
what is a special problem at a school with our close
Church relationship. I would especially caution you about
treating sacred matters lightly. This is always in poor taste
at BYU. Most students resent it, and tell me; others are
confused and write home about it. Parents, it seems, are
never amused, and they write President McKay. We are
embarrassed to explain that apparently the whole thing
was a rather heavy-handed joke. We hope that most of you
are more responsive than this to student expectation and
responsible enough to the dignity of your position to avoid
light-mindedness that is unworthy of you.

     In his campaign for election President Nixon made
much of the rather poignant plea: Bring us together. I
don't think it appropriate or necessary for me to ask for
unity in a group which has more basic "oneness" than any
other major university faculty in the nation. Rather, I
would ask that we move forward in our shared conviction.
If you disagree with University policies, help us try to see

them your way. Your department chairman, your dean, the academic vice-president and I *will* listen. You must grant us the right to be unconvinced, but there have been changes, major changes, in University policies, and procedures over the years. While granting the right of dissent, we do not exercise that dissent in our Church by running to the newspapers and criticizing our bishop or stake president. Rather, if responsive to revelation, we go to him privately and express our views and come to an understanding. That is the policy the Brethren prefer at BYU. I know there are some who measure the success of a university by the amount of controversy that exists on the campus. In one of the criteria adopted by the Board of Trustees, that thesis is rejected for this University. Instead the Brethren urge us in their language "to operate in the spirit of the gospel, which is love and unity rather than contention and controversy." If we follow that injunction we will together make a University which will fit the dream of its founder.

SUPERIOR TEACHING

(*Conclusion of an address to the Brigham Young University faculty at the Pre-school Conference, September 13, 1965*)

As we go into the new school year, I submit that it is incumbent on all of us to dedicate ourselves to an improvement in teaching, in scholarship, and in every aspect of our university life.

As members of the BYU faculty, our first opportunity and duty is that of being superior teachers. In this respect I need merely point out that each member of the faculty has an opportunity greater than did Karl G. Maeser to mold the lives of students; in the days of Brother Maeser, there were only 29 students on the campus, but each teacher today will have direct contact with many more students than that.

Obviously, the first and foremost function of a university is to impart knowledge to inquiring minds. To accomplish this, superior teaching is imperative. As a matter of fact, the quality of teaching determines the real status of the institution. How many students attend or graduate from a university is not nearly as important as how many have learned and benefited by their attendance. The question is not how many students have gone through the University, but how many students have had the University go through them.

I think that at BYU we must have a serious goal of seeing to it that students succeed rather than creating frustrations and taking pride in their failures. Good teaching requires that students be motivated to achieve and to accomplish the purposes of their learning.

Our graduates should remember their experiences here as successful and pleasant ones. True, a faculty member may be outstanding as a researcher, writer, artist, scientist, etc. But this is not sufficient at BYU—every member of our faculty must first of all be an outstanding teacher.

Good teaching inspires, motivates, encourages, and imparts knowledge. Student lives are thereby changed for the better. Poor teaching, no matter how fine a person the teacher is, results in just the opposite effect—students are uninterested, lack motivation, become discouraged, and learn little or nothing except to avoid such a teacher in future classes. Several experiences like this usually result in failure, and eventually the student becomes a drop-out.

We have always had a reputation for good teaching on this campus, but I see evidence at times on the part of certain faculty members that they are failing in this primary obligation. The questionnaires, for instance, which were received from seniors graduating last year gave some very serious criticisms regarding the performance of some of our teachers.

Now may I say with respect to those comments that no one is going to be a popular teacher on this campus by being "easy" or by passing everyone in his class. Over the years graduating seniors have given the highest ratings to those teachers who are known to be exacting and demanding in their work, but who at the same time are loud in their explanations and understanding with their students.

Based on the senior questionnaires and a wealth of other experience, a very competent faculty committee has come up with the following Ten Commandments for superior teaching at BYU:

1. He must be punctual; keep his appointments with students, and be in his office during office hours.

2.   He must be able, willing and eager to communicate well with his students. This means not only in the classroom but in conferences with them. He must give clear and adequate instructions.

3.   He must have his course and lessons well-organized.

4.   He must be well informed on the subject matter of his course.

5.   He must stimulate his students and cause them to think.

6.   He must be courteous and considerate of students, and not cut them by sarcasm. He should remember that he has a great advantage over the student who cannot answer in kind.

7.   He must make assignments that are meaningful and balanced throughout the year.

8.   He must be prompt and thorough in handling students' paper work.

9.   He must give fair tests and grade fairly, and should have no favorites (no matter how good looking she is.)

10.   Most important, he must spiritually inspire his students and lift them to new heights. In the words of Karl G. Maeser, "There is a Mt. Sinai for every child if only he can be inspired to climb it."

This means also that at BYU there should be a constant conscious effort on the part of each teacher to integrate the known facts of his particular discipline with the spiritual truths of the gospel. Indeed, the only justification for the existence of BYU is that the gospel will pervade every class and every activity of this campus. Unless that is a reality, we might just as well substitute Institutes for BYU. If anything I say today needs more emphasis than anything else, it is this. We must enlarge the spiritual vision and testimonies of our students and motivate them to better living in every class. Unless a teacher does this at BYU he is failing. I therefore ask each of you to examine your own teaching and conduct with this in mind.

I well remember that a few summers ago we had on our faculty one of the distinguished teachers of the University of California. After he left the campus he wrote me a letter in which he observed that he was happy to find remaining among the great institutions of learning a university where the main emphasis was still placed on good teaching. It seems that in addition to visiting several classes, he even had taken a course in Mormon theology. Of his theology teacher he had this to say: "His methods are the most effective I have seen in academic teaching in a very long while. His powers of analysis are the keenest, his logic the most incisive, his humor the most infectious, and his urbanity the most compelling that I have ever encountered in a theologian of any persuasion without loss of spirituality. I wish we had men like him at California to infuse new life into our teaching."

I hope that what this distinguished teacher from California said with respect to one of our faculty members we may be able, at the end of this year, to say with respect to every teacher on the campus.

Indeed, may I say that the *number one project* of the administration this year will be to examine the quality of faculty teaching at BYU. In doing this we certainly do not intend to make snap judgments, but to avail ourselves of all criteria possible for mature judgments as to the competence of each teacher. We will therefore expect careful reports from the chairmen of each department, from the dean of each college, and we will also carefully study student questionnaires, knowing their limitations. To that end, a very distinguished committee of the faculty this summer, after contacting 100 other institutions of higher learning and studying their methods of teacher evaluation, has devised a student questionnaire, which will be given to all students this fall. This committee found that 34 of these institutions are now using student questionnaires to help evaluate teaching. The committee which has carefully prepared this questionnaire and the administration wants to make it plain that this questionnaire will be only one of the indices to be used in determining the actual effectiveness of a teacher. We will, of course, also take into consideration the judgment of department heads, deans, fellow teachers and all other proper criteria.

But we do not believe, as it is sometimes claimed by certain teacher organizations, that it is impossible to determine the quality of a teacher. I remember that in this state, for instance, certain officers of the dominant teacher organization contended that merit pay was impossible because there was no way of telling the difference between a good and bad teacher. Yet the very next year these same officers were complaining that because of the teacher salary level in this state, the good teachers were leaving the state.

I cannot conclude this subject of effective teaching without noting that one of the best tests of whether you are a good teacher is that of whether you enjoy teaching, or whether you consider it a drudgery, or something monotonous. If you fall in the latter category, I frankly suggest that in your own interest, as well as that of the Brigham Young University, you should decide on a change of employment.

The proper attitude is that illustrated by George Herbert Palmer, eminent Harvard philosopher, who said: "Harvard pays me for doing what I would gladly pay it for allowing me to do. . . . In my mind, teaching is not merely a life work, a profession, an occupation, a struggle, it is a passion. I love to teach. I love to teach as a painter loves to paint, as a musician loves to play, as a singer loves to sing, as a strong man enjoys running a race." Now you may not have the funds to pay BYU, but you should love teaching in the same way as George Herbert Palmer, in the same way that Janie Thompson loves to produce "Curtain Time, USA," or Crawford Gates loves to compose music, or Herald R. Clark likes to bring the world's best orchestras to Provo.

I close with a prayer posted on a church in St. Agnes, New York:

> Give us a good digestion, Lord,
>   And something to digest.
> Give us a healthy body, Lord,
>   With some sense to keep it at its best.
> Give us a healthy mind, good Lord,
>   To keep the good and pure in sight.
> Which, seeing sin, is not appalled
>   But finds a way to set it right.
> Give us a mind that is not bored,
>   That does not whimper, whine, or sigh;
> Don't let us worry over much
>   About that funny thing called I.
> Give us a sense of humor, Lord;
>   Give us the grace to see a joke—
> To get some happiness from life.
>   And pass it on to other folk.

May the Lord give us wisdom, strength, and the will this year to improve our accomplishments of past years, and may we have fun and joy in so doing, I ask in the name of the Lord Jesus Christ. Amen.

VALEDICTORY

Section 7

Dr. Ernest L. Wilkinson, president of BYU, flips switch which starts machinery to lift 4 million pound roof of Activities Center at the Provo campus.

Dr. Wilkinson *acknowledges standing ovation of faculty and students after his address at the opening assembly of 1970. Mrs. Wilkinson is beside him.*

A PARTING MESSAGE

(While this talk to the Brigham Young University faculty is not the latest in time sequence in this volume, it is included logically as a part of the valedictory. It was given February 20, 1964, after Dr. Wilkinson had entered the political race for a seat in the U. S. Senate, and in it he offers his farewell to the faculty, for he did not know at that time that he would return.)

Sister Wilkinson and I appreciate the opportunity to meet with you today. We had intended to announce my resignation to the faculty before it was announced in the newspapers, but events over which I had no control permitted the newspapers to get the news first, which I regret very much. This is the first faculty meeting since that time I have been free to attend. During the 13 years we have been here I have been chided a lot about quoting Karl G. Maeser, but in this, our valedictory to the faculty, I am going to quote him again. Brother Maeser said there are two times when a person ought to be brief in what he says: (1) when he is assuming a new position, and (2) when he retires from it. I hope to follow that admonition today.

At the outset I want to thank my wife for the loyal support and encouragement she has given me. As a student here it was my good fortune to manage the campaign of the "Blue Party" for student officers for the succeeding year. The candidate of that party for student body president was A. Ray Olpin and for vice-president, Alice Ludlow. I had been editor of the "Y" News (now the Universe) and Ray had been the associate editor. I had previously hardly known Alice, although there were less than 300 students in the student body.

We held a rally on the lower campus at which the candidates mounted the fountain in front of the main building and gave speeches. I don't remember what Alice said in that speech but it was the best one given, and I decided I would have to pay more attention to her, and not merely as a candidate. Her persuasive powers extended beyond that of successfully garnering votes as vice-president of the student body.

That spring I left the campus to teach at Weber College. She stayed in Provo either attending BYU or teaching at Provo High School. But it was less than 100 miles from Ogden to Spanish Fork where she lived, and I soon learned every turn in the road. It took me two years to convert her, but it was the most important contract I ever entered into, and what little accomplishments I have attained are due in large part to the affection, inspiration and loyal support I have received from her.

Four of our five children have graduated from this institution, three by way of their formal graduation exercises, and the other by way of BYU matrimony before scholastic graduation. Three of these four were students here before I was appointed president. The fifth is now a junior at BYU and after going on a mission this summer expects to return and graduate from here. So, entirely apart from our position here, we are very much indebted to this institution. If our children turn out to be good citizens and faithful Church members, as I believe they will, it will be due to the fact they had an understanding and observant mother, and that they were exposed to the influence of this great school. They have had little personal attention from their father.

Sister Wilkinson had some doubts as to whether I should accept the position of president. Knowing my restless nature she thought I would never be satisfied in my academic atmosphere. But she and I agree that the 13 years we have spent here have been the most satisfying and rewarding years of our lives. We are deeply grateful for them.

Instead of events being monotonous to me, these

years have been full of excitement, adventure and toil, and
we hope some small accomplishment. Indeed there have
been so many things to be done that we have continuously
regretted that we have never been able to have the social
life with members of the faculty which at the beginning
of each year we planned, only to abandon for lack of time.
My main criticism of the "Creation" is that the good Lord
didn't put more waking hours in each day. My dual duties
as president and either as administrator or chancellor
have consumed all of my time, and my wife has been
equally as busy in doing her duties as a wife and either
being president of the Relief Society of the BYU Stake
when we had only one stake, or as a member of the General Board of the Relief Society. Being accustomed all her
life to being a "widow" a good part of her time, because
of my preoccupation with other matters, she is now getting some measure of revenge by attending stake quarterly
conferences in many parts of this country and leaving me
as the "widower."

We both apologize that we have not had more socials
for the faculty, but it has not been because of a lack of
desire on our part. The loss has been ours, and the absence
of the frequent faculty gatherings by departments and
otherwise, that we contemplated will always be our chief
regret on leaving this campus.

Our main purpose in coming here today is to express
our deep appreciation to you as a faculty for your support
over the last 13 years. We are aware that the tremendous
growth of our institution during that period has created
problems and work and difficulties for you, as it has for us.
But you have not only met the challenge, you have made
notable achievements as a faculty during that period. I
cannot hope to enumerate all of them in this short talk,
but let me be specific as to some of them. The exclusion of
others does not mean they are unimportant.

In the first place, may I thank you for your full and
enthusiastic cooperation in integrating the religious and
intellectual lives of our students. The creation of 3 stakes
and 43 wards on our campus has denoted more than one

milestone of progress and these are nearly all presided over
by members of the faculty, without any diminution of their
academic load. Since 1956 over 255 members of the faculty
have either been bishops or members of the high council
on this campus. We are indebted to all of you who have
thus served.

(Editor's note: In 1971 the Church organization on
campus had grown to ten stakes and 98 wards.)

In the second place, may I thank you for your cooperation in our plan of holding classes campus wide from 8 a.m.
(many as early as 7 a.m.) to 5 p.m. including the noon
hour. This has meant that you have had classes in the
afternoon as well as the morning and have permitted us
to have a better utilization of all academic buildings (classrooms and laboratories) than any large university in the
country. This year on the basis of a 44-hour week that
approximates 100%, which means some classrooms and
laboratories are used in excess of 44 hours. The Board of
Trustees has been particularly gratified at this evidence
of your industry and spirit of cooperation.

In the third place, may I thank you for making unusual progress in improving the scholarship of this university. This is obvious on every hand. The raising of standards of admission, the creation of eleven, as compared
with the previous five colleges, the institution of a univer-
sity-wide Honors Program, the upgrading of graduation requirements, a 1000% increase in use of the library, or 300%
even after allowing for the increase in size of the studentbody, a doctoral program in many disciplines, the coopera-
tive plan between the College of Education on the one
hand, and the other colleges on the other, whereby students
may prepare to be teachers in any of our eleven colleges,
and an improved scholarship objective throughout the
campus, have all contributed to that end. Whereas at one
time BYU was thought of as a local institution (presided
over by a local Board of Trustees), it is now recognized, I
am sure, as the university of the entire Church, and does
not need to defer to or apologize for its scholarship to any
other university. In the process it has definitely been estab-

lished as the head of the Unified Church School System, which I hope and trust will be a permanent arrangement.

In this growing process also there has been increased recognition of the great service, apart from the normal academic pursuits, which this University may render to the Church. Examples of these are the Motion Picture Studio, which has already produced 47 motion pictures for the Church, the Data Processing Center which has a number of assignments from the Church, increased reliance by the Brethren on members of our faculty for basis research in support of the basic beliefs of our Church, the 44 Education Week programs (formerly Leadership Weeks) given throughout the Church, greatly expanded adult education program which now reaches over 81,000 people, and in particular, the great missionary training program on our campus. The BYU will be very wise if it finds other means of serving the Church, which I am sure it can do.

Finally, may I thank you for being faithful members of the Church, and for your loyal support of the administration of this school and the General Authorities of the Church. If there is one reason more than any other which over the recent years has prompted the Brethren to build for us one of the greatest campuses in the country, it is because the Brethren have felt that with rare exceptions this faculty was loyal and that the students were here obtaining and developing their testimonies as to the divinity of this Church. Loyalty begets loyalty and faithfulness has its own reward, which in the case of this institution means greater commendation and support from the Brethren. In my judgment this has been the key to the growth of this University, and will be the key to its improvement and pre-eminence in the future. I salute you as the greatest faculty in the world and I think this institution, because of its composite spiritual and secular teaching is the greatest university in the world.

I am happy that during my incumbency the Board of Trustees has been able and willing to increase the average salary of faculty members nearly 100%. I am happy over other programs for the financial benefit of the faculty authorized by the Board of Trustees, such as increased salaries for summer teaching, extra compensation for research, a liberalized sabbatical leave program, a major medical and hospital and group life insurance program, a tax sheltered annuity program, the LDS Teachers Loan Fund, additional compensation for travel study directors, and miscellaneous other benefits. Some of these so-called fringe benefits (actually this is a misnomer) which are measurable in dollars and cents cost the University nearly $600,000 last year. I appreciate that many of you are still teaching for much less than you could make elsewhere. I congratulate you on this monetary sacrifice and only hope that it is more than compensated by added intellectual and spiritual satisfactions.

I have been told, now that I am in politics, I must go easy on my praise of the BYU, but I have resolved that regardless of the outcome I am still going to extol the virtues of this institution.

I would not have you think that I believe that the judgments of your administrators have always been infallible. I know they have not, and that in particular I have made mistakes. But they have been mistakes of judgment and not of the heart. If any of you have been wronged I apologize—actually no wrong has been done intentionally.

And now, having expressed the gratitude of Sister Wilkinson and myself for your contribution to this University and to our personal lives, may I confess that we leave with heavy hearts, for we have enjoyed our work, and our affection for the University and you will always abide with us. Our decision to resign in order to run for political office was the most difficult decision we have ever made in our lives. Many of you know that at one time I was urged to run for governor, and at other times for United States senator. I declined their invitations because I had only been at BYU a relatively short time and I did not feel that it would be fair to the institution to resign in the midst of a large building program. Further, I thought the incumbents were entitled to be re-elected.

This time I made the decision to resign and enter the uncertain, unpredictable and hazardous game of politics because, right or wrong, and I could be wrong, I am seriously concerned over the welfare of our country. As I stated to the student body on Tuesday this is not the place to give a political speech and I intend today to follow the practice I have always practiced as president, of not engaging in political proselyting on the BYU campus, or as a part of my duties as president.

I will not, therefore, today attempt to support my political views, and each of you has a perfect right to disagree with them, but in order that you may understand the reasons for my decision, I merely say that my deep political concern (and this is not an attack on one party as against the other, for you know I have been critical of trends in both parties) arises from the fact that I fear we are losing our spiritual moorings in this country and worshiping the false god of materialism; that our reliance on government is becoming so great that we are attempting to replace God, the plan of creation and individual responsibility with worship of the state; that we seem to think the ills of the world can be cured by the expenditure of vast sums of money; that instead of talking in terms of principle or national honor we now speak of the Gross National Product; that we seem to think friendship for ourselves and freedom for others may be obtained by ransom and purchase; that as a nation we are attempting to substitute ease of living for hard work, and security for adventure, opportunity and freedom. I think this trend, if continued will be fatal to us as a nation, for in the wise and prophetic words of Somerset Maugham:

A nation that wants anything more than freedom will lose its freedom, and the irony of it is, if it is comfort and security it wants, it will lose them, too.

I am concerned that in our worship of materialism our country now has an indebtedness of over $5,000* for every man, woman, and child. I am concerned that we have

*This includes the amount owed for goods already delivered and services already rendered, even though some of these are payable in the future.

in effect abandoned the Monroe Doctrine as our safeguard for ultimate protection of this hemisphere, and that,
partly as a result, we are threatened with communism,
not only in Cuba, but in South America and now in
Africa as well. If the Constitution is to hang by a thread
in this country I want to be one to help preserve it.

With this concern, coupled with continuous entreaties
to run, my conscience would not permit me to say "no,"
for I have always taken the position that as Americans we
have a responsibility and obligation to respond to the call
of our country. Whether there is a "call" in my case will
depend upon the electorate, and I will willingly abide the
result. Should I lose, my conscience will at least be satisfied, even though I will then belong to the vast army of the
unemployed.

This decision was easier for me to make now than in
1956, 1958, or 1962, because our building program has
progressed to the point where I thought I could leave
with good grace. Buildings which will cost nearly $25,000,-
000 are now in the process of construction, and when they
are completed we will have a pretty good campus. In
particular, I am going to be gratified over the completion
of the Franklin S. Harris Fine Arts Building which will
compare with any in the country. I am also very happy
that the construction of the Physical Education Building
is now under way, and that this is to be named in honor
of the late President Stephen L Richards. My gratification
over this name arises from the fact that in the late thirties
President Richards (then a member of The Council of
the Twelve) was instrumental in having a local Board of
Trustees for the BYU replaced by the First Presidency and
Quorum of the Twelve. This made the BYU a Church-
wide institution and made possible the growth we have
had recently.

I do not mean by this to say that we will not need
other buildings. I have already represented to the Board of
Trustees that even if it should limit enrollment to some-
where around 15,000 students, we still need *at least* four
more academic buildings:

1. A life science building is indispensable;
2. A modern building to house together our College of Education and our Training School Laboratory is necessary for an institution which now boasts of training more teachers than any institution in the country.
3. If our engineering sciences are to grow we must have an enlarged and modern engineering building; and
4. We need a general utility classroom building for classes in various disciplines which cannot be housed elsewhere.

I regret, of course, that these buildings were not constructed during my incumbency, but Herald R. Clark tells me I shouldn't complain—that having 3 academic, 5 student housing buildings and a stadium under construction at the same time ought to make me feel pretty good. It does, but as one never completely satisfied, I do hope you can get started soon on a life science building. In saying this I want it understood that I am aware of limitations on funds available to the Board of Trustees and am not complaining about what that Board has done. The building funds made available to this institution over the last 13 years have exceeded any expectations I ever had in mind. I am sure we are all grateful for what has been done and that other buildings will be made available when circumstances permit. In the meantime let's be patient.

In conclusion, may I say that win or lose in my political venture, my heart will always be with you and I have told President Crockett that I will be happy whether I am in the Senate or unemployed to assist in obtaining contributions for a large endowment program for this University. You have a great future and I still hope to help you even though in a small way. I intend to later meet with the Administrative and Deans Councils to express my appreciation to them.

We have not yet determined when we will move from

the campus. The Board of Trustees has said that in exchange for my 13 non-salaried years of service we may remain in the home until we decide where to move permanently for the convenience of our son who is now enrolled in school. We may, however, open another home in Salt Lake also for I am there 6 out of 7 days. But we hope to see all of you frequently. If I should become unemployed we may have the glorious privilege of seeing you more in social gatherings. We pray that the blessings of the Lord will be with each of you always and that this institution in time will be recognized by all as the university of destiny. In this respect I remember a conference which I had with Dr. John A. Widtsoe as he lay on his death bed. I visited him in 1952, I believe, to tell him the Board of Trustees had just voted $10,000,000 for a building program. His eyes sparkled and he said, "Thank God the BYU has at last come into its own."

I think I should here acknowledge that John A. Widtsoe and Albert E. Bowen were largely responsible for persuading me to accept the presidency of this institution. Dr. Widtsoe, as you know, had been president of the USU and U. of U. Brother Bowen had at one time been offered the presidency of Brigham Young College at Logan, but could not accept because of professional legal obligations he had undertaken.

Now I would not have you think that buildings have made or will make this institution a great university. Its influence will continue to expand only as it breathes through the faculty the spirit of intelligent and humble faith. May the Lord help all of us to contribute to that end, I ask in the name of the Lord Jesus Christ. Amen.

A COMMITMENT FULFILLED

(This address was given by President Wilkinson March 9, 1971, to a capacity audience at an assembly in George Albert Smith Fieldhouse, at which President Harold B. Lee, first counselor in the First Presidency of the Church, announced that the BYU Board of Trustees had accepted President Wilkinson's resignation, effective at the end of the school year. President Lee also read a resolution of appreciation from the Board of Trustees, and Dr. Neal Maxwell, Church commissioner of education, gave a brief tribute to Dr. Wilkinson. It was announced also that Dr. Wilkinson had been assigned a major role in the establishment of a new J. Reuben Clark College of Law at BYU, to open in 1973.)

May I first of all, for the benefit of the news media, report that between five and seven this morning I had a number of calls asking if I was retiring. The answer was a resounding no. And that was a correct answer, for I am not retiring. I am merely changing jobs. There is a difference between *resigning* and *retiring*. They are spelled differently; they have a different connotation; and they are different. If those of the news media had asked the right question, they might have gotten a different answer.

Fortified Against Flattery

I, of course, appreciate what has been said by President Lee and Commissioner Maxwell. And I might fall for some of this flattery except for the advice of the late President J. Reuben Clark, Jr., who was the greatest realist I have ever known, and whom I deeply respected. On one occasion he said to me, "Ernest, never believe all that you hear at a funeral or at the time of one's resignation or retirement."

I remember also the story he told me of a lowly government employee who one day burst into the office of a cabinet member, indignant over what had happened in his department. The cabinet member looked at him and said, "Sir, you have forgotten rule 2104." The indignant employee inquired as to what that rule was. The cabinet member replied, "Don't take yourself too dang seriously."

My wife, in her discreet and subtle way, has fortified me against taking what has been said this morning too seriously. Knowing what was to take place, she, last night, reminded me of the story of a United States senator who, on his retirement from the Senate, was honored by his political friends with a very sumptuous banquet. There he was lavishly praised by his friends. So many good things were said about him that he was almost literally walking on air. As he and his wife started home, holding hands, he commented, "Dear, just how many great men do you think there are in the world?"

After a pause she replied, "I really don't know, but I am sure of one thing—there is one less than you think there is."

I am not yet ready, nor do I desire, to be taken up, for I now want to start a third career. And I hope the good Lord will permit me to finish that third career.

Expression of Appreciation

To begin with, I would like it understood that most of the credit I have received for the progress of this University over the last twenty years has been due not to me but to others. President Lee has already alluded to the creation of the 10 stakes and the 98 wards. That in my mind has always been the most satisfying accomplishment during the time I have been here. When I was appointed president there was only one branch of the Church on this campus. And while I had a modest part in urging the creation of the ten wards and first stake, of which Antone Romney—who sits in front of me—was president, the decisions to create them, as well as all subsequent stakes and wards, were decisions of the General Authorities of the Church. They are also responsible for appropriating the millions of dollars which have made it possible to build this great campus—considered by many educators and others to be the most beautiful campus in America. And, finally, they are responsible for the overall policies governing this institution, which have caused it to be recognized throughout the country as a citadel of academic excellence, law and order, and Christian charity and integrity.

The development which I next consider to be the most important, to which President Lee has also alluded, is the improvement in scholarship. A freshman student recently came to my office greatly disturbed over our high standards of admission. Looking me straight in the face, and thinking he would get an argument, he said, "If you were applying now, you wouldn't be admitted to this institution." I avoided an argument by admitting it. The main credit for this improvement in scholarship goes to the devoted faculty of this institution, most of whom are as dedicated in their academic responsibilities as they are in their callings in the Church. In fact, helping to educate young Latter-day Saints is a very sacred calling. At this University we have never forgotten President Brigham Young's original injunction to infuse all that is taught with the Spirit of God.

I want also to express my deep appreciation to my associates in the administration, for without their loyal help it would have been impossible to administer the complex affairs of this institution. When I first came here twenty years ago, I was able to supervise personally almost every activity on campus. And even then I well remember a telephone call to my home after I had been here just a week. One of my sons answered the telephone; the person on the other end wanted to ask me a question. In a rather surly voice my son commented, "He won't know. He is only the president of this institution." I learned the next day it was a member of the Council of the Twelve who had called. With our remarkable growth I have of necessity been compelled to delegate many duties to my associates. I am grateful to them for their competent advice and faithful performance.

Students Without Peer

President Lee this morning has alluded again to the fact that we have no disturbances or riots at this institution. My reply to those who give us credit for this is that you students are without peer in the world. Most of you come from fine homes where gospel principles are thankfully accepted. All of you have agreed to be examples of Christian conduct at a time when many students appear unwilling to accept any restraints. Your spiritual maturity makes it possible for you to accept discipline without sacrificing individuality. Your response to law is that of reasonable men and women who know that a better world must be created and not merely demanded. You recognize that violence is always undiscriminating and never more than an expedient. With 7,500 returned missionaries in our student body, some of whom have themselves been the targets of riots, one would not expect violent confrontations here. Again I say that you are the greatest student body on earth; and the reputation of this school will grow in direct proportion to your conduct and later accomplishments, both as students and as alumni. You are the ones who are entitled to the largest credit for the character of this institution, and you should be anxious to show other student bodies what the gospel of Jesus Christ can mean in the lives of young adults.

Support of Sister Wilkinson

Finally, I would be remiss on this occasion if I did not acknowledge the loyal and loving support of my sweetheart whom I first met on this campus fifty years ago, and who, by her graciousness, tact, and talent, induced me to propose an eternal marriage. She really proposed it, but I didn't recognize it at the time. That of course has been the greatest blessing of my life. With all the intuition of a woman, she did not readily say yes, but had me repeat the proposal more than once.

I first met her in my senior year when I was managing the campaign of the nominees of the Blue Party for student body officers for the coming year. She was the candidate of that party for vice-president of the student body. I'd never met her before. In one of our campaign rallies I remember calling on her for an extemporaneous speech. I was so impressed with her response that I decided to ask her for a date. Very soon admiration and respect ripened into love, then marriage, then parenthood. I recommend this sequence of events for all of you.

I know that during my tenure as president I have often made enemies, but she has always made friends. I am indebted to her for our five children, for their training, discipline, scholarship, Church activity, and testimony, and I am grateful that no one of them, by his or her conduct, has ever been anything but a blessing to us.

New Perspectives

As always happens on a university campus, which are hotbeds of rumor—and BYU is no exception—there will be many rumors as to the cause of my resignation. In fact, there have been rumors for the last ten years. May I lay at rest all of these rumors by saying that after twenty years of endurance I thought the time had come when I should pass the baton to someone else who could get a fresh start and tackle the problems that are still unresolved. For while we have made considerable progress, there are many things yet to be done, both of a spiritual and intellectual nature.

With a student body of 25,000 (24,000 of whom are members of this Church) there are many things which can and should be done by this student body to build the kingdom of God. There are also many improvements that may be made in the pursuit of knowledge on this campus which are now ready for formation and implementation. I wish that my time and energy had been such that I could have been instrumental in creating new programs to accomplish these purposes, but they will have to be left to my successor.

When I tendered my resignation last June, I had in mind several alternative careers on which I could embark, for I confess I am one of those individuals who gets more satisfaction out of anticipation than I do out of ultimate realization. When something is completed I am not nearly as interested in it as I am in starting something new. I confess that while I have reviewed the plans for all buildings on this campus before they were erected there are still two of them I have not had time to visit since completion.

When, however, the decision was made to establish a law school on this campus and give it the name of J. Reuben Clark, and I was asked by the Presidency if I would take over the administrative work in its founding, this appealed to me very much. I decided to stay on to accomplish that objective as well as to complete certain other unfinished projects.

Distinctive Goals

May I comment with respect to this new law school which I am honored in having a part in getting into operation. I hope it will be just as different and distinctive from other law schools as Brigham Young University is different and distinctive from other universities. I hope that it will be a law school that will have as its foundation the divinity of Christianity, dedication to the Constitution of the United States, allegiance to the concept of free agency, and a belief in the nobility and integrity of man as an individual, not as a creature of the state. This, in my judgment—and I was happy to hear President Lee say the same thing—will be one of the ways in which the youth of Zion will save our country, which, we were informed by the Prophet Joseph, will someday hang by a thread. And that is a day that many think is either fast approaching or is already upon us.

This does not mean that the students at this law school will not get the same relevant subjects as at any other law school. It does mean, however, that we may begin with different premises and therefore we may get different answers.

In view of the erosion of constitutional concepts today, this college of law could well take for some of its guiding philosophy a quotation from Mr. Justice George Sutherland, one of the first students of this institution (not a member of our Church) and the only man from this state to ever be elevated to the United States Supreme Court. This quotation is on a plaque on the first floor of the Abraham Smoot Administration Building. It was contained in a speech given by him to the Association of the Bar of New York City when he was president of the American Bar Association, before he was elevated to the Supreme Court.

> Property, per se, has no rights; but the individual—the man—has three great rights, equally sacred from arbitrary interference: the right to his life, the right to his liberty, the right to his property. . . . To give a man his life but deny him his liberty, is to take from him all that makes his life worth living. To give him his liberty but take from him the property which is the fruit and badge of his liberty, is to still leave him a slave.

This short response would not be complete without my testimony as to the divinity of this institution. I came to this hallowed hill, then known as Temple Hill, first, not as a student, but as a young soldier during World War I in the uniform of my country. Nearly all of the male members of the student body had enlisted in the service of their country. I am happy that I was nurtured in the patriotic sentiment of that time rather than in the unpatriotic and sometimes treasonable climate we find today. Because nearly all of the men had enlisted, the girls didn't see any purpose in attending the University, so BYU as an educational institution was closed.

A Commitment Fulfilled

During my relatively short time here as a soldier (and you'll be interested that Dr. Charles Hart of our College of Physical Education was my second lieutenant), a dread influenza epidemic spread across the country. More American citizens died in that epidemic than American soldiers died on the battlefields of Europe. In Utah County alone hundreds of citizens lost their lives. I was the second person in our company of infantry to be stricken by this frightening disease. Before the epidemic was over most of our company had also been stricken. Nearly all of us, however, were holders of the Melchizedek Priesthood, and in between times of our individual illnesses we would go around and lay our hands upon each other's head and beseech the blessings of heaven.

And, while school was not in session, I became so attached to the ideals of this institution that I promised my Heavenly Father at that time that if he would restore me to normal health if ever I could be of service to this institution I would respond. Little did I realize that some thirty-three years later I would be invited to return here as its president, and I hope you can imagine my deep feelings when I returned to find that my office was in the same room where as a soldier, through the power of the priesthood, I had been raised from my bed of affliction.

I hope I have kept the commitment I then made to the Lord, for in the language of the revelation given to Joseph Smith, I deeply believe that our Church is the only true and living church upon the face of the whole earth with which he, the Lord, is well pleased. And I believe that this University is a part of that Church and has the same divine mission. It was established under the direction of Brigham Young and is now directed by a Board of Trustees presided over by President Joseph Fielding Smith.

Karl G. Maeser once said that its influence would extend to every hearthstone of the Church. I still believe the utterance of Karl G. Maeser will be fulfilled: first, by BYU being the heart of the Church's educational system; second, by the services of loyal members of our faculty diligently helping to establish religious programs for the entire Church; and third, by creating programs not yet formulated, for this student body, that will give guidance and inspiration to young people throughout the world. I leave to my successor the accomplishment of these aims, and I invoke the Lord's choicest blessings upon him.

In undertaking my new assignment I recall the advice of Oliver Wendell Holmes:

Look not always back,
Leave what you've done for what you have to do,
Do not necessarily be consistent, but be simply true.

RESOLUTION OF APPRECIATION

A Resolution of appreciation, Brigham Young University Board of Trustees, March 9, 1971.

Whereas, Dr. Ernest L. Wilkinson has served with distinction as the President of brigham Young University during the years 1951-71;

Whereas, Dr. Ernest L. Wilkinson has also served concurrently, and with distinction, as chancellor of the Unified Church School System during the years 1953-64;

And whereas, Dr. Ernest L. Wilkinson has given unselfishly of his time, talents, and his means in the unprecedented development of Brigham Young University;

Be it therefore resolved that the Brigham Young University Board of Trustees, at a special meeting held on March 9, 1971, accepts Dr. Wilkinson's resignation as President of Brigham Young University, to be effective during the summer or on August F1, 1971;

With deep appreciation to him for his deep and lasting contribution to Brigham Young University and to education in the Church education system; with acknowledgment of the thousands of lives affected by his leadership, and special appreciation for his devotion and his vigor in pursuing quality as well as growth."

INDEX

Webster, Daniel, on liberty, 55
welfare, Lyndon B. Johnson on, 39
welfare programs, 48-49
welfare state, 61; change of America to, 30-55; denounced, 33; trends of, 41-47; termed socialism, 30
welfare rolls, 40
Widtsoe, John A., on BYU, 318
wife, tribute to, 21-22
Wilson, Woodrow, on government, 54; on greatness of America, 28, 64; on liberty, 59
Wirthlin, Joseph L., on political apostasy, 47
work, habit of, 13; learning to, 205-07; modern contempt of, 26
woman, 116-24

Young, Brigham, denounced socialism, 35; on Constitution, 36; on education, 113-14; on prophets, 31
youth, dreams of, 196-99